CLEMATIS
The Complete Guide

CLEMATIS

The Complete Guide

Ruth Gooch

The Crowood Press

First published in 1996 by
The Crowood Press Ltd
Ramsbury, Marlborough
Wiltshire SN8 2HR

British Library Cataloguing in Publication Data
A catalogue record for this book is available from the British
Library.

ISBN 1 85223 928 X

Dedication
To Jimmy, a friend and fellow clematarian

Acknowledgements
Thanks to my husband for all his help and support. Without him
this project would not have been possible. Thanks also to Jimmy
and Ann James for their encouragement and editorial assistance.
Finally, thanks to my parents – to my father for infecting me with
the gardening bug and, together with my mother, for helping me
to establish a business from our hobby.

Picture Credits
Photographs by Jonathan Gooch and Anne Green-Armytage.
Line-drawings by Claire Upsdale-Jones

Typeset by Dorwyn Ltd, Rowlands Castle, Hants
Printed and bound in Great Britain by
WBC Book Manufacturers, Mid Glamorgan

CONTENTS

INTRODUCTION

I grew up with gardening in my blood. My father, a keen amateur gardener, grew almost everything from vegetables to tender summer bedding plants, shrubs and, of course, clematis. Therefore my interest in plants and flowers began at an early age.

About twenty years ago I became increasingly aware of the diversity of clematis. Until then, like many people, I was blissfully unaware of the existence of other clematis beyond 'The President' and 'Nelly Moser'.

My sincere hope in writing this book, is that I may be able to inspire other gardeners to 'open their eyes', not only to the vast range of clematis available today, but to the many different ways there are to grow them.

It is possible to have clematis in flower in our gardens almost all year round, beginning with the evergreen *C. cirrhosa* and its varieties in early spring, followed by *C. armandii* (also evergreen) in spring. The *alpina* and *macropetala* groups bloom through to early summer, when a wealth of colourful varieties take over until late summer. In the autumn *C. rehderiana* and 'Bill MacKenzie' come into their own, and finally *C. cirrhosa* 'Freckles' takes us up to Christmas, while all through the winter we can also appreciate the pretty seedheads left by the season's blooms.

The flowers vary in size considerably, from the 'dinner plates' of 'W. E. Gladstone' down to the tiny, scented, star-like flowers of *C. flammula*. Not only does the size of the bloom vary but so does its growing habit. There are the almost miniature *C. integrifolia* or *marmoraria* types, growing usually no more than 2ft (60cm) tall, then there are the rather vast montanas which can grow to around 40ft (13m). The majority of clematis are deciduous, but a few are evergreen; most are hardy, whilst a few are tender.

I have already mentioned two of the most popular large flowered clematis, but there are many more commercially grown varieties to choose from. Amongst these is an intriguing range of species and many of these 'wild' clematis make excellent garden plants.

Clematis are generally thought of as climbers; there are however several varieties of non-climbing clematis which can be grown as herbaceous plants. They are versatile plants and can be used to clothe walls and fences, to adorn pergolas, to beautify containers, and to enhance other climbers, roses, shrubs and trees – their uses are many. I much prefer to grow clematis this way, scrambling into and over other plants; they look so much more 'at home' growing with a living host as they do in the wild.

For many years clematis has been used world-wide for its medicinal properties, to cure such things as headaches and fever, as a laxative and diuretic, as well as for raising blisters! The wild *Clematis vitalba* was one of thirty-eight different plants discovered during the 1930s by Dr Edward Bach to possess healing properties. He used the individual plant remedies to treat the patient's emotional outlook rather than the physical condition they were suffering from. These 'Bach Flower Remedies' are still available today from health stores, as licensed homeopathic medicines.

Clematis belong to a family of plants called *Ranunculaceae*, which includes the buttercup and anemone, whose similarity in flower shape reveals the family likeness. The clematis however is the only climber within this family which ranges from a humble weed to the towering spires of the delphinium.

Clematis are extremely labour intensive plants to produce on a nursery, and occasionally I wish we grew something easier if less beautiful! But when I see the result of our labours, and talk to other clematis enthusiasts, then I remember why we do it.

The following pages have been compiled from experience gleaned over the years from growing and admiring these plants. The book is written for gardeners – not botanists. I have covered the sometimes confusing subject of nomenclature in Chapter 1, trying to keep the matter as simple and yet as accurate as possible.

I prefer not to take sides in the lasting dispute about the correct pronunciation of 'clematis'. In numerous parts of the British Isles, the pronunciation of cle-**may**-tis has stood many a gardener in good stead. Probably the most common pronunciation, and that favoured by dictionaries, is **clem**-u-tis. Usage indicates they are both understood and accepted. You can take your choice and still be given the plant you want! I have even been asked for a cle-**matt**-is and correctly interpreted the meaning.

To those readers seeking further knowledge of clematis I would recommend joining the British Clematis Society. Its members meet throughout the year, across the country, with visits to gardens and specialist nurseries, as well as talks during the winter months. The society's address can be found at the back of the book.

The writing of this book has been a new experience for me and it will be rewarding if some of the information and ideas offered encourage you to add to, or begin, a collection of clematis of your own. The 'companionable clematis' is justifiably fast becoming as popular as it was in its Victorian heyday. Jim Fisk rightly called it 'The Queen of Climbers'.

1
HISTORY

The word clematis comes from the Greek 'Klema' meaning 'vine-like' and while this makes the flower seem very ancient, little was written about this 'vine' until the 1500s. For centuries the rose has been immortalized by poets, artists and sculptors, but not so the clematis.

Clematis vitalba, the only clematis native to the British Isles, is still referred to by the name John Gerard, an apothecary and surgeon, gave it in his *Herball* of 1597: 'Travellers Joy'. Nowadays it is also often referred to as 'Old Man's Beard'. In 1548, in *The Names of Herbes*, William Turner (physician to the Duke of Somerset, Lord Protector at Syon House) had referred to *C. vitalba* as 'Hedge-Vine', possibly because of its growing habit.

THE INTRODUCTION OF THE SPECIES

The first clematis introduced to Britain from abroad, *C. viticella*, came from Spain in 1569, during the reign of Queen Elizabeth I. Clematis were then referred to as 'Virgin's Bower' in recognition of the fact, it is thought, that Elizabeth liked to be called 'The Virgin Queen'. *C. viticella* then became known as the 'Purple Virgin's Bower'.

During Elizabeth's reign and onwards, interest in plants developed and, increasingly, new clematis species were introduced to Britain from abroad. By the latter half of the 1500s four species had been introduced which are still grown today: *C. cirrhosa* and *C. flammula* in 1590 from southern Europe, together with *C. integrifolia* in 1573 and *C. recta* in 1597 from eastern Europe. There was then a spell during the 1600s when clematis introductions ceased, until the early part of the 1700s when once again new species were brought to Britain. *C. crispa* and *C. viorna* came from America in 1726, and the *C. orientalis* or 'Yellow Indian Virgin's Bower' from northern Asia was introduced in 1727.

Probably one of the most significant clematis discoveries was introduced to Britain from China in 1776. This was *C. florida*, and was to become one of the four main parents of our modern day hybrids. Two more valuable introductions were made in the late 1700s: that of *C. alpina* or 'Alpine Virgin's Bower' from the mountain ranges of north-east Asia and central Europe in 1792, and that of *C. cirrhosa ssp balearica* from the Mediterranean in 1783.

During the 1800s many other clematis species were introduced to the British Isles. *C. campaniflora* was introduced from Portugal in 1820, and in 1831 Lady Amherst introduced what was to become one of the most popular clematis species ever, *C. montana*, from the Himalayas.

C. heracleifolia, a herbaceous clematis which bears clusters of hyacinth-shaped flowers, was introduced from China in 1837, while three years later in 1840 *C. paniculata*, a species from New Zealand, came to Britain.

Two rather unusual species were introduced during the 1800s and are still grown today: *C. fusca* came from north-east Asia in 1860 and *C. aethusifolia* was brought from northern China in 1875. The former has woolly, brown, urn-shaped flowers which in some respects look more like seed pods than flowers. The latter has carrot-like foliage and clusters of the prettiest little creamy-yellow, bell-shaped flowers.

A very significant introduction was made from America in 1868, this being that of *C. texensis*, the species which was eventually hybridized to produce *C. texensis* 'Gravetye Beauty', *C. texensis* 'Etoile Rose' and others. In the eighteenth and nineteenth centuries clematis of other American species were introduced to Britain: *C. addisonii*, *C. columbiana*, *C. douglasii*, *C. fremontii*, *C. occidentalis*, *C. pitcheri*, *C. tenuiloba*, *C. versicolor*, *C. verticillaris*, and *C. virginiana*.

In 1898 another of today's popular species was introduced from central Asia via Russia: that of *C. tangutica*.

In fact, many of the original species are still being grown, although over the years a number have been re-named. This re-naming has caused great debates in the plant world and has often led to confusion.

PLANT COLLECTING

During the 1800s plant-hunting expeditions became more common. As travel became easier, while commercial and missionary work opened up the Far East, more and more expeditions set forth in a bid to satisfy the voracious appetites of plant collectors and botanists back home.

Many of these expeditions were fraught with terrible danger, and some plant hunters, such as the Scotsman David Douglas, even lost their lives in the course of their adventures.

Philipp F. von Siebold (1796–1866), a German medical man and naturalist, was employed as a doctor by the Dutch community in Japan, from where he introduced numerous trees and shrubs as well as clematis.

Robert Fortune (1812–1880) was born in Berwickshire. Fortune spent some time at the Botanic Gardens in Edinburgh until, in 1841, he moved on to the Horticultural Society's garden at Chiswick as superintendent of its 'hothouse' department. In 1843, following the opening of China to westerners, the Society sent Fortune there to collect plants for them. He returned to England in 1846 and was appointed curator of the Chelsea Physic Garden but stayed for only two years before returning to China to transmit the tea plant to the hill regions of India. It was largely as a result of his work that the tea industry in India flourished. Fortune continued to visit China, and later on Japan, collecting and studying their native plants, some of which were clematis.

Ernest Henry Wilson (1876–1930) was one of Britain's most famous plant hunters. Wilson was born in Gloucestershire and worked, first of all, at the Botanic Gardens in Birmingham. In 1897 he moved on to work at Kew. Wilson visited China a number of times collecting on behalf of subscribers, the first two being Messrs. Veitch and Harvard University. While in China in 1910, Wilson and his party were caught in an avalanche of stones, one of which broke his right leg. He had to be carried for three days before any medical help was obtained. Following his accident he travelled to America, from where he was later sent to Japan and the Far East. In 1927, Wilson was appointed 'Keeper of the Arnold Arboretum' and it was in America that both he and his wife were killed in a motoring accident in 1930. A sad end for one of the world's most famous plant collectors. It has been said that Wilson's services to horticulture were probably greater than those of any other collector. He introduced some 1,200 species of trees and shrubs and collected over 65,000 sheets of herbarium specimens, many of which were clematis.

George Forrest (1873–1932) was born in Falkirk and made seven expeditions to China and Tibet during his twenty-eight year career as a plant collector. He had a very nasty experience, which he recorded in 1910. While on the border of Tibet and China he was hunted for over a week by 'bloodthirsty bands of Lamas'. Hiding from them by day and travelling by night, he eventually managed to get to the city of Talifu in China, having lost two French missionaries from the expedition to the Lamas.

Each of these famous men (there were of course many others) made a tremendous contribution to our plant collections in Britain and around the world. Without them we would not have had anything like the number of plants we now take for granted in our gardens, nor would we have our wonderful collection of clematis.

Many species of clematis take their names from famous plant hunters, in recognition of their work:

C. armandii – after Père Armand David the French missionary and plant collector.
C. douglasii – after David Douglas.

C. fargesii – after Paul Farges.
C. forrestii – after George Forrest.
(C. napaulensis) – after George Forrest.
C. fortunei – after Robert Fortune.
C. florida 'Sieboldii' – from Siebold's nursery.
C. tibetana vernayi 'Ludlow & Sherriff' – after F. Ludlow and G. Sherriff.
C. mont. var. wilsonii – E. H. Wilson.

While this 'frenzy' of plant collecting was taking place abroad during the 1800s, nurserymen in the countries to which the newly collected species had been introduced, began hybridizing them.

THE EARLY HYBRIDS

Mr Henderson of the Pine-apple Nursery, St John's Wood, made one of the first ever clematis crosses in around 1835. His cross was made between *C. viticella* and *C. integrifolia*, and resulted in the plant known as *C. x hendersoni*, which was later renamed *C. x eriostemon* 'Hendersonii', and which we still grow today.

There were other particularly important species introductions as well as the aforementioned *C. florida* (1776) and *C. viticella* (1569). These were introduced from China and Japan: the large-flowered *C. patens* and *C. lanuginosa*, together with *C. Fortunei* and *C. Standishii*. These last two were introduced from Japan by Robert Fortune during the mid 1800s, and were widely used in hybridizing, but their parentage has always been in question. *C. Fortunei* was described as being creamy-white and semi-double; both this and *C. Standishii* are now widely thought to be varieties of *C. patens*.

C. patens was introduced in 1836 and *C. lanuginosa* in 1851. Both of these species, as well as the aforementioned *C. florida*, had large flowers. This no doubt created great excitement, and plantsmen in Britain became increasingly keen to experiment with hybridizing.

Isaac Anderson-Henry of Edinburgh was one of the first to achieve success in hybridizing a beautiful large-flowered clematis. During the 1850s he crossed *C. patens* with *C. lanuginosa* and produced two large-flowered clematis, a white which he called *C. x henryi*, and a mauve named *C. x lawsoniana,* both of which we still grow today.

Meanwhile, George Jackman and Sons of Woking, Surrey were also busy crossing clematis. One of their first and certainly one of their most famous crosses was *C.* 'Jackmanni' (now spelt 'Jackmanii'). This was the result of crossing *C. lanuginosa* by *C. Hendersoni* (*C. x eriostemon* 'Hendersonii') and *C. viticella atrorubens* during 1858. The first blooms of this cross were seen in 1862; two plants were selected for naming, one C. 'Jack-manni', the other C. *rubro-violacea*. They both received 'certificates of merit of the first class', when shown in 1863. 'Jackmanii' is probably one of the best-known clematis in the world.

Two other nurseries in Britain were also hybridizing clematis at this time: Cripps and Sons of Tunbridge Wells produced 'Lady Caroline Nevill' in 1866 and 'Star of India' in 1867; while in 1869, Charles Noble of Sunningdale introduced 'Miss Bateman' and 'Lady Londesborough'. All four of these clematis are still grown.

Famous nurseries throughout Europe also experimented with hybridiz-ation, producing excellent crosses. The names of some of the clematis they produced are still familiar to us today.

Initially for my own interest, I decided to note down all the old clematis I could find recorded, which were hybridized during the last century, and are still being grown and sold today. Bearing in mind the majority of these varieties are over 100 years old, I am sure you will also find the list to be of interest.

'Belle Nantaise'	Boisselot	1887
'Belle of Woking'	Jackman	1875
'Countess of Lovelace'	Jackman	1871
'Duchess of Edinburgh'	Jackman	1875
'Durandii'	Frères	1870
x *eriostemon* '*Hendersonii*'	Henderson	1835
'Fair Rosamond'	Jackman	1871
'Gipsy Queen'	Cripps	1877
'Henryi'	Anderson-Henry	1855
'Jackmanii'	Jackman	1858
'Jackmanii Alba'	Noble	1878
'Jackmanii Superba'	Jackman	1878
'Lady Caroline Nevill'	Cripps	1866
'Lady Londesborough'	Noble	1869
'Lawsoniana'	Anderson-Henry	1855
'Lord Nevill'	Cripps	1878
'Madame Baron Veillard'	Veillard	1885
'Madame Edouard André'	Veillard	1893
'Madame Grangé'	Grangé	1875
'Marcel Moser'	Moser	1896
'Miss Bateman'	Noble	1869
'Miss Crawshay'	Jackman	1873
'Mrs Cholmondeley'	Noble	1873
'Mrs George Jackman'	Jackman	1873
'Nelly Moser'	Moser	1897

'Otto Froebel'	Lemoine	c. 1865
'Perle d'Azur'	Morel	c. 1885
'Proteus'	Noble	1876
'Star of India'	Cripps	1867
'Duchess of Albany' (*tex.*)	Jackman	1890
'Sir Trevor Lawrence' (*tex.*)	Jackman	1890
'The President'	Noble	1876
x *triternata* 'Rubromarginata'	Jackman	1863
'Victoria'	Cripps	1870
'Etoile Violette' (*vit.*)	Morel	1885
'Ville de Lyon'	Morel	1899
'W.E. Gladstone'	Noble	1881
'William Kennett'	unknown	1875

The list turned out to be far longer than I had anticipated and it is quite possible more could be added. Many of these old clematis are still favourites today ('Victoria' and 'Durandii' are the two I would take to my desert island).

By 1877 Jackman's Nursery listed 343 varieties of clematis. This reflected the popularity appeal of clematis at the time, and the response to the hybridization boom in the wake of the finds of the plant hunters.

The almost fanatic plant collecting persisted until the outbreak of the First World War, with both Wilson and Forrest bringing numerous treasures back from China. Between the beginning of the twentieth century and the first weeks of war, many more new species were introduced. Among the most important were *C. armandii* and *C. montana* var. *rubens* in 1900, *C. rehderiana* in 1908, *C. spooneri* in 1909 and, in 1910, *C. chrysocoma* and *C. macropetala*, then in 1911 *C. fargesii*; all were from China. In 1908 the unusual 'rush-stemmed' *C. afoliata* came from New Zealand.

Since 1918 there have been few new species introduced, and the onset of 'clematis wilt' caused a decline in clematis interest between the two world wars. Despite this, the twentieth century has seen many beautiful hybrid clematis produced. William Robinson, along with his head gardener, Ernest Markham, at Gravetye Manor, Sussex, were between them largely responsible, I feel, for the re-awakening of interest in clematis. In 1914 at Gravetye, Markham planted clematis seedlings which had been raised by Morel of Lyons. Markham also raised many seedlings himself, one of which was originally called *C. macropetala* var. 'Markhamii', now known to us as *C. macropetala* 'Markham's Pink'. Two viticella varieties were also raised by Markham: 'Blue Belle' and 'Little Nell'. The well known texensis variety 'Gravetye Beauty' is also a tribute to these two gentlemen. Following Ernest Markham's death in 1937 (two years after that of Robinson), Markham's remaining seedlings were given to Jackman's Nursery in Woking, who named a magenta seedling from the batch 'Ernest Markham'. These are all varieties you will currently find available.

In the early 1800s American gardeners were growing few clematis, and were largely confined to growing their own native species. This developed further with the introduction of some large-flowered species from China and Japan, which were exhibited in Boston and Philadelphia in the mid 1800s.

As in England, American nurserymen began producing clematis during the late 1800s to satisfy the eager gardeners who were keen to grow these plants. By the early 1890s Parson's Nursery of Flushing, Long Island, listed seventy-three varieties. It was J. E. Spingarn who, following a visit to England in 1927, and with his enthusiasm to grow clematis, encouraged American gardeners. He believed that every garden should contain ten or twelve specimens – he aimed to make America 'clematis-conscious'. By the mid 1930s Spingarn had collected and planted around 250 species and cultivars of clematis in his garden in Amenia, New York, and was considered at the time to be America's only clematis specialist. Spingarn's enthusiasm for these plants led him to write a chapter in Ernest Markham's book *Clematis* (1935), on clematis in America.

In 1895, Frank L. Skinner moved with his family to Canada from Scotland. His keen interest in horticulture led him to breed hardy clematis suitable for coping with Canadian weather conditions. Among his many crosses he used *C. macropetala* and *C. alpina* to provide hardiness, and produced 'Blue Bird', 'Rosy O'Grady' and 'White Swan'. His clematis 'Blue Boy', raised in 1947, was a cross between *C. integrifolia* and *C. viticella*, and is said to be extremely hardy. One of his first crosses was thought to be lost to cultivation but it is said that 'Grace' is in fact alive and well in Holland. Let us hope that it will, in the future, again be generally available. This dedicated plant hybridist was honoured in 1943 with an MBE.

Many of the clematis we grow today were produced back in the late nineteenth and early twentieth centuries by various enthusiastic French nurserymen. The names of Boisselot, Frères, Grangé, Lemoine, Morel, Moser and Veillard will go down in the history of clematis for producing some of the most beautiful of our large-flowered hybrids. 'Marie Boisselot', 'Durandii', 'Madame Grangé', 'Etoile Rose', 'Perle d'Azur', 'Nelly Moser' and 'Madame Baron Veillard' are but a few of the famous names produced by these nurserymen.

It was not until after the Second World War, with the availability of new fungicides to combat the dreaded 'wilt', that interest in clematis was renewed. With new awareness created by magazines and gardening programmes, clematis received a new lease of life. Nurseries again began to specialize in clematis and once more new cultivars and species were introduced from around the world by enthusiastic growers.

Clematis have proved very popular in Europe. Earlier this century, two of today's favourite varieties, 'Lasurstern' and 'Elsa Späth', were hybridized in Germany.

Mr Jan Fopma of Boskoop in Holland is one of Europe's greatest exporters of clematis today, sending plants to Canada, Sweden and the United Kingdom and specialising in producing clematis which will withstand the extremes of climate, besides introducing new varieties.

Other countries with comparable, equally dramatic weather conditions are those of the former Soviet Union, Latvia and Estonia, and also Sweden and Poland. In these countries, clematis breeders are busy working to produce clematis which will withstand temperatures down to $-30°C$, which they must regularly cope with during the winter months.

To enable clematis to overwinter in such a harsh climate, it is normal for them to be hard pruned down to one or two buds during the late autumn, then mulched with peat to insulate them against the frost. Snow cover also helps to insulate the crowns of the plants from the most severe frosts. In the spring, the mulch is removed and the clematis are once again ready for their summer blooming.

Japan and New Zealand are countries from which we have also seen some stunning varieties of clematis introduced in recent years. Of particular note from New Zealand are 'Allanah', 'Prince Charles' and 'Snow Queen', and from Japan, there are 'Pink Champagne' ('Kakio'), 'Haku Ookan', 'Asao' and 'Wada's Primrose'.

America is home to one of the largest specialist clematis nurseries in the world today. Arthur Steffen Snr became interested in clematis in the late 1950s, having previously grown geraniums for the wholesale market. Arthur 'Bing' Steffen Jnr joined his father in the late 1960s. Bing Steffen has been instrumental in promoting clematis throughout America. The nursery at Fairport, New York, was producing around one million clematis plants a year, until disaster befell following the use of a fungicide. The nursery was closed for almost three years while the devastating problems were resolved, but, like the phoenix, it has risen from the ashes. Some of their own hybrids introduced in recent years are 'Perrins Pride' (1987), 'Sunset' (1988), 'The First Lady' (1989), 'Cotton Candy' (1991) and 'Juliette' (1992).

The late Walter Pennell from Lincoln did much, in hybridizing and increasing the numbers of large flowered clematis. Many of his introductions remain some of the most popular available today. They include 'Vyvyan Pennell', 'Richard Pennell', 'Walter Pennell' and 'Veronica's Choice', also 'Charissima', 'Herbert Johnson', 'H. F. Young', 'Kathleen

Wheeler', 'Lincoln Star' and 'Mrs N. Thompson'. John Treasure, another great clematarian of this century was also responsible for introducing and popularizing clematis. Tom Bennett, writing about John Treasure in *The Clematis* 1994 (the Journal of the British Clematis Society), wrote: 'In the years when clematis were in the doldrums, John established, with fore-sight and determination and entirely from scratch (and, initially, in collab-oration with Christopher Lloyd), Treasures of Tenbury, a nursery which was soon to become a mecca for all clematis devotees'.

Jim Fisk from Westleton in Suffolk has for many years been one of the 'famous names' in the clematis world. Not only has he raised and intro-duced his own plants, but he has been instrumental in bringing to Britain clematis from all over the world. Without his influence we would quite possibly be lacking many of the best clematis we have today. 'Dr Ruppel' which Mr Fisk introduced from Argentina in 1975, has to be one of his best large-flowered 'discoveries', along with 'Prince Charles' (small-flowered) from New Zealand. Another strong connection Mr Fisk has is with Poland, whence came such beautiful flowers as 'Niobe' in 1975, 'General Sikorski' in 1980, 'John Paul II' in 1982, and 'Warsaw Nike' (pronounced 'nee-ka') in 1986. He also introduced 'Haku Ookan' from Japan in 1971. Many other 'English' clematis were introduced by Mr Fisk. Among them the ever popular 'Hagley Hybrid' in 1956, 'Kathleen Dunford' in 1962, and 'Alice Fisk' (named after his mother) in 1967. There followed 'Margaret Hunt' in 1969, 'Gillian Blades' in 1975, 'Louise Rowe' in 1984, and *montana* 'Freda' in 1985. Jim Fisk, now in his eighties, has been a great influence to numerous gardeners for very many years – I am one of them.

Raymond Evison has had an equally distinguished career introducing new varieties of clematis from abroad. Many of these recent introduc-tions, including some hybridized at his own nursery, have been chosen specially for today's modern gardens, where very compact, free-flowering clematis are required. Amongst these are 'Anna-Louise', 'Arctic Queen' and 'Royal Velvet'.

Hybridizing is still thriving today. In recent years we have seen some really good new varieties coming from Barry Fretwell in Devon, and also from Vince and Sylvia Denny in Lancashire. Vince and Sylvia are respon-sible for the 'Seed Exchange' of the British Clematis Society and are keen to encourage other 'would be' hybridizers to 'have a go'. Two of their own introductions include 'Sylvia Denny', a double white which has become very popular and is widely grown, and an excellent new montana called 'Broughton Star', a semi-double, deep dusky pink.

So, from the very old to the very new, we have looked at many different clematis. Just for a moment I would like to reflect on the 'old' clematis books, particularly that of Moore and Jackman, and wonder

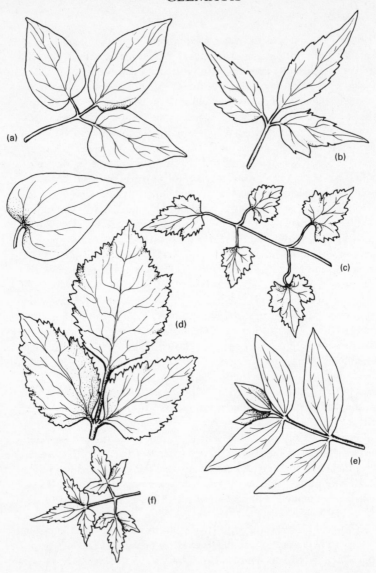

The foliage of clematis can vary tremendously in size, shape and texture. The selection shown here are drawn to scale: 25 per cent of actual size. (a) The well-known large-flowered hybrid leaf is usually a dull dark green, occasionally born singly but more commonly in threes. (b) The serrated-edged leaf of the Montana variety. (c) The light- to mid-green toothed leaves of C. rehderiana, which are soft and hairy to the touch. (d) The very large, coarse leaf of the herbaceous C. heracleifolia. (e) The smooth 'clean' leaf of another herbaceous type, C. integrifolia. (f) The very attractive toothed leaves of the early-flowering C. alpina.

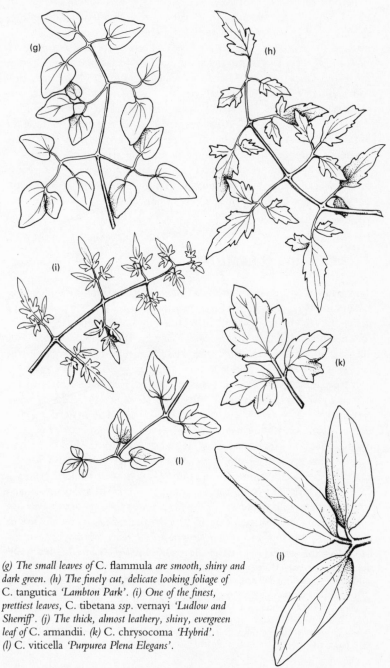

(g) The small leaves of C. flammula *are smooth, shiny and dark green. (h) The finely cut, delicate looking foliage of* C. tangutica *'Lambton Park'. (i) One of the finest, prettiest leaves,* C. tibetana *ssp.* vernayi *'Ludlow and Sherriff'. (j) The thick, almost leathery, shiny, evergreen leaf of* C. armandii. *(k)* C. chrysocoma *'Hybrid'. (l)* C. viticella *'Purpurea Plena Elegans'.*

'where are they now?'; some of the clematis they mentioned, as far as I am aware, are no longer around. Their names conjure up wonderful pictures: so who were 'Annie Wood' and 'Clara'? I also wonder who might have inspired the naming of 'Maiden's Blush'? Perhaps we will never know. We can however be grateful to Denny and Harry Caddick from Cheshire for re-introducing some old clematis which, with their appealing names, had seemingly been lost to cultivation. Thanks to them we have re-gained 'Otto Froebel', 'Colette Deville' and 'Bagatelle'. I have no doubt that as a result of their enthusiasm we will gradually see many more of the old clematis once again sharing the stage with their modern counterparts.

Clematis are clearly back in favour with gardeners and therefore nurserymen. This genus of lovely versatile plants, as it did in the nineteenth century, again captivates the imagination and senses of all keen horticulturists. The continued production of new cultivars can be anticipated with excitement.

THE CLEMATIS FAMILY

The genus *Clematis* is part of the *Ranunculaceae* family, which includes a wide variety of garden plants, from the winter-flowering aconite and hellebores, to the spring-flowering buttercups and anemones; from the summer-flowering delphiniums and aquilegias to the autumn-flowering Japanese anemones and, of course, the clematis the only climber in the family, which can be found in flower almost all year round.

It may seem odd to find clematis in a family group which includes the buttercup and the delphinium, but if we look closely at the different genera within the family we can find similarities. The main thing they have in common is their need for a rich, fertile soil and a moist yet well drained situation in which to grow. If you compare individual flowers of, perhaps, the Japanese anemone and the early-flowering *Clematis montana* varieties, the shape, colour and texture of the flowers in both genera is very similar. Also if you look at the leaves of the Japanese anemones and compare them with the leaves of the herbaceous *Clematis heracleifolia* you will again find similarities. Compare also the individual double flowers of the delphinium, with the double flowers of *Clematis* 'Beauty of Worcester', 'Royalty', or 'Vyvyan Pennell'; or the *Aquilegia* 'Nora Barlow' with the spikey double-flowered clematis 'Multi Blue'.

Some members of the family take their names from other family members, for instance *Aquilegia clematiflora*, being an aquilegia with clematis-like flowers, so once again, similarities can be found.

Clematis are the most diverse members of the *Ranunculaceae* family. The majority of clematis are climbers, using their petioles (leaf stalks) to cling on to whatever is available. There are also non-climbers within the genus, such as the integrifolias and heracleifolias, whose identity is based more on herbaceous, clump-forming plants. Then there are the tall, but non-clinging varieties such as 'Durandii' and *C.* x *eriostemon* 'Hendersonii'. Clematis also differ from the other genera within the family in that their height can vary tremendously, from the really short *C. marmoraria*, only a few inches high, to the really tall montana types, some of which can grow to around 50ft (15m). Even the shape and size of the flowers

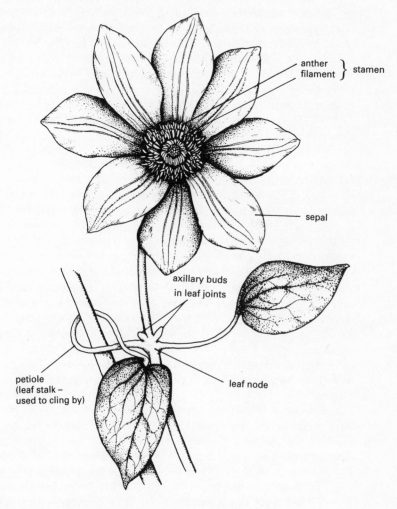

Clematis flower and leaf.

within the genus vary greatly, some varieties have small, hanging, bell-shaped flowers, whilst others have what we think of as those of a typical clematis, large, flat, star-shaped flowers.

The leaf shape, size and texture of clematis also varies. It can be found to have large, coarse, hairy leaves, typical of the *heracleifolia*s, or long, oval, leathery leaves typical of the evergreen *armandii*s. Some clematis produce finely cut leaves which appear more like ferns, rather than like the leaves we normally associate with clematis.

Not only do the growing habit, flowers and leaves vary within the genus, but so too do the type of roots. While the large-flowered hybrid clematis have quite thick, spaghetti-like, pale orangey-beige-coloured roots, the species clematis have a much more fibrous root system.

Unlike other members of the *Ranunculaceae* family, clematis do not have petals, but instead have brightly-coloured sepals. Sepals are the part of the flower which normally enclose the petals and fold back completely to allow the petals to open, as with roses for instance. The illustration on page 13 shows the main structure of a clematis flower and leaf more closely.

NOMENCLATURE

Family   –   *Ranunculaceae*
Genus   –   *Clematis, Delphinium, Aquilegia* and so on.
Species   –   *alpina, montana*, and so on.
Variety   –   *sibirica, wilsonii*, and so on.
Cultivar   –   'Helsingborg', 'Broughton Star', and so on.

Nomenclature can be a difficult topic to cover satisfactorily, as plant names seem to be constantly changing. However, with the help of Wim Snoeijer's *Clematis Index*, The *Plant Finder* (*see* Bibliography), and the Royal Horticultural Society, some naming has been clarified, although we cannot hope to be perfect yet. Publications such as the *Clematis Index* are mainly of interest to the professionals, while the majority of gardeners are quite happy simply to locate a particular clematis, regardless of what it is called.

It often proves difficult though to find a certain clematis which may have been listed under one name, but is more often found under another. Let us take *C. alpina* 'Helsingborg' as an example: previously this clematis would normally have been found listed alphabetically under the 'A's as *alpina* 'Helsingborg'; it can now be found listed under the 'H's as purely 'Helsingborg'. The latter is correct due to the origin of this clematis being a cross. Because I feel that for most people this could be quite confusing, I have continued to list clematis under the species group commonly associated with that plant. For example, the *texensis* varieties now known as 'Duchess of Albany', 'Ladybird Johnson', and 'The Princess of Wales', will be found under 'T', as *texensis* 'Duchess of Albany' and so on, rather than under 'D' for Duchess.

Until recent years, many of our large-flowered hybrid clematis had been classified under their species names as well as under their cultivar names. This stemmed from the first hybridizers using *C. patens*, *C. lanuginosa*, and *C. florida* in their original crosses. Hence 'Mrs George Jackman' would be listed as being of the *patens* group, and 'Mrs Cholmondeley' from the *lanuginosa* group. During the last 100 years or so these original hybrids have again been crossed many times, so that it has now become difficult to identify their origins. We therefore now identify many clematis solely by their cultivar name, for example 'Louise Rowe', 'Sealand Gem', or 'Dorothy Tolver'.

As more and more cultivars are introduced, many having a complex parentage, it will become increasingly impracticable to use the species in the name. This does not seem to be a problem for other families of plants, such as roses, where cultivar names only are used for normal description and listing in catalogues. However, the use of the group type after the name may be a useful guide to details such as its habit, pruning and flowering time. For example, *C.* 'Helsingborg' (*alpina* type). This system of identification is becoming increasingly popular: the *Plant Finder* uses abbreviations of the type or group to which the variety bears the closest resemblance.

Another aspect of clematis names which can be misleading is where one cultivar can be listed under two quite different names, for example 'Marie Boisselot' and 'Madame Le Coultre' are the same plant. Here I have listed them under their most commonly known names, with cross references given where necessary. It is hoped that in the future clematis hybridizers will register their new varieties, and thereby fix the true name, before further confusion is caused for the poor gardener who has to become a detective in order to track down the correct identity of some varieties.

2

SELECTING YOUR CLEMATIS

Selecting and planting are probably the most important aspects of clematis cultivation and there are several vital questions to be taken into consideration:

1 **Which** plant do I buy?
2 **Where** do I site it?
3 **When** do I plant it?
4 **Why** do I want it?

The selection of the correct plant for the position chosen is so important with clematis because of the wide variety of types. The range of heights, flowering times, pruning needs, colours and so on give scope for good planting design but, by the same measure, scope for mistakes. I hope that the following guidance will help you to avoid too many of the mistakes!

WHICH? – PURCHASING A PLANT

When selecting a plant always choose a mature clematis from a reputable source. By a mature plant I mean one that is probably eighteen months to two years old. It will have *at least* two good strong stems, although if it has more, so much the better. Check also to make sure it looks healthy: one infested with greenfly, whitefly, red spider mite or mildew would be best avoided.

Try to make sure the plant is not terribly pot-bound. Do be careful though if you decide to upturn the pot, not to tip compost all over the place. If you pick up a pot and find a few roots coming out of the drainage holes at the bottom, do not be too alarmed. When plants are grown on gravel or sand beds they will send roots down to find moisture and will quickly root into whatever is underneath. If, however, there is a large mass of root growing out of the pot then this could indicate an old or pot-bound plant. There may be times when this is unavoidable if you are looking for a particular variety, but it is useful to avoid these potential problems if you can. The plant to reject would be one where the roots can be seen on the surface of the compost as this would indicate, in all probability, that it was badly pot-bound. It is also advisable to make sure that the stems are not damaged above the soil, as this could be a possible site for the clematis wilt fungi to enter the plant.

Other plants I would avoid, unless you are happy to re-pot and grow on, are what are known in the trade as 'liners'. These are nothing more than rooted cuttings, potted and pruned down. Liners are often bought from other nurseries, they are potted on into larger pots, usually two or three litres, and grown on under cover until saleable. This can take another year. Occasionally you will find nurseries and garden centres offering liners to the unknowing public, at very reduced prices. They are a good bargain – IF you are prepared to pot on and wait for them to grow until they are strong enough to be planted out. Unfortunately, many people are not aware of this and plant liners straight out into the garden where their chance of survival is governed largely by luck.

Other clematis to be wary of are some of those found on supermarket shelves and market stalls. Again, if you are tempted, do take it home, but if it is small and weak be prepared to pot on and wait for a few months before you risk planting it out in the garden.

A well-grown mature clematis will, of course, be more expensive to buy in the first place, but it is well worth paying the extra for a quality plant and be more sure of success in the long run. As is often said, 'you get what you pay for'.

You should also find that buying a clematis from a specialist grower who can give you all the advice you need regarding selecting, planting, pruning and after-care will be well worthwhile. An awful lot can be gleaned from his knowledge and experience.

WHERE? – POSITIONING THE PLANT

The aspect of your chosen planting position is an important consideration when selecting your clematis. For instance, if you have a chain-link fence between you and your neighbour and this is exposed on all quarters to the wind and the weather, then do avoid the evergreen clematis which require a sheltered south or south-west aspect in which to flourish. Instead, choose a variety which will cope with an exposed site and you will have that live green barrier in no time at all.

If the situation is very shady, take into account the fact that very deep, dark coloured flowers will just not show up. The dark blues and purples will be wasted in a shady position, so choose instead one of the lighter, brighter colours, perhaps a pink, light blue or white. These will really cheer up a dull wall or corner of the garden. If your shady site is a very open, exposed north-facing aspect, careful selection will again be needed to find a variety which is not only the right colour but which will also cope with an exposed situation.

Another site you need to be very careful with when it comes to selecting a clematis is a south-facing aspect which is in full sun all day long, or for the greater part of the day. You will need to bear in mind that some of the very pale-coloured flowers will lose their colour almost completely if exposed for many hours each day to the sun. Taking 'Nelly Moser' as an example, if you grow this clematis in full sun the colour will bleach out very quickly, whereas if it is grown in full- or semi-shade, the colour will last and give a magnificent display. Whilst considering the most suitable position for your new plant, it is worth bearing in mind the need to provide them with a cool root system. Clematis do need to have cool, moist roots and therefore, very open, sunny sites can be a problem. The sun will dry the soil out very quickly, leaving the roots to bake. Providing shade is as easy as regular watering, so you may like to choose a spot in the shade of another plant or a wall or fence. Careful consideration of the exact location will often enable you to provide your clematis with ideal growing conditions.

It is wise to be aware of the fact that the later-flowering clematis need a good deal of sun to encourage flowering before the frosts halt them prematurely. Some late-flowering varieties that are best grown in full sun are *C. rehderiana*, 'Allanah', 'Huldine', 'Ernest Markham', 'Madame Baron Veillard' and 'Lady Betty Balfour'.

Selecting the colour of your plant to suit the background against which it will be growing is also an important matter for deliberation. Walls are often a problem: I once planted *C. montana* 'Freda', which has deep carmine-coloured flowers and bronze foliage, on a red brick wall – it looked awful. I then moved the plant along to where the wall is painted cream and the effect was amazing. Freda's bronze foliage and carmine flowers took on a whole new appearance; instead of looking drab merging into dull brickwork, it is now radiant in its new position. Another mistake I made was when planting a clematis against the wall of our dog shed, which is black. Again, I did not take everything into consideration. The clematis I chose was a very deep dusky pink and, of course, I should have realised that the black wall and dark clematis just did not complement one another.

Another matter requiring your attention when you have decided where to plant is the height and type of growth the clematis will eventually make. One day I overheard a lady saying to her friend that the *C. integrifolia* she was looking at, which was in full flower at the time, would look lovely growing up her wall. I then explained that the *integrifolia* types usually only make around 2ft (60cm) of growth and are not climbers. It is this sort of information that is so easily overlooked. Another mistake that is often made is planting very tall or very rampant clematis in a confined space. *C. montana* varieties which can grow to thirty or forty feet (ten or twelve metres) will be unsuitable for growing on a bungalow's walls unless careful training and pruning are carried out.

WHEN? – TIMING THE PLANTING

Clematis can be planted almost all year round, provided the ground is not frozen solid, in which case it will be almost impossible to plant anything, let alone a clematis.

The best times to plant are late winter to early- or mid-spring, and early- to mid-autumn. During the late winter and spring the ground will be moist and the soil will be starting to warm up as the days get longer and we see more sun. This is a good time to plant and will allow your clematis a chance to establish before the heat of the summer. Remember that later on in the spring it can be very dry, so do keep your new plant watered. If the soil dries out completely and the summer winds bake the foliage, your clematis will be far from happy.

During early to mid-autumn the soil will, again, be moist and will still be quite warm after the summer sun. Provided you can plant at this time your clematis will have the best possible chance to establish before the worst of the winter comes along. I do feel however that varieties which are a little on the tender side, such as the *armandii*, *cirrhosa* and *florida* types, would be far better planted in the spring. This would allow them the maximum opportunity to settle into their new positions and establish a good framework of ripened growth before winter sets in. Planting these clematis in autumn would not allow the essential ripening to take place.

Planting clematis during the heat of the summer is, of course possible and many of us do just that. You must, however, realize that not only will the sun bake the earth, but the warm winds will dry the foliage, so be prepared to give copious watering.

Alternatively, planting in the middle of winter, provided the ground is not frozen and is workable, is quite acceptable. It will mean though that you will need to be particularly sure that the clematis you have purchased is alive and thriving. During the rest of the year your new plant will be in leaf and possibly in flower, but in winter there will be no leaves unless it is one of the few evergreen varieties. Accordingly, attention must be paid to the buds in the leaf joints. By checking these you should be able to tell the state of the plant. If no healthy viable buds can be found in any of the leaf joints I would leave well alone and look for a plant showing some signs that spring is on its way. To check the newly formed buds in the leaf joints, *carefully* brush them with a finger-tip. If they feel papery and 'give' to the touch they are most likely not viable, but if the buds look fat and feel firm, then they should sprout forth in spring, producing a good plant.

Having checked the buds in the leaf joints, look down at the base of the plant, near the compost. Very often during the winter and early spring you will see new shoots coming from low down, even from below the soil level. These will give another indication as to how well your new clematis will grow on. Do not worry though if these shoots are not apparent, as long as the buds in the leaf joints are viable.

WHY? – PURPOSE BEHIND THE PURCHASE

Is your new plant to be a companion plant to add to an established shrub, tree or rose? Is it to become a screen either from your neighbours or to hide an ugly building? Or is it, perhaps, to add extra colour to a part of the garden that needs brightening at that time of the year? It may even need to perform a mixture of these tasks.

You may be thinking of using clematis as companion plants in the garden. Over the years they tend to have been grown on their own as specimen plants on pieces of trellis against the wall of the house. While they can look very attractive grown in this way we need to remember that there are many alternative ways to grow clematis, 'companion planting' being one. There are almost endless opportunities to use clematis to enhance the plants already in our gardens. I will suggest a few ideas to you here. There are more ideas in Chapters 6 and 7.

Planting in association with other plants can work extremely well. I have a passion for old roses and grow many different varieties in my own garden. Each has a clematis running up through it and this helps to provide additional interest in that part of the garden. Further opportunities can be found by using clematis to enhance another shrub which is in between flowering and berries and is lacking interest. For example, a summer-flowering clematis grown through a pyracantha or cotoneaster will provide extra colour for either of these shrubs. Having first flowered in the spring, they later produce a spectacular autumnal display of coloured berries. Some friends of ours have a *Cotoneaster watereri*, grown as a single-stemmed tree, and this is host to a clematis which flowers during mid to late summer, called 'Star of India'. The cotoneaster is an ideal host, showing the clematis flowers off to near perfection. Later in the season when the clematis has finally finished flowering, the cotoneaster comes into its own with a glorious display of red berries.

Clematis can also be considered suitable for use as screens, or perhaps for disguising an ugly old outbuilding. As was mentioned earlier in the section on where to plant, the evergreen types can make an excellent screen, particularly the *C. armandii*s which can form quite dense growth. But do remember that evergreen clematis dislike cold, biting winds. If you require a screen therefore in a very open, exposed area it would be wise to avoid these varieties. Where there is harsh exposure to the elements, I would use one of the alpinas or macropetalas for screening purposes. Although these are not evergreen, they will hold their leaves well into the winter and in no time at all the spring will be here and they will be in leaf again, together with a wonderful display of flowers. During the winter the old vines alone provide a surprisingly effective screen.

Where the screen just has to be evergreen and the site is exposed, you could try, as I have done, growing a selection of decorative ivies up livestock netting. This will soon form a dense, practically wind-proof screen, up which you could then grow a selection of clematis to add colour throughout the spring, summer and autumn months.

The varieties of the *montana* group really do come into their own when you need to disguise an outbuilding. Beware though – a small garden shed could become buried under a *C. montana*! So, for smaller areas, choose instead a *C. macropetala*, or *alpina*. Neither of these will require much pruning other than a tidy-up when flowering has finished. We use *montana* varieties to camouflage our large, open-fronted car shelter which is made out of old electricity poles and floor boards. It was quite a transformation from an unsightly wooden structure to a rounded, green and altogether more subtle shape, with just enough space to drive the cars in and out. In the spring it becomes a pink and white flowering mass.

Conclusion
The choice of clematis can be an extremely difficult one to make. By now you have probably narrowed it down slightly after taking into account the site, flowering period, ultimate height and so on. Now comes the fun part – buying your plant. If you are lucky enough to have a well-stocked garden centre locally, or a specialist clematis grower nearby, all is well and good. If you have neither, do not despair. Nowadays plant hunting can be done from the comfort of your armchair. First of all obtain a copy of the modern plant-hunter's yellow bible, entitled *The Plant Finder*. This useful paperback book is published each spring and lists literally thousands of plants and where to buy them, including of course clematis. You may even find a copy in your local library. In *The Plant Finder* you will find listed several hundred clematis. Listed next to each variety is a code for the nurseries supplying that particular one. You then turn to the page of the nursery code index and there you will find all the details for that nursery, including its address, telephone number, opening times and whether or not a postal delivery service is available. It could not be easier!

You have now not only chosen a clematis but managed to buy one. Next you must set about planting it well, to give it the best possible chance to flourish in your garden for years to come.

3

PLANTING

Having selected your clematis and decided on the best position for it in the garden, you now need to plant it.

The secret of successful clematis growing is in the soil which, if poor, will have to be improved. A good source of food and humus for your new plant will be needed, such as manure, good garden compost, leaf-mould, old grow bags or, if none of these are available, some potting compost. The better the growing conditions, the better your clematis will grow and flower.

You could simply dig a hole and put the clematis in; with luck it might grow, and with more luck, it might even do well enough to flower. However most of us have to work much harder to achieve success in the garden. I am sure you will get greater satisfaction from planting your clematis well. It is always worth taking the time to do the job properly at the outset, rather than spending years afterwards nurturing a once healthy plant back to life.

PREPARING THE SOIL

Unless your soil is in absolutely tiptop condition, do give it a really good forking through, mixing in as you go, any of the soil conditioners already mentioned. The one I recommend is manure. Nowadays it is not necessary to live beside a farm in order to have a plentiful supply; it is now available in garden centres, ready bagged.

If you are unfortunate enough to garden on pure clay, you are probably used to incorporating almost anything that will help to break up this difficult soil. I would recommend, before planting a clematis in clay, not only to fork in manure, garden compost or peat, but also a large amount of coarse grit – probably two or three good spadefuls per plant. If you are lucky enough to have a gravel extraction pit in the area, it may be obtainable from there. Otherwise, visit your local garden centre for they often sell coarse grit, already bagged, for you to take home. We are fortunate in having light, free-draining soil which is much easier to work than heavy clay. On the other hand, we do have the problem of trying to get it to hold moisture. When we plant in our garden it is essential to dig in compost or peat and manure, to add water-retaining humus and to provide feed. Artificial fertilizers are a convenient source of instant feed but they do nothing for the structure of your soil.

If your soil is already in good condition you will still find that your clematis benefits from having a layer of manure put into the bottom of the planting hole, with a 2in (5cm) layer of soil on top so that it does not burn the roots.

ACID OR ALKALINE?

I am frequently asked whether this group of plants prefers acid or alkaline growing conditions. This is a tricky question to answer. When considering this topic, we should bear in mind where nature puts clematis. If you visualize the only clematis native to the British Isles, *Clematis vitalba*, and then analyse the soil it grows in, you will find it prefers to grow on chalk or limestone. In Norfolk there are odd patches of *C. vitalba* growing wild, although it is not particularly common in East Anglia. In parts of Britain where chalk or limestone are commonplace, you will find *C. vitalba* in abundance. On a sunny day in autumn, driving through the Cotswolds and Gloucestershire, or along the M25 south of London, where a good view of the North Downs can be had, one can see miles of vitalba making a shimmering display of silvery seedheads.

This observation may lead us to believe that clematis would really only be happy growing in very chalky conditions, which is certainly not the case. While it is true to say that many clematis will cope with quite chalky conditions, they will also cope with growing in acid conditions alongside rhododendrons, camellias and heathers. A friend who gardens in Kentish woodland and grows all the acid-loving plants which we are unable to grow in our limey soil, has a camellia hedge through which an abundance of clematis is growing happily. He finds that the majority of clematis will do very well growing in this acid clay. In fact it is quite possible that most of the clematis we grow in our gardens would prefer growing in moist acid clay, rather than in too freely drained, pure chalk.

For clematis, moist, free-draining soil is the critical factor, more than any particular level of acidity. I think it is fair to say that clematis, like most plants, will grow quite happily whether your soil is acid or alkaline – provided the soil is in good condition. Gardeners should perhaps be less worried about pH, and more concerned about improving the general condition of the soil they are expecting their plants to grow in. So, whatever type of soil you have, whether it is acid or alkaline, light or heavy, do prepare it first.

POSTAL DELIVERY AND HARDENING OFF

If you have bought your clematis via a postal delivery service it is quite likely to be mid-winter when you receive your plants. This is because most nurseries prefer to post the plants in a dormant state, and at a time when the nursery is not busy taking cuttings, potting-up etc. They will usually only dispatch plants when the weather is reasonable, rather than during periods of severe frost. However we all know that our English weather can change unexpectedly, so I would suggest that if your parcel arrives during a period when the ground is completely frozen, you delay planting until the weather improves and the ground thaws out. Remove the plants from their packaging and check to see if they are dry. Sometimes delivery can be delayed, and your plants will suffer if they have dried out and *you* do not water them when they arrive. It is then a good idea to keep the clematis in a cold glasshouse or cold conservatory, or even by the window in a garage or garden shed until you are able to plant out.

Another delay in planting could occur when a plant is purchased during the early spring from a nurseryman who has produced his plants under cover. It is quite common to find clematis being sold from a cold glasshouse or polythene tunnel, but do remember that when the sun shines during late winter and early spring, the temperature under the cover soars and the plants will be encouraged to put on a lot of tender young growth. There is no harm in this, as long as you are aware of the danger in planting these clematis immediately. To avoid setting the plants back, do harden them off well before planting out. Hardening off involves standing your plants in a sheltered position during the day, then moving them into either a cold glasshouse, conservatory, garage or shed overnight, remembering to stand them out again the next day. This may sound a real chore, but is only the same as you would do with tender bedding plants later on in the spring. Remember to water your clematis while hardening them off. They will not require any feed during this time, as nowadays nurserymen use slow release fertilizers in the growing compost. It would be a good idea to follow this pattern for up to two weeks, but the weather will eventually dictate the best time to plant your new possession.

HOW TO PLANT

You will not only have to dig a hole big enough to accommodate the root ball, but it must also be deep enough for the clematis to be planted about 4–6in (10–15cm) deeper than it was in its pot. By planting at this depth, it will allow one or, better still, two sets of leaf joints to be buried below the surface of the soil. It is often believed that this will stop clematis wilt. In fact, it will not necessarily stop clematis wilt, but if the plant does wilt, it will stand a far better chance of recovery. (Clematis wilt is discussed in Chapter 10.) What the clematis will do if it has been planted deep is re-shoot from the leaf joints which were buried when you planted it.

By planting deep, you will safeguard the life of your clematis. If it gets damaged, clematis will always re-shoot if given time. I have known of over-enthusiastic garden strimmer owners giving clematis an untimely hard prune and being totally distraught afterwards. When damage has occurred I suggest pruning down hard any damaged stems, keeping the plant watered, and waiting. It can sometimes take months for the plant to shoot out, but ninety-nine times out of a hundred it will do so and go on to give a magnificent display of flowers for many years.

Check the depth of the hole before taking the clematis out of its pot, because if the depth does need adjusting the plant will take less harm if it is still in its pot. If your land tends to retain water in winter, it is a good idea when planting clematis to put a good thick layer of large stones or broken crock into the bottom of the hole. This will allow the clematis a better chance of survival, as they cannot bear to be standing in water. This may seem odd because this is a plant which prefers a lot of moisture, but there is a large difference between moist and waterlogged soil. Having put in the stones (if necessary), add a layer of soil and consider this new level as the bottom of your hole. I would suggest you avoid planting clematis in an area of the garden which is waterlogged during the winter as the roots will rot.

If you have no need to add stones for drainage purposes, do make sure to fork over the bottom of the hole to loosen the soil. This will ensure the plant is able to send its roots down. Into this loosened soil mix one good single handful of bonemeal. Bonemeal, I find, is the best additional feed to use for clematis as it is slow acting. This is particularly important if planting in early spring, so as not to force too much tender growth on to the plant too early in the season before the frosts have finished. Fish blood and bone would be suitable to use if planting during the summer months, however we use bonemeal all year round.

As your final preparation before planting, give your clematis a thorough watering. If it is very dry it would be a good idea to soak it in a bucket of water for about two hours.

Do make sure to remove the pot when planting. This advice may sound silly, but you would be amazed at the number of people who still think that you plant the pot as well! Nowadays clematis are generally grown in rigid plastic pots which **must** be removed. Even the thin plastic bag type of pots are not designed to be buried with your plant. To remove the pot without damaging the plant, put your flat hand across the top of the pot, with the clematis stems and cane between your second and third finger. Grasp the pot firmly in your other hand and upturn it. By carefully squeezing the sides of the pot and then giving a sharp tap on its bottom, it can easily be removed from the root ball. This is a procedure that needs to be done extremely carefully, because it is only too easy for the clematis stems to detach themselves from the roots. Having removed the pot, check the roots before putting the plant into the ground. If the roots spiral round very tightly together tease a few of them out very carefully, so that when placed in the hole, some roots will be free from the mass and will be better able to grow down into the loosened soil. After carefully placing your plant in the hole, check to make sure the roots are spread out a little, then be sure to remove any ties from around the clematis and cane which will be below soil level, otherwise the plant will strangle itself.

Now replace the soil which you dug out of the hole and firm this down very carefully using the heel of your boot, making sure you do not damage the stems. When replacing the soil into the hole, it is a good idea to leave a slight well around the base of the plant (see diagram opposite) which, when the plant is watered, will allow the moisture to seep straight down to the roots where it is needed. If you left the soil at the base of the plant raised in relation to the surrounding soil level, when you watered, the plant the area for several feet around would be wet, but the poor clematis would be left quite dry. You can sink a pipe, or perhaps a bottle with the bottom cut out, beside your clematis and then water into this so that the moisture gets down to the roots. I am not keen on seeing bits of pipe or plastic bottles planted in the garden; they are not terribly attractive and are quite unnecessary if you adopt the method I have suggested.

Water the plant in well as this will make sure the soil has settled around the root ball and that there are no air pockets left. You will find that a newly planted clematis will require fairly regular watering if planted during late spring or summer, especially if the soil is free draining. Make absolutely sure you water a new clematis if there is a prolonged period of drought. Often during these conditions clematis can suffer terribly, as they will lose a great deal of moisture from the foliage in the warm, drying winds. Even well-established plants suffer in droughts and, while it may be impracticable to water often, do try to give it a watering-canful now and again just to keep it 'ticking over'.

If the clematis you bought was full of flowers at the time of planting, but seems to spend the summer sitting there with no intention of growing, in order to encourage it to start making new growth it is a good idea to dead-head it as the flowers die off. Otherwise the plant will use all its energy to develop and ripen the seed heads rather than produce fresh growth. Dead-heading is not always necessary, or practicable, on a mature clematis, but it will help a very young plant to concentrate on the important task of producing strong stems. It is always tempting to buy the plant with lots of flowers on, but it will need this extra attention after you have finished enjoying its flowers.

PLANTING AGAINST WALLS

It is a good idea, when planting a clematis against a wall, to plant as far out from the wall as you are able. If possible, plant about 18in (45cm) away, leaning the clematis towards the wall on its cane. The soil close to a wall is always very dry, partly because the brickwork soaks up a lot of moisture, and also, depending on the prevailing wind direction, the wall will keep the rain off the soil up to about 2ft (60cm) away.

PLANTING NEAR MATURE TREES AND SHRUBS

When planting a clematis to grow into trees or over large, mature shrubs, remember that the host plant may have totally drained the surrounding

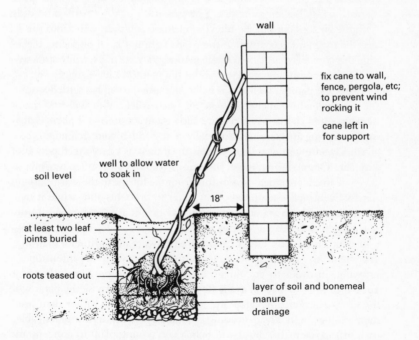

Planting against a wall.

soil of nutrients. It is essential in this sort of situation to improve the soil before planting, as was previously described, and also to be aware that regular watering will be necessary until your clematis is well established.

If at all possible, when planting against trees, position your clematis on the north side of its host. This will enable the host plant to shade the root system of the clematis. The clematis will then naturally grow towards the light. It can be quite difficult planting near mature trees as they can have a vast root system. This can make it difficult to dig a hole large enough to accommodate the clematis with a good layer of manure in the bottom of the hole. Therefore it is often necessary to site your clematis several feet out from the trunk of the tree, just to find sufficient root-free ground to plant into. (See diagram opposite).

When planting a clematis to grow over a shrub, again, plant on the north side if possible and also out on the 'drip line' of its host (see diagram opposite). Bear in mind if the shrub has dense foliage, that when it rains the water will run off its leaves and down to the ground at the outer edges of the shrub, leaving the ground underneath it bone dry. If you plant out on this drip line, however, the clematis will be well watered when it rains.

When planting a clematis in a position which is exposed to full sun for most of the day it is advisable to shade its root system from the worst of the baking heat. You can do this by using some stones, gravel, bark chippings or perhaps a small paving slab or roof tile. These can be placed at the base of the clematis and will provide the plant with a cool root run. Alternatively, you may prefer, as I do, to plant something else in front of the clematis. Depending on the space available, you could use lavender, cistus, ornamental sage (either bronze or variegated) or ground cover plants such as helianthemums, artemisia, diascia etc. Many of the hardy geraniums or pinks would also be suitable. There are many different plants you could use for this purpose, but check that they can cope with a hot, sunny position.

To Summarize

Clematis prefer a rich, well-drained soil with plenty of moisture. They also require a cool root system and deep planting. Thoughtful pruning and additional feeding really are well worth the trouble.

QUICK PLANTING GUIDE

1   **Prepare soil** – manure, garden compost and so on.
2   **Dig deep hole** – check depth before removing pot.
3   **Stones** – for drainage if waterlogging may occur.

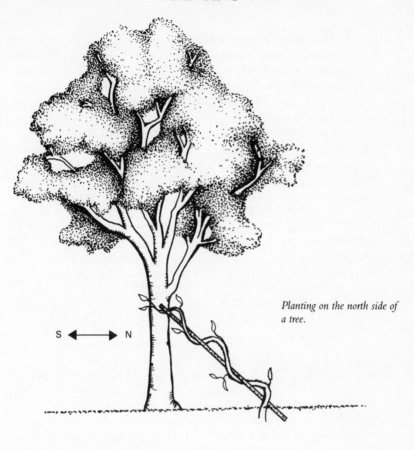

S ← → N

Planting on the north side of a tree.

S ← → N

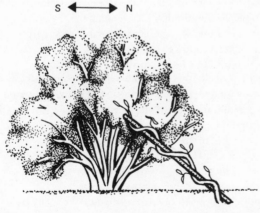

Planting on the north side of a shrub.

4 **Loosen soil** in bottom of hole.
5 Add one big single handful of **bonemeal**.
6 **Remove plant ties** low down.
7 Tease out **roots**.
8 Bury at least one, preferably two **leaf joints** below soil level.
9 Firm down soil, leaving a **well**.
10 Water in and **keep watered** during dry weather.

MOVING CLEMATIS

There can be a number of reasons why a clematis requires moving from its original planting position. The aspect may be too sunny, too shady, or too exposed. You may be moving house and wish to take a favourite clematis with you. Or there may be colour clashes in your planting schemes that need correction.

Transplanting a clematis needs to be carried out with forethought and care. The best time to move a clematis is when it is dormant, during the late winter or early spring, but while the ground is open and workable. In fact, pruning time is ideal.

First prepare the new siutation well, with manure, compost and bonemeal, exactly as you did when first planting the clematis. A larger hole will be required this time, to allow for deeper planting. The root ball needs to be 4–6in (10–15cm) deeper than it was originally, to allow for the burying of at least two leaf joints below the surface of the soil. A hole 18in–2ft (45–60cm) square and deep must be prepared.

Before digging out the plant, reduce the top growth in size to make the job more manageable. Hard prune the clematis down to about 2ft 6in (75cm) above the soil. This need not be done too exactly as final pruning will be carried out when replanting has been completed. Before digging begins, ensure that the vines remaining on the plant are cut free from their original support. Dig out the root-ball no less than 1ft (30cm) square and 1ft deep, to allow for minimum root disturbance which in turn should ensure the operation is successful. Once loosened, the root-ball can be lifted out onto a piece of thick plastic or sacking which can be carried or dragged to the new planting position. The plant can then be slid into the new hole and bedded down into place with fresh compost. Use your heel to firm around the hole, and then drench it with a can of water.

Once this has been completed final pruning can be carried out. Starting at soil level, work up each stem and prune off just above a good set of buds in the leaf joints.

If you are moving house, the clematis can be placed in a large plastic flower pot where it can remain until you can plant it in the new garden.

Do not allow the transplanted clematis to dry out completely during the first year following its move. Treat it as you would a new clematis and it will recover and flourish.

Certain varieties, *montanas* and *armandiis* for instance, do not take kindly to moving after having been planted for two or three years. They make a very woody base in their early years and will not readily respond to the required pruning and interference of transplanting. However, if the move is judged essential, it is a risk worth taking. The same goes for transplanting a clematis at the wrong time of the year, rather than the late winter or early spring. If you do have to move a clematis during the height of summer, then frequent watering will be essential. Again, if the move is essential it is worth the risk.

AROUND THE WORLD

Clematis gardening in parts of America, Canada and Northern Europe is somewhat different than in the British Isles. Here, the temperature varies between winter and summer only marginally, compared to the extremes witnessed in other countries where gardeners have to cope with severe climatic changes from dry heat in summer to from minus 30° to minus 40°C in winter. Some clematis will cope better with this than others, particularly if planted deep to protect the crown. The viticellas cope admirably, as do many other hard prune types which can be cut down and thickly mulched in autumn to insulate against the frost. Final pruning can be carried out at the onset of better weather, when the mulch can be removed. The macropetalas and alpinas are quite robust and will also survive harsh climatic conditions and are well suited to northern latitudes, where their early flowering on mature wood means they do not require long summer days to produce their flowers. Their display of blooms in the spring must be a welcome sight after a long, hard winter.

4

FEEDING

Providing additional feed for your clematis can be as simple or as complicated as you, the gardener, wish to make it. Feeding is essential for the growth of the plant – a healthy plant is better able to resist disease and attack by pests.

Let us assume you planted your clematis in well-prepared soil, with plenty of nutrients added, to enable the plant to have the best start possible. If you now give up thinking about feed, after two or three years, when the clematis has exhausted its early supply of food, it will survive only by luck. If it does survive, it will probably not be as floriferous as it would have been if you had encouraged it to a better performance with the addition of extra feed.

The busy gardener may not be able to afford what can amount to a considerable amount of time to provide additional feed. Regular liquid feeding, particularly, can be most time consuming. The solution we use in our garden, where time is limited, is a handful of bonemeal worked in around the base of each clematis using either a small hand fork, or fingers. If done at pruning time, this will allow the plant to tick over gently. This is a slow acting feed that will provide nourishment over a long period. Bonemeal in spring followed by a mulch with manure during the autumn, will be quite adequate for most clematis – and is work enough for most gardeners.

If you do have the time, interest and inclination, to provide further food for your clematis, then the subject of feeding will need to be researched. Additional fertilizers need to be checked as to their suitability for clematis, and the time of year to apply them. For instance it would be unwise to use a feed that would encourage the clematis to put on an enormous amount of lush, tender growth too early in the year, before the worst of the frosts had finished.

You need to look at the individual feeds to see exactly how your plants will react to them. On the fertilizer packaging you will find an indication of the contents' chemical formula, which is a guide to its use. This will be expressed in terms of 'N', 'P' and 'K', where 'N' is Nitrogen (this puts on leafy growth), 'P' is Phosphorus (which is a root feed), and 'K' is Potassium (potash) (this promotes flowers and fruit). The relative quantities of these nutrients are expressed as numbers, for example, 10:5:10. By looking at this information on the labels of the different feeds, you can decide which would be best to use and when.

Bonemeal contains 3.5 per cent N and 7.4 per cent P (or 3.5:7.4:0). A small amount of nitrogen is best early in the spring to encourage the plant gently into growth, but not too quickly. The extra phosphorus will benefit the roots, which of course are an essential part of the plant. Without strong, healthy roots, the rest of the plant has a poor future. Note that bonemeal has no potassium to help with the production of flowers. This, however can be remedied using Sulphate of Potash (potassium sulphate).

Sulphate of Potash This improves the flowers, not only in terms of quantity, but also in their size and depth of colour. This can be used in addition to bonemeal, about one month later, during mid-spring. Again, one single handful worked in around the base of the plant will be adequate. Like bonemeal, do water it in if you are not expecting rain. An excellent natural source of potash is wood ash, or bonfire ash. Do remember though, that anything other than wood will usually produce an ash that will be very toxic to plants. A reliable supply of bonfire ash would be useful when mulching, which is described later in this chapter.

Some other fertilizers are: fish blood and bone (6:7:6), Growmore (7:7:7), Phostrogen (10:10:27 plus trace elements), Osmacote (14:13:13), and Osmacote tablets (10:11:18 plus trace elements).

One application during late spring or early summer of any of these should be sufficient. All the fertilizers mentioned above have a high rate of nitrogen. I would therefore recommend using any of these on your clematis from late spring onwards when the chance of severe frosts is reduced. Fish blood and bone, and Growmore are excellent, well-balanced feeds for use during late spring and early summer if you wish. Phostrogen can be used either as a granular feed, sprinkled onto the ground, or as a liquid feed. Either way, wait until late spring to use this.

Liquid Feeds Again, I would only recommend liquid-feeding clematis from late spring onwards, once the weather has improved. If you have the time to do this your clematis will most certainly benefit. The best liquid feeds for clematis are those with a high potash content. This helps produce an abundance of flowers and enriches their colour. The liquid tomato feeds are very good. Phostrogen is another liquid feed which has a high potash content and is an excellent alternative to the tomato feeds.

When liquid-feeding, do be careful not to over-feed. A fortnightly liquid feed from late spring onwards is adequate for most clematis. It is far more important to keep your plant regularly watered, than to add liberal amounts of liquid feed, so concentrate your efforts on watering, with the occasional addition of liquid feed. If you over-feed clematis, the outcome will be a clematis with incredibly healthy, lush foliage and few, or no, flowers. It is not uncommon for fuchsia and pelargonium growers to produce clematis like this. They give their clematis the same treatment they apply to their fuchsias and pelargoniums – that is, to liquid feed every time they water!

Do not use liquid feeds once the clematis have budded up or are in flower. This is because liquid feed boosts the plant and pushes it on, therefore if liquid feeding is continued, instead of the flowers lasting for eight weeks, they may well be over in four. The plant needs to slow down and begin a period of dormancy during the autumn. So I would suggest you stop liquid feeding by early autumn, thus allowing the plant the rest it needs.

Liquid feeding in many gardens is hardly necessary if the soil is in good condition and well maintained. There is one time in the year however when liquid feeding in the garden is always beneficial. If you grow any of the large-flowered clematis which have a double flowering period, that is, they flower in late spring and again in early autumn. I would suggest that after the early flowers have died, you dead-head the plant. Then apply one or perhaps two doses of liquid feed about a week apart, to encourage the plant to grow and produce better flowering wood, instead of sitting there making unnecessary seed-heads. The seed-heads can be very attractive but I prefer a better second crop of flowers. I would certainly recommend this treatment.

Hoof and Horn Although not a liquid feed, this also has a very high nitrogen content, so if you are particularly keen to use it, wait until early summer and then a single application will be sufficient.

FOLIAR FEEDING

The liquid feeds are also excellent to use as foliar feeds, particularly if you have a variety of clematis that is prone to yellowing leaves. For plants that are suffering from chlorosis (yellow leaves) the application of a liquid feed containing the trace elements (micro-nutrients) Magnesium and Iron, (written as Mg and Fe on the packets) will improve the leaf colour to a healthy green. Remember a healthy plant is much more capable of overcoming pest and disease attack. Mix the feed, as recommended, in a hand sprayer and liberally cover all the leaves once a week at sundown for perhaps three or four weeks and you should see a great improvement. Foliar feeding is especially useful if you are growing clematis permanently in conservatories. This application will not only keep the foliage in good condition but it also seems to help keep down the 'bugs' which can be such a nuisance under glass. This reduces the need to use insecticides (see Chapter 10).

FEEDING CLEMATIS IN POTS AND CONTAINERS

Feeding plants that are kept permanently in pots and containers is absolutely essential, as the feed which was in the compost at planting time will be quickly exhausted. I would therefore recommend you apply one good single handful of bonemeal at pruning time, then wait until the frosts have finished to begin liquid feeding. Obviously plants kept in containers will have to be watered, so a fortnightly addition of liquid feed is simple to incorporate into this routine. Stop feeding while the clematis is in flower, or at least reduce the quantity of feed added to the water by half, then stop feeding altogether by early autumn.

Instead of using liquid feeds in your containers you can apply the new 'plug' feeds, which slowly release fertilizer over a period of months. You will need to work out the quantity of compost your container holds and from that, you will be able to calculate the number of plugs to use, as recommended on the packet.

MULCHING

Having prepared the soil well and given your clematis a really good start, the nutrients which were incorporated when planting will soon be used up. It is then a good idea to mulch clematis to top up the nutrients in the soil, which in turn will revitalise our plants. Mulching is an excellent means of providing several important things for clematis. It will help to hold in moisture, provide additional feed and also shade the root system from the baking sun, all of which are equally important.

There are many different materials you can use for mulching, but the one which I consider by far the best is manure, as this will provide all three of the important aspects of mulching. Other mulches you could use are good garden compost, leaf mould or potting compost. They will not help quite as much regarding the provision of food, but will help to retain moisture and provide shade for the roots. Leaf-mould is the mulch nature provides for itself and if you are able to collect leaf sweepings in autumn, you can easily make your own. Composting leaves for a few months in a black dustbin liner works very well.

Mulching is best done during the autumn, when the soil is already moist from the autumnal rains. First of all, add a good single handful of bonemeal to the soil around the base of your clematis. Work this in using your fingers or, if you prefer, a short hand-fork. A thick layer of mulch can then be added on top to a depth of about 3in (7cm). If you use manure, do make sure it is well rotted. Also, when using manure, leave a gap of about 3in (7cm) between the clematis stems and the mulch, as manure could cause the stems to rot. Spread the mulch over an area of about twelve inches (30cm) around the stems.

When pruning in the spring, you can gently fork the mulch into the soil surrounding your clematis, at the same time adding another good single handful of bonemeal.

Mulching was referred to in Moore and Jackman's book of 1872 *The Clematis as a Garden Flower*, where they recommended annual manurings with horse or cow manure, to keep up the vigour of clematis. They also recommended a dressing of leaf-mould to be beneficial on heavy soils. This advice, although over 120 years old, is still relevant today.

We tend to think of cocoa-fibre as a modern development in the horticultural world, but Moore and Jackman suggested the fibre of the 'cocoa-nut' would be a suitable substitute where mulching with manure would be objectionable.

SUMMARY

Basic Feeding Programme
- Bonemeal at pruning time (late winter to early spring). One good single handful worked in around base of clematis
- Mulch in autumn – preferably manure

Complete Feeding Programme
- Bonemeal at pruning time
- Sulphate of potash mid to late spring
- Dead-head early large-flowered varieties and apply one or two doses of liquid feed one week apart
- Mulch in autumn – preferably manure

5

PRUNING

The main aim in pruning clematis is to make the plant tidy after the winter season, to improve its shape and overall appearance and, of course, to encourage it to display a mass of flowers.

Pruning clematis always seems to cause concern, whether the gardener is an experienced horticulturist or an amateur. Of course it does help if one can keep the name labels on the plants, or else a note of which varieties are planted where.

It is important to know the variety or type of clematis when it comes to pruning because, as with roses, the pruning method varies according to type. The secret of successful pruning is to start by planting your clematis deep. Burying some of the leaf joints below the surface of the soil will produce many more stems, ensuring in future years you will have something worthwhile to prune.

I have set out below the pruning guide that has become standard with clematis growers in recent years, that is by organizing the different clematis into pruning groups. The groups used are as follows: (1) tidy after flowering; (2) light prune; and (3) hard prune.

These are all explained in depth below. Wherever I suggest the pruning time as being late winter or early spring, bear in mind that in different areas the seasons vary greatly. In the south of England, for example, January would not be too early to begin pruning in most gardens, whereas further north pruning could well be delayed until April. Take this into account when pruning, and to a large extent allow the plants to be your guide.

PRUNING YOUNG CLEMATIS

Most clematis will grow quickly after planting, especially if they have been planted well, as previously described, and have been kept well watered. Although the plant will look wonderfully healthy above ground, however, unfortunately this rapid growth will sometimes hinder the production of a good root system. The roots of course, are the all-important part of the plant and without a strong root system the plant will invariably fail to thrive for very many years. Hence there is a need to check this rapid growth above ground in the first spring after planting. Therefore I suggest hard pruning **all** varieties of clematis after their first winter, probably

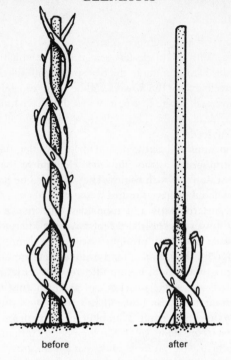

before   after

Pruning a young clematis.

during late winter or early spring. This would apply whether they are normally tidied, or lightly or hard pruned.

The technique to apply is to work up from soil level and leave at least two good sets of buds in the leaf joints, then prune off all stems just above the second set of buds. Having halted growth above the ground the plant will be encouraged to make and spread its roots, thus in future years having a strong root system to sustain vigorous growth. This hard pruning should also encourage your clematis to break new shoots from the leaf joints that were buried when planted deeply.

I have sometimes found that the 'light prune' varieties of clematis (group 2) are reluctant to grow strongly, so I have hard pruned them again in the second, and sometimes even the third spring. Eventually, with this encouragement, they will give up resisting and grow well, giving a magnificent display of flowers.

Do bear in mind one or two points regarding this initial hard prune. For example, the double-flowered varieties of clematis such as 'Vyvyan Pennell', 'Sylvia Denny' and 'Proteus' only flower double on the old ripened wood. Therefore, by pruning these varieties hard, the double flowers will have to be forfeited for this first year. Some compensation is gained though in that a good display of single flowers will be produced in the late summer. With the single-flowering varieties which are normally lightly pruned this hard pruning in the first spring will still allow them to flower equally well, except the flowers will be approximately six to eight weeks later than usual. In the first year, when they have finished flowering remove the dead heads. This will then allow the plants to grow instead of making seeds.

With the armandiis and cirrhosas and their varieties, allow them to flower in the first spring, as they flower at the end of the winter well before the new season's growth begins. They can then be hard pruned in their first year when they have finished flowering.

The alpinas, macropetalas and montanas, like the armandiis and cirrhosas, only flower on the old ripened wood. Therefore, to enjoy the flowers, leave the hard pruning until early summer when the flowers will have finished. If you hard pruned these types in late winter or early spring you would have no flowers at all the first year. Although these early-flowering varieties can make an enormous amount of growth in their first year I would still strongly recommend hard pruning if they have not made a number of stems from the base. A montana with two bare stems 4ft (1.2m) long before it branches out will look ridiculous.

With all these early-flowering clematis, namely the *armandii*, *cirrhosa*, *alpina*, *macropetala* and *montana* groups, once they have been hard pruned they will make vigorous new growth during late spring, summer and autumn. These new stems can be trained during these seasons, and the growth will then ripen during the late autumn and winter to produce flowering wood for the following spring.

GROUP 1 – TIDY AFTER FLOWERING

C. armandii, *cirrhosa*, *alpina*, *macropetala* and *montana* groups

All the very early flowering varieties of clematis flower only on their old wood. When the flowers have finished, they will produce many new shoots which, if not pruned off, will ripen over the autumn and winter to produce flowers themselves the following spring. After their initial hard prune the first spring, the new growth which is produced each year can be trained into its support and, especially in the case of montanas, the plant will grow, not only vigorously in length, but also in stem diameter, becoming very thick and heavy if left untended. All these varieties are ideal for covering up unsightly buildings, sheds, garages, barns, and so on, but the armandiis and cirrhosas require a sheltered site as these evergreen clematis will not cope with very bitter, cold winds.

When your clematis has managed to fill its allotted space, and is in danger of becoming a mess or a nuisance, then the time has come to take charge of the situation before it gets out of hand. You need to prune off all the stems that have just flowered, back to the original framework of stems which were tied into their support. This needs to be carried out immediately after flowering. While your plant is in its early years this tidying up is best done with secateurs, but when the plant has matured, this process will take far too long. The job can instead be done with a good pair of garden shears. Make sure they are really sharp before you start, as shears which have been used on hedges may not be at their best, and are likely to tear the clematis rather than cut it. As these are such strong-growing varieties, and so much growth may need removing, there is no need to be too particular about cutting each stem above a leaf joint. However, it would be unwise to become too carefree with your shears. No more is needed than a 'good haircut', to tidy up the loose tendrils. Having done this the plant will quickly sprout new shoots which can then be trained in to cover any bare patches which may have developed over the years.

Montana varieties are quite capable of lifting roof tiles and blocking guttering. If space for this type of clematis is severely restricted, try pruning down most of the wood which has flowered, in late spring. This will allow the plant to make new growth in time to ripen for flowering next spring. This type of control will be suitable for most of these varieties, but a few may not appreciate it. Only experimentation will tell you. If the plant does object it would be advisable to move it to where it can be allowed room to develop fully.

The day may come when your plant, despite years of careful regular tidying, eventually does need a drastic prune – but be careful! If the plant has some good buds and leaves to prune down to, the job will be less fraught with danger, but if there is no apparent sign of life in the old gnarled trunks, do avoid pruning into this wood.

If, by necessity, one of these varieties of clematis has to be pruned right down, give it some encouragement to re-grow by applying a mulch of well-rotted manure and plenty of water. If manure is not available, try two doses of liquid feed, followed by generous watering, and it will stand a better chance of survival.

The pruning of these varieties is very much concerned with controlling the quantity of growth. The timing is important because if pruned in late winter or early spring you would lose the flowers for that year. Do then ensure some flower buds remain on the over-wintered wood. As each year passes your experience will help you to modify your technique to gain the exact effect you desire.

GROUP 2 – LIGHT PRUNING

Early Large-Flowered – including Double-Flowered Varieties

The early large-flowered hybrids will generally begin their first flush of blooms sometime during late spring, through to mid-summer. This display can be a magnificent sight, especially if the plant has been well pruned earlier in the season.

Light pruning needs to be carried out around the end of winter or early spring, depending on the weather and on where you live.

Remember the best flowers will be produced early from the previous season's ripened wood. Therefore, if you hard pruned these varieties in the early spring, the first blooms would be lost, so pruning must leave a quantity of old but viable wood. After the initial flowers have died it is well worth dead-heading the plant to encourage new shoots to be produced during the summer. A far better second display of flowers can then be enjoyed during the late summer or early autumn. If you keep your plant well watered during the summer, with an occasional liquid feed, around once a fortnight, then the later display of flowers will be greatly improved. In the case of the double varieties, which normally flower double from the old wood in late spring and early summer, single flowers will be produced from the new wood later in the year.

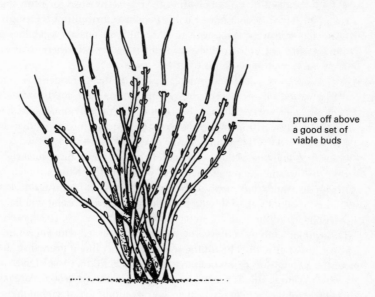

prune off above a good set of viable buds

Light pruning – group 2.

Having produced a strong base to your clematis by hard pruning the young plant in its first year, you can begin light pruning each spring. Light pruning consists mainly of removing the dead wood and making the plant tidy, but to do a really good job more is required.

When you begin pruning, first of all carefully remove all the dead material. You will be amazed at the amount of dead wood you will get off a mature clematis, so have a wheelbarrow ready! Start at the top of the plant – a step-ladder may be needed for some of the taller-growing varieties – and taking each stem in turn, trace it from the very top of the growth down to where there is a noticeably good set of buds in the leaf joints. This may be as much as 3ft (1m) back along each stem. Having reduced the height considerably and got rid of all the old dead tangled top growth, the plant will start to look better.

Continue to work down the whole plant, taking each stem in turn. You will find that each stem that produced a flower the previous year will be dead about 12–18in (30–45cm) from the tip, so, working down from each tip, prune off again just above a good set of buds. This is the part which will really test your patience. It is very often the case that having pruned one stem carefully you will later accidentally cut through it lower down! Do not despair, there is usually another set of buds you can prune down to. You may also find that however careful you are at untangling your plant, inevitably at some point a good stem will be damaged. Do not leave a damaged stem on the plant; it will be much better to prune down to a good set of buds below where the damage occurred. Having removed all the dead wood, now look to see if there are any weak, spindly stems. These will be best removed right down to soil level. This will encourage new stronger stems to grow low down.

After several years of light pruning a plant, do then consider at pruning time removing one or two of the very old stems right down, almost to soil level. This sounds drastic, but it will help ensure a continual regrowth of stems from below the soil. Having taken the plunge and pruned through an old stem, all the attached growth will then need to be removed, which is rather a tedious task to perform, but the result will be well worth it.

You may well feel inclined, having read this, to avoid buying any clematis which requires light pruning, but what I have described would be the ultimate in light pruning. Of course, this type of pruning can be adjusted to the amount of time available, but try to find time to remove the dead tangled growth from the top of the plant. If you can do no more than that, your plant will still look better than if you had ignored it completely.

The clematis in this group will also benefit from dead-heading after the first display of flowers has finished each year. This is described in Chapter 4 under 'Liquid Feeding'.

GROUP 3 – HARD PRUNING

Late Large-Flowered plus *texensis, viticellas, orientalis* and *tanguticas*

Hard pruning is more or less as previously described for young clematis, but will change slightly as your plant matures. Pruning should be carried out around late winter to early spring.

These varieties begin flowering some time after midsummer and flower at the tips of the current season's growth. This means that if the ultimate height of the plant is 8ft (2.5m), following its hard prune in the spring, the plant will grow around 8ft before flowering.

With the 'hard prune' varieties it is a good idea to prune down as hard as possible, bearing in mind these clematis normally only flower on the current season's growth. Consequently, if you fail to hard prune, the old wood will start to send shoots out from about 3–4ft (1–1.2m) off the ground. The plant will then grow another 6–12ft (2–4m) depending on variety, before it begins to flower. If the plant is not pruned again, the same thing will happen the next year, until the only local inhabitant able to enjoy the flowers will be the sparrow sitting on the guttering.

To begin hard pruning, start at soil level and work up each stem, leaving at least two good sets of buds in the leaf joints, and prune off just above the second set (see diagram below). On an old clematis make sure the buds in the leaf joints are viable. If the buds are green or a good,

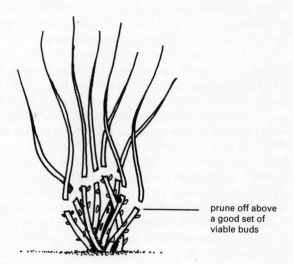

prune off above
a good set of
viable buds

Hard pruning – group 3.

healthy-looking red-brown, it should be fairly obvious. If, however, you cannot be sure of their state of health, touch the buds carefully: if they feel firm they will be viable, whereas if they feel papery or soft, they are not healthy and you will need to work further along the stem until a good set of buds is found. Take each stem in turn and prune it off and, when all the stems have been cut through, you can enjoy pulling down all the old growth, and consign it to the bonfire.

There are, as always, alternatives to the basic rules. After pruning as hard as possible for at least two or three years, you can adjust your hard pruning to get the plant to grow and flower to even better effect. If some stems are not pruned down as hard as others, the clematis will have stems of varying length – some pruned to 6, 12, 18 or 24in (15, 30, 45 or 60cm) and so on. By doing this, when the plant flowers it will produce blooms over a greater area, and give you a far better display of flowers overall.

I would suggest however, that each year you lower the stems which were not pruned so hard the previous year. This will encourage new shoots to grow from low down, so that the plant will always have new wood to replace the old.

We have in our garden a tree stump which was left after an old Christmas tree had the top and branches removed when it became an eyesore. The stump is about 8ft (2.5m) tall, and up it we have grown a C. flammula. This clematis would normally make a good 15ft (5m) a year after hard pruning. I wanted this clematis to grow to the top of the stump each year and cascade its masses of tiny white, scented blossoms down towards the ground giving the impression of a waterfall. However, because our land is very light and free-draining, and we do not have the time to water each of the 300 or more clematis in our garden, the plant fails to make the quantity of growth required if hard pruned. What I have found works well is to prune a few stems down hard to about 9–12in (20–30cm) from the ground, and the rest to about 4–5ft (1.2 to 1.5m). By doing this I am able to remove all the previous season's flowering wood, while gaining a few feet of growth to help towards my goal. This goal has been reached this past few years, proving to me that you can, by giving thought to the variety of your clematis and growing conditions, adjust your pruning to produce the overall effect you wish to achieve.

It is a good idea when growing 'Group 3' clematis (which require hard pruning) into trees, to hard prune in the first two or three years, to enable the plant to make a good number of stems low down. After this has been achieved, only hard prune down as far as the lowest set of branches on the tree. By doing this you will save yourself the trouble of having to train the clematis up the trunk of the tree each year. Once the clematis is able to grow into the branches of the tree it will wind around them and grow in the most natural way.

Last year a customer was enquiring why his clematis was not flowering. He had hard pruned it correctly and had fed and watered it well. This had me really puzzled until he explained that the fence his clematis was growing on was 6ft (2m) tall and his plant was just growing too tall. Each time the plant reached the top of the fence he pruned it 'to keep it tidy'. Of course, what he was doing each time he 'tidied' it was to remove the flowering growth. Had he instead trained the stems sideways as they grew throughout the year, or else when they reached the top of the fence, trained them back down again, the plant would have had a wonderful display of flowers. The lesson to be learnt from this is that once you have hard pruned your clematis in the spring do not prune it any more until the flowers have finished, then you can tidy it up if you feel it is necessary.

The *texensis* varieties all require hard pruning each year, although you will find that after a really mild winter there will be live buds in the leaf joints well up the plant. Prune these down to about 12–18in (30–45cm) from the ground. During very severe winter weather the old top growth will die down completely and you will have to rely on the new shoots growing from below soil to provide the flowering growth for that year. One of the species we grow in our garden dies down completely each winter. This is *C. aethusifolia*, and it always amazes me when, in late spring, it shoots again from below the soil level. Two of the most rampant varieties of clematis which require hard pruning each year are the *orientalis* and *tanguticas*. They not only grow very tall, but make very deep, dense growth, smothering anything and everything which gets in their way. I would not recommend growing either of these clematis if space is limited in the garden. However, if space is not a problem, these are enchanting plants to grow, with their hundreds of bright yellow lantern-shaped flowers displayed all summer long. These, in turn, leave a host of silvery seedheads, adored by the birds in winter. During the early years, prune these varieties really hard, down to about 12–18in (30–45cm), then after that, if space really is unlimited, prune back to the framework of old stems. This can be done quite easily with shears, especially as there is no need to prune just above a good set of buds. The *orientalis* and *tanguticas* in our garden are growing quite close to other varieties of clematis and climbing roses, therefore, because space is limited, we need to prune down very hard every year. Again, we use the shears and prune all stems down to approximately 18in (45cm). All that is left is a collection of dead sticks. After a session like this, you might think you have killed your clematis but in a few weeks its new growth will prove you wrong.

OPTIONAL PRUNING

Of course, for some of the clematis in Group 3 you could take your pick regarding hard or light pruning, depending very much on where they are growing and when you want them to flower. You may find that if they have been hard pruned, the very late flowering clematis will not make enough flowering wood to bloom before the frosts take them. Whereas if they are lightly pruned, sufficient to remove the previous season's flowering wood, you will find that the plant manages to flower a few weeks earlier, thus allowing them the chance to display their flowers before the frost brings a premature end to your enjoyment.

During the last few years I was becoming rather disillusioned with a few of the later-blooming large-flowered clematis which require hard pruning. Most of the references I have consulted regarding these clematis suggest that they should be hard pruned. There will always be one or two plants which bend the rules. I refer to clematis 'Allanah', 'John Paul II' and 'Huldine', all of which were regularly hard pruned but were reluctant to flower. I must have become so disillusioned with ours that last spring their pruning was completely overlooked. Late in August all three came into flower and were still in flower in early October. I would therefore suggest that if you have any of the late-flowering clematis that are shy of flowering, try, one spring, giving them only a light prune and wait to see what happens.

These examples show what can be achieved with a bit of extra thought before going into the attack with your secateurs.

PRUNING HERBACEOUS CLEMATIS

Integrifolias, C x eriostemon 'Hendersonii', 'Durandii', heracleifolias, jouinianas, rectas and so on

The pruning of these herbaceous varieties is very simple. They tend to grow in two different ways. the integrifolias and eriostemons die right down in winter, while 'Durandii', the heracleifolias and jouinianas, make quite woody growth and leave some good buds low down on the stem.

When you want to prune the integrifolias and eriostemons around late winter or early spring, you will find that the old flowering stems from the previous season will be completely dead. This growth can all be pruned off, as close to the ground as is practical, bearing in mind not to prune so low that you cut off the tips of the new season's shoots as they are emerging through the ground.

With the 'Durandii', heracleifolia and jouiniana you will find that the majority of the old growth will be dead wood. Start at the base of the plant and work up each stem pruning off just above the second set of leaf joints. If the clematis was planted deeply enough, the new season will see new shoots appearing from below ground.

You will find with this group of clematis, that if you are tidying herbaceous beds during the late autumn and early winter you could prune off about half the previous season's growth, leaving the final pruning until late winter or early spring. This can help to avoid damage to the base of the stems caused by severe winds tearing at the old top growth.

PRUNING CLEMATIS GROWN IN HEATHERS

Among our winter-flowering heathers we grow a mixture of 'hard prune' and 'lightly prune' clematis, but these are **all** hard pruned. Varieties which would not be suitable are the doubles, and any which only flower on the old wood, for example, the *alpina* types. Because of the hard pruning you would never have any double flowers or old ripened flowering wood.

We hard prune clematis in our heather beds, not in late winter or early spring, as would normally be done, but during late autumn. Because the clematis are dormant at this time of year, there is no need to prune off carefully above a leaf joint. The growth can be cut through with shears approximately 18in (45cm) from the soil level, then all old top growth is removed. This lets light and air in, and the heathers' flowers and foliage can be appreciated over the winter months. During late winter and early spring, when you are pruning your other clematis, check the plants which were pruned in the autumn. You should find that the clematis have healthy buds in the leaf joints at this time and you will easily be able to prune out any old wood which is not shooting.

When the heathers have finished flowering, run the shears lightly over them to remove the old flowering stems and in a few short weeks your clematis will be up and flowering again.

PREPARING FOR WINTER

During the autumn, before the weather turns wintry, inspect your clematis. If there is a great deal of very heavy top growth, which is likely to be knocked around in high winds, this could cause unnecessary damage to the plant and possibly to its support as well. Damaged stems can be a source of infection, which can also cause the stems to rot.

Whether the clematis is normally lightly or hard pruned, it is therefore a good idea to remove any large mass of tangled growth from the top of the plant. Do, however, leave alone the main stems which are tied into the support, and complete the pruning in the normal way during late winter or early spring.

MILD WINTERS – ADDITIONAL PRUNING

During a mild winter some clematis will be encouraged to put out lush new shoots far too early, long before the worst of the winter weather can be declared over. While I strongly feel the main pruning of clematis should wait until late winter or early spring, it would do no harm to 'check' this sudden surge of boisterous spring behaviour during midwinter. Simply reduce each stem which has put out a long new shoot back to a more dormant set of buds. This should help to discourage the clematis from premature growth and to preserve its strength for when spring arrives.

PRUNING UNKNOWN VARIETIES OF CLEMATIS

If you have the misfortune to lose a name label, or if you move house and inherit an unknown clematis, and therefore do not know the pruning required, give the plant a simple light prune in late winter or early spring and then sit back and wait for it to flower. A very rough guide, but one well worth remembering, is that if it begins flowering **before** the longest day then **lightly** prune it. If, on the other hand, it begins flowering **after** the longest day then in future springs **hard** prune it.

Prune and Feed

Always apply a good single handful of bonemeal when you have pruned your clematis. Work it into the soil around the base of the plant and if the spring is very dry, water it in. I would recommend that you use only bonemeal at pruning time as it works nice and slowly. Leave the other fertilizers until after the frosts have finished as you do not want to encourage too much fresh growth too early in the season.

BASIC PRUNING GUIDE

1   When planting, make sure to plant deep – bury at least two leaf joints.
2   Lightly prune – start at the top and work down.
3   Hard prune – start at the bottom and work up.
4   Feed with bonemeal.

FINAL THOUGHTS ON PRUNING

I hope this pruning guide will be of use to you and has given you confidence to experiment with your pruning techniques. If you are new to clematis growing, and pruning still seems a mystery, try starting with the hard prune varieties. This is a relatively simple procedure and should give you the confidence to try a clematis from one of the other groups.

Since our nursery has been open to the public we have found that the biggest question mark over the cultivation of clematis is the pruning. We decided, because of this, to hold clematis pruning demonstrations each spring. You will find that most specialist clematis nurseries now hold clematis pruning demonstrations in the late winter or early spring. It would be worth enquiring at your nearest specialist nursery if you are interested in seeing a demonstration − or contact the British Clematis Society, whose address is at the back of this book, and who should be able to give you the relevant details.

6

WAYS TO GROW – USING ARTIFICIAL SUPPORTS

To grow clematis in certain positions in the garden it will be necessary to provide them with some support. They will climb, but they need something to climb up or over.

The majority of clematis are climbers and will cling onto the stem, twig or branch of another plant as they do in the wild. The way they do this is to wrap their petiole (leaf-stem) around whatever is available. Unlike ivies, which can attach themselves directly on to brickwork, clematis require a support of some kind before being able to climb. Clematis will happily clothe walls, fences, screens or pergolas, providing this additional support is given for the clematis to attach itself to.

You can use clematis to cover arbours, gazebos, obelisks and arches, perhaps in conjunction with other climbing plants such as roses, honeysuckle and wisteria. They can also be grown as festoons, pillars or as standards. More than one plant of a particular variety can be grown, or several clematis of differing colours can be grown together to form a free-standing pillar of colour.

Another interesting way to grow clematis is as 'trained' ground-cover. Instead of allowing the plants to scramble freely, they are given support and trained into shape. The ideas are almost endless, but we should first look at those already suggested, in greater detail.

WALLS AND FENCES

These can be considered together, as the methods of support are applicable to both. Clematis, being unable to cling directly onto brickwork or wood, need trellis or wires around which they can wrap their leaf stems. A variety of these supports is commercially available as fancy wooden or plastic trellises, and these come in an array of shapes, sizes and designs. The wooden trellises are usually made of hardwood and will last for many years. Plastic trellis, although good at the outset will, after a few years of scorching heat in summer and freezing temperatures in winter, gradually break down. I prefer wood to plastic. The wood can quite easily be treated with a 'plant friendly' preservative, and will last a very long time. When treating wood in the garden near plants, avoid using creosote, as its fumes will quickly kill plants. For ease of transport, you can also buy trellis that expands. It can even be bought ready-shaped to cover a drain pipe!

When fitting trellis ensure that a gap of about three-quarters of an inch (2cm) or more, is left between the wall and the trellis. This will allow the clematis room to scramble up and be trained and tied in, whilst also giving the leaf stems anchorage points. Small blocks of treated wood can be fixed onto the wall to which the trellis can then be screwed. When fixing, I would recommend using screws, rather than nails, as they can more easily be removed if necessary. If the wall is colour-washed for instance, then every few years the clematis and trellis will need removing for essential maintenance to the wall. This is best done either at pruning time, when the clematis could be hard pruned, or later in the season, after the clematis has flowered, when the plant can be cut down and the trellis removed for the painting. The occasional hard prune during early autumn for this purpose will not do a clematis any harm. It may, depending on the variety, simply mean a less impressive display of blooms the following year.

Whilst ready-made hardwood trellises can be attractive, they can also be expensive. You could try making trellis, using bamboo canes, to your own design. I have seen a fan-shaped trellis made of canes and also a large, oblong design with 'windows'. Both were very attractive, making effective use of natural material.

Clematis netting is also available for use on walls and fences as support. This is usually plastic-covered wire mesh and can be bought by the yard (or the metre). This is very useful, quite cheap to buy, and comes in a range of colours, usually brown, green, or white. Care is needed to match the wire colour with the intended site: brown against a red brick wall would be fine, as would white against a pale colour-washed wall. Without this consideration the netting would detract from the beauty of the plant.

The method I prefer to use for training a clematis on a wall or fence, is simply to use nails and wire. Nails with a large head are ideal. For brick walls use masonry nails or 'vine eyes', whereas for fences, almost any large-headed nail will do. You can then train your clematis wherever you wish. Knock in a few nails, leaving about a three-quarter inch (2cm) gap between the head and the wall then, using a reel of training wire, twist the wire around the first nail to anchor it, and stretch it tightly to the next nail and twist, and so on. You can make shapes or you could train your clematis around a window or a door – there are endless possibilities. As the plant grows, if it runs out of space, knock in another nail, twist another piece of wire and the clematis will continue its growth. This is a simple and cheap method of support, which will quickly be covered by the clematis. If you do not like nails driven into the brickwork of a house, use only sufficient to support the outer edges of the plant.

When there is a low wall or fence in need of softening by clematis, its 'height' can be trained sideways to grow horizontally. With a few nails and some wire, even a rampant montana can be trained along, rather than up. Near our nursery is a low boundary wall in a front garden. In the spring the wall is completely covered with montana flowers and is a really wonderful sight. Then during the summer, the appearance of the brick-work is softened by the foliage. With the additional planting of summer-flowering varieties of clematis into the montana, the season of blooms could be extended right through the summer. The montana may not grow to 30ft (10m) in height, but it travels just as far horizontally.

SCREENS AND PERGOLAS

These are effective means of displaying clematis and providing the site is not too exposed to the wind and weather, many different types can be grown.

Usually a screen is built to hide or disguise something unsightly from the house or sitting-out area of the garden. Often these are used to hide fuel tanks, compost bins and garden storage areas, or to be used as a dividing screen between the flower and vegetable gardens.

When building a screen or pergola with wooden posts, treat the timber with wood preservative. You can buy poles ready-treated, but it is quite simple to treat them yourself. The bottom 2ft (60cm) of the upright posts is best treated with a suitable long-life preservative, as this part will be in the ground and therefore vulnerable to rotting. The rest of the pole should be treated with a 'plant friendly' product (not creosote). If your poles were ready-treated, check with the supplier what preservative was used.

Dig a hole about 18in (45cm) square and 2ft (60cm) deep, and stand the pole in the middle, wedging it with some large stones around the base or a few inches of concrete to stop the pole 'giving' in a high wind. The hole can then be filled in with a mixture of good top-soil, manure, garden compost, leaf-mould and so on, ready for planting.

The poles of our pergolas and screens are not sunk into the soil at all. To prevent rotting, each pole has been stood on a house brick and then bolted to a piece of iron from our scrap metal merchant. The iron has been driven into the ground to a depth of 2ft (60cm) leaving approximately 18in (45cm) above ground to which the pole can be bolted or wired.

This works well for our pergola because, although it stands exposed to the prevailing wind, the two long sides are bolted or wired together by the poles across the top, making it a very stable structure. However, the screens we first built in our garden were not quite so successful because of the open, windy situation in which they stand. During high winds in the first winter the screens bent over to a most precarious angle. This problem was solved by using wooden posts, driven into the ground at an angle, their base supported on a brick, with the top nailed to the top of the screen. This strengthening use of braces has now been in place for several years and has proved most effective.

Another alternative to burying the poles in the ground is to buy metal post holes. These are available from fencing suppliers and are basically metal tubes with long spikes at one end. You drive the spike into the ground and sit the pole in the tube. The pole and the metal tube can then be bolted together to make the structure more rigid.

If evergreen growth is required on a screen or pergola then the armandiis or cirrhosas are ideal for this purpose, provided the position is not open to the biting cold winds. These varieties will only flourish in a sheltered position. Where a screen or pergola is in a very exposed position and evergreen plants are required, I would recommend using ivies or evergreen honeysuckles as a base of foliage and, when they are established, to interplant with clematis for added colour. Montanas, although not evergreen, do keep their foliage for most of the winter, and only seem to shed their leaves shortly before the flowers are due. It could mean putting up with a few 'bare' weeks; this is a minor drawback set against the advantages.

Pergolas tend to be sited in the middle of gardens, rather than tucked away in sheltered areas. If the position is open and windy, avoid tender clematis and choose from the vast number of 'toughies' (those clematis which specialist growers will recommend for any aspect). From this range of clematis you can have a succession of blooms from early spring right through to early winter. Our pergola stands exposed to the south-westerly winds and some clematis planted by it have not thrived. We are now replanting using varieties that should cope better with this situation. Early and late flowerers are planted alternately, and we will endeavour to keep the stems of each from intertwining with one another, to facilitate pruning. It is not impossible to prune one clematis out of another, but it is a fiddly, time-consuming occupation requiring a great deal of patience. Many clematis do survive well in an open site, and all will flourish in a sheltered position.

ARBOURS, BOWERS AND GAZEBOS

These decorative structures are popular in many gardens, and afford numerous opportunities to grow climbing plants and form a shelter in which to sit and admire the garden. The *Oxford English Dictionary*'s definition of an arbour is: 'Bower, shady retreat with sides and roof, formed by trees or lattice-work covered with climbing plants.' All three structures comply with this definition, despite their differing romantic names.

The arbour when positioned in a sheltered part of the garden can be adorned with almost any clematis. If, however, it is situated in an open, windy site, it would be better to use the tougher clematis. In a windy aspect the plants may be required to form a windbreak, keeping the seats sheltered. For this purpose I recommend the montanas or macropetalas to form a permanent dense back-drop and then, once they are established, to inter-plant some summer-flowering clematis. This will give maximum colour and coverage to the arbour and should provide months of pleasure.

If the arbour is in a sheltered position it would be an opportunity to use any of the evergreen *armandii* varieties as the main back-drop. On mild spring days, when the sun encourages sitting out, the perfume from the clusters of flowers can be appreciated.

Using Scented Clematis

Perfume is an essential ingredient in a garden, and is particularly pleasing when scented flowers are placed near a seat. I have mentioned the scented armandiis as being suitable for a sheltered position but, for a windy aspect, try one of the scented montanas such as 'Elizabeth', 'Odorata', or wilsonii. For perfume later in the summer, try growing *C. flammula* or *C.* x *triternata* 'Rubromarginata' near a seat. *C. flammula* has clouds of tiny, white star-shaped flowers, with a very pleasant hawthorn-like fragrance. *C.* x *triternata* 'Rubromarginata' has the most wonderful almond-like perfume, and has to be my favourite amongst the scented clematis. Again, like *flammula*, it has small, white star-shaped flowers, but those of the *triternata* have deep red tips – very pretty flowers, as well as being highly scented. Further scented clematis can be identified in the alphabetical listing in Chapter 11.

An arbour covered with a mixture of perfumed clematis, fragrant old-fashioned climbing roses and honeysuckle, is my idea of a perfect place to sit and rest when the weeding is finished.

ARCHES

Arches are also splendid structures on which to display clematis. Again, scented varieties are a welcome bonus especially when the arch spans a pathway. Avoid choosing clematis of rampant growth if the arch is small or narrow. We know of a gentleman who planted 'Bill Mackenzie' to grow over a small arch. Once the clematis was established, he was unable to walk through the arch for half of the year, because the plant completely filled the gap! On the other hand 'Bill Mackenzie' would be marvellous planted against the pillar of a large arch.

Two or more different varieties of clematis can be grown together, depending on the size of the arch, and these can be selected to complement a colour scheme. A combination of white with light or dark blue such as 'Henryi' with 'H.F. Young' or 'Miss Bateman' with 'Elsa Späth' would make a pleasing spectacle when grown in tandem against an arch. Alternatively, combinations of colours can be selected through shades of pink, red or purple. If a real impact of colour is desirable at a specific time of the year, then to grow more than one plant of the same variety together would establish the effect more quickly.

My preference for an arch is to grow a highly scented climbing rose with a clematis, whose colours complement each other. Some roses have very few or no thorns, which is an asset close to a path; a few suggestions are:

Rose	Clematis
Zéphirine Drouhin (cerise pink)	vit. 'Alba Luxurians' (white) or 'John Huxtable' (white)
Kathleen Harrop (soft shell-pink)	'Elsa Späth' (deep blue) or 'Venosa Violacea' (white/purple)
Mme Alfred Carrière (pinky-white)	'H. F. Young' (blue) or 'Lasurstern' (blue)
Goldfinch (golden yellow to primrose)	vit. 'Royal Velours' (reddy-purple) or 'Jackmanii' (bluey purple)
Alister Stella Gray (yellow to creamy white)	'Etoile de Paris' (blue) or 'Madame Grangé' (reddy-purple)
Claire Jacquier (yolk-yellow)	'Gipsy Queen' (purple) or 'The President' (purple)

FESTOONS, OBELISKS, PILLARS AND POLES

Each of these gives structure to the garden, and their height readily accommodates clematis as climbers. Festoons can be used to divide the garden into smaller sections or, beside a path, as an alternative to

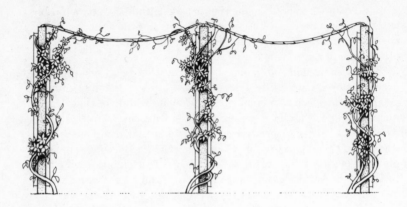

Festoons.

a pergola. Obelisks, pillars and poles, are attractive additions almost anywhere in the garden and provide tall columns of colour, in flower beds and borders. They add a new dimension to areas of low planting.

Each of these will require treated poles placed in the ground as supports.

Festoons are built using a row of poles, each 6–8ft (2–2.5m) tall, placed about 8–10ft (2.5–3m) apart. Between each pole is slung a length of sturdy rope, wire or linked chain which is allowed to hang slack. The taller growing clematis can then be trained up each pole on wires, and tied in along the chain to form garlands.

If the festoon is placed at the back of a border, the base of the poles will be discreetly hidden by other plants and you can use clematis varieties that will grow to 12–16ft (4–5m) tall. Varieties such as 'Henryi', 'Marie Boisselot', 'Mrs Cholmondeley', or 'William Kennett' would be ideal in this situation. If, however, the base of the poles is visible, plant two clematis at each pole, one taller-growing variety with one which will flower low down. A combination of 'William Kennett' with 'Miss Bateman' or 'Asao' for example, would look splendid. If you prefer hard prune varieties, try the taller-growing 'Victoria' or 'Star of India', twinned with 'Prince Charles', 'Pink Fantasy' or 'Carnaby'.

Ornate obelisks made from metal can make an impressive feature in a garden. If placed where they are likely to catch the prevailing wind, it would be advisable to cement the structures into the ground. Once in position an assortment of clematis can be grown through them. On the obelisks in our sunken garden I have used a combination of roses and clematis, trying to find complementary colours, textures and flowering seasons:

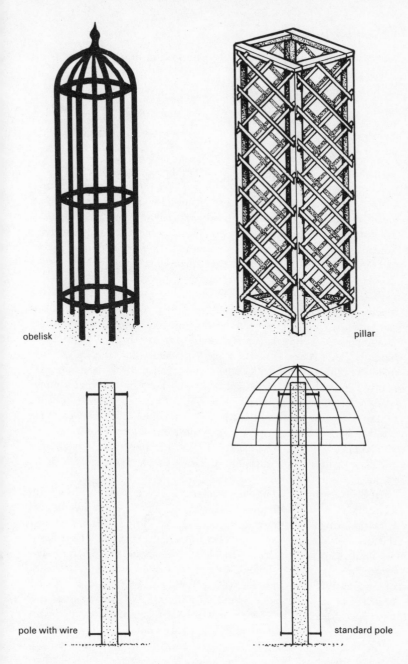

obelisk

pillar

pole with wire

standard pole

Obelisks, pillars and poles.

Clematis	Rose
'Lady Caroline Nevill' (double and single, mauve)	'Surpassing Beauty' (dark red)
'Will Goodwin' (pale blue)	'Ghislaine de Féligonde' (light orangey-yellow)
'Sylvia Denny' (double and single, white)	'Eden Rose '88' (white/lavender/pink)
'Rouge Cardinal' (dark red)	'Sombrueil' (white)

Wooden pillars can be constructed using four treated poles, and four pieces of diamond trellis measuring 6ft × 2ft (2m × 60cm). Erect the poles in a square 2ft (60cm) apart, leaving 6ft (2m) out of the ground. The trellis can then be nailed onto the poles to form a tall, square column. Before planting with clematis, fill the central square with several inches of bark chippings or gravel to prevent weed growth.

Four clematis can then be planted, one along each side. If you have a special colour scheme in that area of the garden, your choice of clematis can blend in with it. In a white border you could use *C. alpina* 'White Columbine' for spring colour, 'Arctic Queen' for early and late summer blooms, 'Edith' for mid-summer and *C. flammula* for late flowers. In a mauve or purple border, try *C. alpina* 'Helsingborg' for spring colour, and 'Lady Londesborough' or 'Louise Rowe' for early to mid-summer blooms. You could also try 'Etoile Violette' for mid to late colour, followed by 'Star of India'. For a pink or red colour scheme try *C. alpina* 'Ruby', 'Bees Jubilee', 'Crimson King' or 'Mme Edouard André' and *C. vit.* 'Rubra', or *C. vit.* 'Abundance'. Experimenting with colour schemes and planting ideas can be great fun, and it is exciting waiting for the plants to flower.

If space is limited in a bed or a border which excludes the use of anything as large as a pillar, you could instead erect a single pole to give height. Having placed the pole in position, drive in eight nails, four near the top and four close to the soil. Two-inch (5cm) nails with large heads are ideal. Knock them into the pole so that about 1in (2.5cm) is left protruding. Each top nail should be directly above a bottom nail. A piece of training wire can then be twisted tightly around the top nail and stretched down and twisted around the bottom nail. Continue to do this with the other six nails. These four wires will then provide the necessary support for the clematis to wrap its leaf stems around. (See Diagram 11.)

Another option would be to grow clematis as a standard, to form a weeping mop-head. Using a single pole, wired as previously described, to which can be added a rose trainer, which looks similar to a large upturned hanging basket. Nail this firmly to the top of the post to make a solid structure. When the clematis has climbed the wires of the pole and reached the top, the growth can be trained over and around the frame. This will allow the blooms to cascade down in a fountain of colour. Again, as with the festoons, you could use more than one variety of clematis. Choose one to give flowers low down (one of the clematis recommended for a container would be ideal) and the other could be a taller growing variety, but with the same pruning requirements (see page 57).

BEDDING OUT

Bedding out clematis was used by Victorian gardeners, over 100 years ago. Some people think of 'bedding plants' as those tender, summer-flowering salvias, alyssum and lobelia, which are not planted out until the risk of frost has passed, and are removed in early winter as the first frosts kill them off.

Clematis however can be treated differently and used as a permanent bedding display, unlike the annuals which are changed each year. Planting clematis in a flower bed without support, and allowing them to ramble where they please would be fine. There are, however, ways to make the planting much more interesting, and which will also help to give some year round colour. An island flower bed of almost any shape can be transformed this way. The use of a circular bed is shown overleaf.

To get the best from clematis in this situation some form of support is necessary to prevent their blooms lying on the bare earth and spoiling. For the design shown you will need nine wooden stakes, each 18in (45cm) long, and a reel of strong wire. Decide where you want the centre of the circle to be and drive a wooden stake into the ground. From this central stake, measure outwards aproximately 3ft (1m) and drive in another stake. Continue this with the other stakes so that they form a circle around the first peg. Each of the surrounding stakes should be driven into the ground about 9in (20cm) and leaning away slightly from the centre. The distances of the stakes from the centre and from the edge can be adjusted to suit the size of your bed. The outer pegs should not be too close to the edge of the bed. The wire can then be put in place, twisting it tightly around each stake. Start at one of the outer stakes, twisting the wire firmly around it about 2in (5cm) from the top then, stretching the wire across the bed, twist it around the central peg and then out to the one opposite the first. Do each opposite pair in turn, and then finally take the wire around all the outer stakes to make a circle of wire. By driving the stakes into the ground at an angle, leaning away from the centre of the circle, the wires

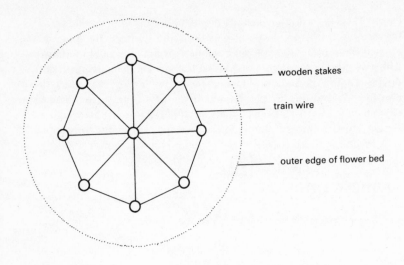

wooden stakes

train wire

outer edge of flower bed

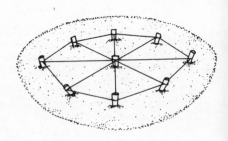

Bedding out.

can be drawn tight enough to prevent them from hanging slack, without the risk of pulling the stakes out of the ground.

This task can be completed in a few minutes. Because it involves tramping about on the soil itself, leave forking in manure and and compost until after the supports are erected and wired. Then the whole bed can be manured and forked over.

This basic structure offers scope to indulge in a range of planting ideas. Place the outer ring of stakes about 2ft (60cm) in from the edge of the bed to allow room for planting 'edging' or 'front of border' plants around the perimeter. In my plan, I have used a colour scheme based on white and various shades of blue and purple. Select the clematis first choosing four or more different varieties to match the size of bed. Clematis can be chosen from both Group 2 and Group 3 – that is, they can be light or hard prune varieties, but all will be hard pruned. By hard pruning the

Group 2 clematis, you lose the early display of flowers from the old wood, but promote a massive display of flowers in mid-summer. By doing this you will have a far greater range of colour, size and form of blooms from which to choose. Avoid choosing a double-flowered clematis which only produces double flowers on old wood, because if this is pruned away, the double flowers will be lost. There are exceptions such as: 'Arctic Queen', 'Kiri Te Kanawa' and *C. vit.* 'Purpurea Plena Elegans'; these will all flower double from new growth, and can be used in this type of planting scheme. I have selected a few varieties to give you some ideas.

Whites	Blues	Purples
Arctic Queen	Ascotiensis	Daniel Deronda
Gillian Blades	Kiri Te Kanawa	*eriost.* 'Hendersonii'
Henryi	Lasurstern	Gipsy Queen
John Huxtable	Perle d'Azur	Jackmanii
Marie Boisselot	Prince Charles	Star of India
vit. Alba Luxurians	William Kennett	*vit.* Etoile Violette

I would choose six clematis, two whites, two blues and two purples, from my suggested list. Mix large- and small-flowered varieties together and also, star- and round-shaped flowers to make a massed collage of shapes and sizes.

Whilst this planting will give a glorious display of flowers throughout the summer months, winter and spring could look rather empty when the clematis are pruned down. This is when other plants can compensate and take over.

In my design I would use one of the silver-blue grasses, the low-growing *Festuca glauca* 'Azurit' is ideal as an edging plant, but requires splitting every other year to remove dead stems. Between the grasses small groups of purple crocuses, snowdrops and grape hyacinth could be planted alternately. The grass would give year-round interest with the bulbs adding to the display during the winter and spring. Within this outer edging, plant an inner circle of dwarf lavender: 'Hidcote' makes a good, compact plant and has rich, purple flowers with a strong perfume. This planting complements the colour scheme, with its silvery-grey foliage and purple flowers – providing interest throughout the year with varying colour, shape and texture.

Having planted the outer edge of the circular bed for year-round interest, the centre of the bed could look particularly bare during the spring once the clematis have been pruned. This gives more scope for further interplanting with spring bulbs, this time perhaps using something taller, such as tulips. Lily-flowered tulips are a favourite of mine and for this colour scheme I would use 'White Triumphator'.

Other variations to this theme could include the use of box hedging or the gold and green variegated grass, *Carex* 'Evergold', which makes an unusual edging plant. Using these 'permanent' plants as edging gives structure to the whole design, and by using various bulbs, colour can be added during a season when the clematis are not in flower.

Imaginative use of artificial supports in the garden can thus provide another dimension to growing clematis. The ideas given can be adapted to suit one's own gardening style. While some are elaborate and quite expensive, others can be simple to create and not be a drain on the gardening budget, yet still achieve the desired effect. Artificial supports are in keeping with a formal gardening style, whereas for more informal planting schemes the use of natural supports for clematis are more appropriate.

7

WAYS TO GROW – USING NATURAL SUPPORTS

Having used all the hard landscaping features, the walls and fences, the pillars, posts and pergolas in the garden to support clematis and felt that the uses of these plants have been exhausted, stop and look again. Numerous opportunities still await for these under-used climbers to add their wonderful array of colourful blooms to the rest of the garden. A myriad of plants already in our gardens are crying out to be given the chance to host a clematis.

Moore and Jackman suggested in their book that clematis could be used to drape a mural ruin or to cover an unsightly bank or slope. While very few people have a 'ruin' in their garden on which to drape clematis, some readers may well have a bank or slope which could house a few clematis to great effect. Every one of us who has a garden must have some other plants through which to grow clematis. Roses, trees and tree stumps, shrubs, heathers and conifers, herbaceous beds and rockeries, are all waiting for you, the gardener, to have the necessary inspiration to transform and enhance their natural beauty.

When our modern clematis' predecessors were growing in their wild state, there was no trellis for them to climb, nor walls, arbours or festoons of rope. Instead, all they had to climb or scramble over was shrubby undergrowth, rocks and trees. In their natural habitat clematis will clamber up and drape themselves over their hosts in a most appealing fashion.

CLIMBING HOSTS

Other climbers will be enhanced by the addition of a clematis – especially if the host plant has a relatively short flowering season, or has no flowers at all, as in the case of ivies.

We have several climbing plants in our garden which are host to a clematis, they include honeysuckle, pyracantha, wisteria, solanum, ivies and roses. Each plant should be allowed to have its own share of the limelight, whilst sharing the centre stage with another great performer.

On the wall of the house, which is cream colour-washed, we grow together *C. montana* 'Freda' with a bronze-leaved honeysuckle. 'Freda' also has bronze foliage and the two together complement one another. The montana begins flowering almost before the leaves are fully open, during early spring, and flowers on almost to the beginning of summer, its cherry-red blooms showing up to good effect against the cream wall. There is then a short break before the honeysuckle begins flowering during midsummer, but it goes on flowering until early autumn.

The east wall of the house is traditional Norfolk red brick and is host to a wall-trained pyracantha. In about eight years the pyracantha grew almost to the eaves of the house and made a perfect situation in which to attempt to grow evergreen *Clematis armandii*. I say 'attempt' because our whole garden stands exposed to the elements, and this east-facing wall is the most sheltered wall of the house. *C. armandii*, being somewhat tender, prefers a more sheltered aspect in which to flourish but we decided that the pyracantha could in turn host the armandii using its own foliage to provide the clematis with some extra protection. This has worked rather well and, although I am sure, given a choice, the *C. armandii* would prefer to be growing with more protection, it has survived for several years and flowers profusely for us each spring.

Our wisteria is trained on the south wall of the house and was planted close to the brickwork before the terrace was laid around its base. In the normal way I would have preferred to plant a clematis close to the trunk of the wisteria, but in this case the terrace was in place before I had considered the possibility of using the wisteria to host another plant. True, a paving slab could have been removed to allow enough room to plant a clematis, but the problem was solved another way.

I had used three terracotta pots to display clematis on our stand at the Royal Norfolk Show. The largest pot held *C.* x *eriostemon* 'Hendersonii', the middle-sized pot contained *C.* 'Prince Charles' and the smallest held a *C. integrifolia*. After the flower show, the three pots were placed in a group on the terrace at the base of the wisteria. The vines of the two taller clematis were then allowed to clamber up into the trunks of their host. The low-growing herbaceous *C. integrifolia* was given no support and is now allowed to drape over the edge of its pot, providing a colourful display of flowers at the base of this arrangement. This makes a good planting combination, with the wisteria making a tremendous display of mauve blue flowers during the late spring and early summer. Then from midsummer through to early autumn, the clematis take over, adding their display of flowers to a plant which would otherwise be devoid of interest until its own flowering period began again the following year.

On the west wall of the house is planted a variegated solanum (potato flower) through which I grow two clematis: 'Royalty' and 'Dorothy

Tolver'. The solanum has rich purple flowers similar in shape to those of a potato, which are in bloom during the summer months. This rich colour is displayed well against the variegated foliage, which also enhances the deep purple flowers of 'Royalty', 'Royalty' is a very compact clematis which flowers low down, ideal for the solanum, but I also wanted to use a clematis to gain a bit of height in this group. For this I planted 'Dorothy Tolver' (named after my mother), a rich, deep mauve-pink, with large single flowers. The whole combination gives a pleasing effect.

In another part of the garden I have used the well-known solanum, *S. crispum* 'Glasnevin' which has purplish-blue flowers, together with the deep maroon-red climbing rose 'Guinée' and the white clematis 'Snow Queen'. This is another group of climbers which, as individuals, are beautiful, but when planted together make a stunning sight.

During 1994 we began a new piece of garden, reclaimed from the end of a paddock. It is about the size of an average terraced house's garden. We wanted this garden enclosed, behind tall hedges, so one could sit in peace and solitude, shut away from the rest of the world. In a relatively small, narrow area a large hedge would be totally impractical as it would take up most of the garden. Someone then had the idea of using ivies, grown up stock netting, to make a narrow hedge 6ft (2m) tall. This makes an almost windproof screen, providing shelter for the plants in the garden and seclusion for those seeking peace and tranquillity. One of the long sides of this ivy hedge has a grass path on the outside running its whole length. This has been a useful place to display some of the species of clematis with small flowers which would be totally lost at the back of a border and need closer inspection to appreciate their delicate charm. By growing these up through the ivies and being able to stand very close to study each individual flower, their appeal is able to captivate the onlooker. The clematis planted here are *C. tibetana vernayi* 'Ludlow & Sheriff', *C. orientalis var. orientalis, C. pitcheri, C. ladakiana, C. thibetianus* and the evergreen *C. cirrhosa*.

ROSES

For me, planting roses and clematis together is one of the best ways to display clematis. Some of my favourite roses are the old-fashioned varieties, their blooms varying from open shaggy heads, to those in tightly packed rosettes. Their colours are usually subtle shades, from creamy whites through shades of yellow, apricot and pink, to deep, almost purple reds. Even the cerise shades are not harsh, but have a gentleness which is very pleasing to the eye, and most have an exquisite, heady perfume.

Many of these old roses have a much shorter flowering season than their modern counterparts, but by interplanting them with clematis, flowers can be enjoyed in that area of the garden for a longer period.

I grow both light and hard pruning varieties of clematis with our roses and find neither are difficult when it comes to pruning. In fact, the pruning of clematis grown with roses can present a golden opportunity to the gardener who, by careful consideration, can manipulate nature to produce flowers at a desired time. The first time this happened in our garden was by sheer chance, but it made me realise there were further possibilities, simply by adjusting the pruning technique. We have a climbing rose, R. 'American Pillar' which is bright pink with a white eye, and has a rather short flowering season during late spring and early summer. For many years this rose has been host to the later-flowering purple clematis 'Gipsy Queen'. The idea of the planting was that the clematis, having been hard pruned, would be flowering during the mid to late summer after the rose had finished. However, one year, on my annual pruning pilgrimage around the garden, I had overlooked the pruning of this clematis. Because of this the clematis flowered several weeks earlier than normal, at the same time as the rose. The dark purple flowers of the clematis with the bright pink blooms of the rose made a pleasing combination. Now at pruning time the clematis, if it is not too 'leggy', gets lightly pruned to tidy it up, and will then flower with the rose. If, however, it has become an unruly mess, it is hard pruned to keep it under control, and will then flower when the rose is over.

I have planted together what might seem an odd combination of clematis with a rose. With the vigorous white rambling rose 'Bobbie James' I have planted two white clematis, the large-flowered 'Marie Boisselot' and the medium-sized flowered 'John Huxtable'. This will seem an incredible feat of pruning to perform, due to the fact that one of the clematis requires light pruning, the other hard. Having hard pruned both clematis for two years, I now only lightly prune both, sufficiently to tidy them up. The effect is rather good, the all-white combination of flowers of varying sizes from the small blooms of the rose, to the large flowers of 'Marie'.

The earlier flowering clematis which have two separate flowering periods are ideal grown with roses. We find in our garden that the early flowers of the clematis are out in bloom at the same time as the roses. When they have finished flowering both can be dead-headed which will encourage them to put on some new growth during the summer. We will then have another flush of flowers during the late summer and early autumn when both the roses and clematis are often back in flower together.

While dead-heading your roses after their early flush of flowers, it is well worth taking the time and trouble to dead-head your clematis at the same time. I appreciate this is a very time-consuming occupation, but even if you can only do some, it would improve your chances of a better display of clematis flowers later in the year.

These are some of the light prune clematis and climbing roses I grow together:

Clematis	with	Rose
Elsa Späth (deep blue)		Handel (white/pink)
Dr Ruppel – (mauve/carmine bars)		Phyllis Bide (pinky-peach)
Proteus (rosy-lilac)		Albéric Barbier (creamy-white)
Lasurstern (lavender blue)		Albertine (pink to gold)
Lady Caroline Nevill (pale mauve)		Surpassing Beauty (deep red)
Vyvyan Pennell (dark lavender)		Gloire de Dijon (buff/apricot)
Will Goodwin (light blue)		Ghislaine de Féligonde (orangey-yellow)
Sylvia Denny (white)		Eden Rose '88 (creamy-pale pink)
H. F. Young (bright to mid blue)		Felicia (pink)
Horn of Plenty (rosy mauve to blue)		Alchemist (pale orangey-yellow)

I also grow hard prune varieties of clematis with our roses. These will begin flowering during mid-summer while the roses are still in flower, and will go on flowering for many weeks through the summer and early autumn after the roses have finished. This is a good way to extend the flowering period and provide colour in that part of the garden while the roses are taking a break.

There are one or two hard prune clematis I would avoid when choosing a clematis to plant with a climbing rose. The *orientalis*, *tanguticas* and *rehderianas* for instance would completely swamp the majority of roses. The only roses which would probably stand up to their competiton would be those such as R. 'Rambling Rector', 'Kiftsgate' and 'Sir Cedric Morris'. Even with these vigorous individuals, it would, however, be wise to allow the rose a few years to establish itself first, before adding the clematis.

These are some of the hard prune clematis and climbing roses that I grow together:

Clematis	with	Rose
Perle d'Azur (azure blue)		Zéphirine Drouhin (cerise to pink)
Etoile Violette (purple)		Casino (yellow)
Venosa Violacea (white/purple)		Sophie's Perpetual (silver/cerise to pink)
Rouge Cardinal (ruby red)		Sombrueil (white)
Prince Charles (light mauve to blue)		Blairi No. 1 (pale pink)
Madame Grangé (reddy-purple)		Paul Léde (apricot pink)
John Huxtable (white)		Paul's Scarlet (scarlet red)
Warsaw Nike (purple)		Compassion-(apricot/yellow/pink)
Gipsy Queen (purple)		American Pillar (cerise pink/white)
vit. 'Rubra' (deep red)		Lady Waterlow (pinky salmon)

The planting of roses and clematis together works very well as both require similar treatment – that is, good, well-manured soil, and pruning at a similar time of year. Do not be too concerned if you find it necessary to spray the roses against black-spot or greenfly as any of the sprays available in shops should not harm your clematis.

We also have a few of the taller-growing, old-fashioned bush roses in the garden and grow clematis through those. Some of my favourite plantings are:

Clematis	with	Rose
Prince Charles (light mauve blue)		Fantin-Latour (blush pink)
'Margot Koster' (deep mauve pink)		Auguste Seebauer (rich rose pink)
Sylvia Denny (white)		Mme Isaac Pereire (purply crimson)
Margaret Hunt (dusky mauve-pink)		Gruss an Aachen (flesh pink to cream)

'Margot Koster' planted with the bush rose 'Auguste Seebauer' makes an interesting combination as the flowers are almost the same colour; the only real difference is the shape. 'Margot Koster' has open, rather gappy sepals that twist slightly as the flower opens and which, seen amongst the blooms of the rose look very pretty.

'Gruss an Aachen' is a very beautiful old bush rose of flesh pink fading to cream and is rather short to host a clematis, growing to only about 2ft (60cm) tall. We grow the clematis 'Margaret Hunt' close by this rose, scrambling across the ground. We allow just two or three stems to wind up through the rose, otherwise the poor thing would be swamped. 'Margaret Hunt' is a deep, dusky pink with medium sized blooms, whose colour enhances the flesh pink in the rose.

Although I am lucky enough to have quite a large garden, it is still not big enough to hold all the combinations of roses and clematis I would like to grow together. I hope my suggestions will inspire you to try growing these two beautiful plants together.

TREES

Trees can take on a whole new appearance when clothed with a clematis. Depending on the size of the tree, many different clematis can be used for this purpose. For example, a very large holly of about 30ft (10m) tall makes a perfect host to the scrambling pale pink montana, which makes a magnificent display of flowers during the late spring.

Leylandii is a very popular tree which, over the years, has been used extensively for hedging and windbreaks. This is probably owing to the fact that it is so quick growing. Unfortunately, unless kept tightly clipped it will eventually become far too large for the average garden. Even when kept under control, a leylandii hedge can be rather boring, so the additional planting of a clematis montana will add some colour and interest. We have used some large conifers, including the golden leylandii and 'Harlequin' as a windbreak between the garden and the nursery. Close to one of these trees stands a large oak half-barrel in which we grow six different hard prune clematis. Each year, following their pruning, they clamber up into the leylandii adding a blaze of colour during the summer months.

The ornamental cherry tree, Prunus 'Amanogawa', which has an upright habit like a column, pale pink semi-double flowers borne during late spring and leaves that turn to shades of red and orange in autumn, provides interest through two different seasons and is a bonus in any garden. Beside this tree the clematis 'Jackmanii', whose lovely purple blooms can be seen high up in the prunus during late summer, adds yet more to the visual pleasure of the garden.

We have an old plum tree which really has seen better days so it is now host to two clematis, one is the species C. tangutica and the other is

C. tritemata 'Rubromarginata'. Having hard pruned both these clematis for two or three years, I now leave them unpruned to do their own thing. By doing this we find they begin flowering early in the summer and continue until the first frosts, leaving the gorgeous fluffy seedheads the tangutica produces to be enjoyed all winter. After a few years, when they become very tatty looking, I will prune both clematis down very hard, thus allowing them a chance to rejuvenate.

When planting a clematis into a tree it is essential not to buy a variety which will outgrow and swamp the tree. A vigorous *C. montana* will only be suitable to grow into very substantial trees where a less vigorous clematis would look lost.

It is also important to improve the soil near the tree before expecting a clematis to grow in these conditions. An established tree will have drained the soil of all nutrients and moisture, so regular watering through the early years until the clematis is also established, will be essential. Further information on this aspect of growing clematis can be found in Chapter 3 under *Planting Near Mature Trees and Shrubs*.

TREE STUMPS

The remains of once proud trees can be unsightly monstrosities if left in the garden with no adornment. They provide a perfect place to grow clematis to make an attractive feature.

If you have to have a very large tree in your garden taken down it is unlikely the stump and root will be removed. This can be put to good use and covered with clematis. First of all you will need to wire the stump to provide some anchorage for the clematis. A piece of chicken or livestock netting nailed over the top would be the most convenient solution. Alternatively, hammer in a few nails around the stump and twist some training wire round each nail head. A few pieces of wire criss-crossed like this would be fine.

When a tree has been felled, it will no longer do any harm to axe through one or two of its roots if necessary, to make a large hole in which to place some manure or good soil ready for planting. Almost any clematis could be used for this, depending on the situation and your personal preferences.

SHRUBS

Shrubs in the garden each play their own part in adding height or width, different coloured foliage, berries or catkins perhaps, and most have a character of their own. While it would be wrong to take away their individuality, their appearance could be enhanced with the addition of a clematis.

Early winter is the best season for the evergreen *Garrya elliptica*, when it is 'dripping' with long, silvery, grey-green catkins, a visual treat to be enjoyed from the warmth of the house on a cold, damp day. During the summer months, when the catkins from the previous winter have long gone, the garrya is a rather boring-looking green bush. But it is a marvellous host for the tiny, bluey-white, bell-shaped flowers of the native Portuguese clematis, *C. campaniflora*, which displays its flowers during the summer. In the autumn the clematis is pruned down to about 2–3ft (60–90cm) to remove the old vines from the garrya, as I feel it would hide the beauty of the shrub's winter display. Then, during late winter or early spring when the worst of the winter weather has passed, the clematis can be pruned down to about 1ft (30cm) from the ground.

Other shrubs with winter interest such as cornus (dogwood), with its colourful bare stems of orange, red, fluorescent green and black, or the contorted hazel, *Corylus* 'contorta' whose cork-screw-like branches are seen to perfection once its leaves have been shed in autumn, all cry out to be adorned by colourful clematis during the summer. The majority of summer-flowering clematis would be successful grown through these shrubs, but I would perhaps choose a variety that requires hard pruning and is not too rampant, a *viticella* would be ideal. I have seen *C. viticella* 'Rubra' flowering in the variegated dogwood (*Cornus alba* 'Elegantissima'), the small, deep red flowers of 'Rubra' looking truly elegant amongst the white-edged grey-green leaves of the cornus. I would suggest that if you try this, you semi-hard prune the clematis when the dogwood beigns to lose its leaves in autumn. This will allow the stems of the cornus to be seen during its finest months, without the old clematis vines distracting the eye. Final pruning of the clematis can again wait until late winter or early spring.

I have also used clematis in various cotoneasters in our garden. The aim is to use a variety which will flower during a period when its host will have little to offer. An early- to mid-summer-flowering clematis would be ideal, whose display would be over by the time the cotoneaster berries were ready to take over the show. We grow a pyracantha as a freestanding shrub, which is host to a spring-flowering clematis *C. alpina* 'Ruby'; this looks fantastic during April and May when the whole shrub is hung with the pinky red bells of 'Ruby'. Unfortunately, the clematis sometimes has a second, almost equally magnificent, display of flowers in the autumn, when the berries of the pyracantha have turned orange. It looks awful! If I had used a blue or a white alpina all would have been well.

The flowering season, or period of interest, has also been extended for other shrubs as well. Our magnolia is host to the pinky red *C. viticella* 'Abundance', whose small flowers show up well against the pale foliage of the magnolia. *Pieris* 'Forest Flame' has been interplanted with 'Serenata', whose purple blooms have an almost cerise bar along the centre of each sepal; they look very attractive together during mid-summer.

Two weigelas in our garden each entertain a clematis. *Weigela florida* 'Foliis Purpureis', which has dull, purplish-green foliage, supports the large, pale silvery-pearl blooms of the clematis 'Peveril Pearl', which really helps to brighten up this rather dull shrub in summer, when its own display of flowers has finished. The variegated *Weigela florida* 'Variegata' plays host to the Polish clematis 'Warsaw Nike', whose rich, reddish-purple flowers are displayed to near perfection amongst the cream and green leaves of the weigela.

There are simply endless combinations of shrubs and clematis which you could try, but you do not have to have them spreading their periods of interest throughout the course of the year – they could be in bloom together. Our ceanothus hosts the lovely pink clematis from Japan, called 'Asao'. The large pink flowers of 'Asao' with the small, fluffy-looking blue flowers of the ceanothus make a wonderful sight together during late spring and early summer.

I hope this has inspired you to try using clematis in your shrubs. Further advice on soil preparation, and planting in shrubs can be found in Chapter 3.

HEATHERS AND CONIFERS

Beds of mixed heathers and conifers became very fashionable a few years ago and we planted three – two island beds and a bank. The tremendous variations of shapes, sizes, colours and textures of conifers is amazing and, combined with heathers for ground cover, they make very attractive features, requiring little maintenance.

Our own soil is on the limy side and is not ideal for many heathers. We have found that with the addition of some peat at planting, the winter-flowering *Erica carnea*, is the heather we can grow most successfully. The *Erica carnea*s are in flower from early winter through to the spring, when they make a wonderful display, but they have little value during the summer months. This is when clematis can take over.

We use a mixture of hard and light prune clematis amongst our heathers and conifers, but all are hard pruned during late autumn. This allows the heathers to have a spell free from clematis vines, so we can then enjoy their flowers over the winter.

There are many clematis that could be used for this purpose, but avoid choosing varieties which only flower on old ripened wood, such as the alpinas, macropetalas and montanas. Because of the need to hard prune each year, there would never be any old wood for them to flower from. Others to avoid would be the double-flowering varieties such as 'Vyvyan Pennell', which only flower double from the old wood. Their single flowers could be enjoyed, but there would never be any double blooms. One of the light prune types we grow through heathers is 'Mrs Cholmondeley'. In the normal way, with light pruning, this would begin flowering here from early summer, semi-continuously to early autumn. Having been hard pruned, 'Mrs Cholmondeley' does not begin flowering until late midsummer, but will still flower well into the autumn. Therefore, by hard pruning these clematis, the early flowers normally produced from the old growth will have to be forfeited.

The light prune (Group 2) clematis we grow successfully in heathers are 'Barbara Dibley', 'Capitaine Thuilleaux', 'Daniel Deronda', 'Dr. Ruppel', 'Guernsey Cream', 'Miss Bateman', 'Mrs Cholmondeley' and 'Richard Pennell'.

The hard prune (Group 3) clematis we use for the same purpose are C. x *eriostemon* 'Hendersonii', 'John Huxtable', 'Prince Charles', 'Pagoda', 'Rouge Cardinal', assorted texensis, 'Victoria' and various viticellas.

Much less suitable are the very rampant varieties from Group 3, such as the orientalis and tanguticas, which could completely smother heathers and conifers, causing them to brown off and develop dead patches.

Apart from the few clematis I have suggested avoiding, there are many varieties to choose from which would be suitable to enhance winter-flowering heathers during their 'dull' season. Simply allowing the clematis to scramble over the heathers and conifers, going where nature takes them, will not only provide extra colour to that part of the garden, but will allow the clematis the freedom to take on a very natural appearance.

HERBACEOUS BORDERS

Wherever they are, herbaceous borders always give me the feeling they should be surrounding an English country cottage. Even the wide herbaceous borders in the gardens of large houses and halls have that 'laid-back', country feel about them. Yet they are very often laid out with swathes of colour, all planned and organised.

How I would like to disorganise a carefully constructed border by lacing a blue clematis through a group of pink lupins! Or perhaps by allowing C. *viticella* 'Alba Luxurians' to clamber up tall blue delphiniums and hang its small white bells from those glorious towers of colour. 'Comtesse de

Bouchaud' could creep its light pink blooms through the silvery-blue ornamental thistle *Echinops ritro*. In fact, anywhere there is a gap in your herbaceous border, where a hole can be dug, try a clematis. Does it really matter about your colour scheme? If it does, then choose a clematis within your chosen colour arrangement; there are so many varieties to pick from.

As with the suggestions for clematis to grow with heathers, I would avoid those varieties only flowering from the old wood as that would limit your ability to prune and tidy, which is essential in the herbaceous border. Also, avoid the orientalis and tanguticas, which could swamp your other treasured plants.

A border would be the obvious place to grow all the herbaceous clematis, such as *C. heracleifolia, C. x eriostemon* 'Hendersonii', 'Durandii', *C. recta* and *C. integrifolia*. Perhaps at the back of the border you could grow the herbaceous *C. x jouiniana* 'Praecox' with some support. The heracleifolias can be planted mid-border to give height, and to display their clusters of hyacinth-like flowers.

Given some support, *C. recta* 'Purpurea', with its wonderful purply-bronze young foliage, makes a marvellous backdrop to other herbaceous plants. I have seen *C. recta* 'Purpurea' used to good effect behind the hardy cerise flowered *Geranium psilostemon*. I have used 'Durandii' with its rich indigo-blue flowers draped through the silver foliage of the curry plant *Helichrysum italicum*. They make a wonderful combination, especially when the curry plant flowers. Its broad clusters of bright yellow flowers held on erect stems, seem to highlight the bright yellow stamens at the centre of *Durandii*'s blooms.

The little herbaceous *C. integrifolia* could be used at the front of the border, either with a few pea-sticks for support, or left to scramble at will. 'Aljonushka', a relatively new pink herbaceous-type clematis could be put to good use growing through the blue spire-like flowers of *Caryopteris x clandonensis* which, with its silvery-grey foliage, makes an excellent border plant.

You don't have to use only the herbaceous clematis in a border; almost any clematis could be used. Any of the hard prune (Group 3) clematis would be suitable, apart from the rampant varieties already mentioned. They could all be reduced by about two-thirds during the autumnal tidying of the border plants, with their final hard prune waiting until late winter or early spring. The clematis will also appreciate the annual mulch which is usually applied to a herbaceous border in the autumn, and will reward you with a glorious display the following summer.

GROUND COVER

Many plants can come under this heading when used by gardeners not only to provide colour and foliage but also to suppress weeds. Three of the herbaceous clematis are ideal for this purpose: *C. recta*, *C. recta* 'Purpurea', and *C.* x *jouiniana* 'Praecox'. Despite the fact they all require hard pruning, they will be back in force, covering the ground by the time the weeds are becoming a problem. They will not stop the weeds altogether, but what few weeds do grow will be weakened by the lack of light under the foliage cover of the clematis and will therefore be easier to pull out. These clematis could be under-planted with daffodils and tulips, which would provide some colour while the clematis are re-growing after their pruning. The *C. jouiniana* makes a particularly attractive display of small, star-like flowers through the late summer and autumn.

ROCKERIES

Although these can be planted up with clematis, there are very few clematis I would consider trying, due to the fact that the majority simply grow too big. In a traditional rock garden, the plants are normally chosen because they are compact and low-growing which, of course, most clematis are not.

There are now, however, a few varieties available which would be ideal in rock gardens. The three I have are crosses between species from New Zealand. *C.* x *cartmanii* 'Joe' is the result of a cross between *C. marmoraria* and *C. paniculata*. *Clematis* 'Moonman' and 'Lunar Lass' are the results of a cross between *C. marata* and *C. marmoraria*. These clematis are dioecious, which means that each plant carries flowers of only one sex, hence 'Moonman' carries male flowers, while 'Lunar Lass' has female flowers.

These plants are not suitable for the 'faint-hearted' gardener to try. Because the climate in their country of origin is quite different to that in the British Isles, they will need to be grown under special conditions, lengths to which perhaps only the dedicated alpine gardener would go. On the rock garden, try growing them in a sunny, sheltered, free-draining position, whilst not allowing the plants to dry out during a drought. You will then, I hope, be successful. They strike easily from cuttings, so it would be worth taking a few to have replacement plants ready if needed.

An easy plant to try on a rockery would be one of the little *integrifolias*, although they are rather sprawling in habit, compared to those previously mentioned.

I hope that these suggestions of different ways to grow clematis, using other plants as hosts, will give you inspiration to try at least one or two. Begin by wandering around the garden during the spring, summer and autumn and discovering which plants you already have that look bare or plain in that particular season. Then, bearing in mind the aspect, and the size of the host plant, careful selection can be made for the ideal clematis to accompany that plant.

COLOUR COMBINATIONS

Careful planning can be used to produce interesting combinations, although many of the best happen by pure chance! Our variegated holly bush is host to the pink, summer-flowering clematis 'Comtesse de Bouchaud' (by design), in front of which is the old purply-cerise rose 'Mme Isaac Pereire'. The three plants together make a glorious display of colour for many weeks through the summer, the rose adding another unplanned, dimension to the effect.

In our previous garden we had the light blue *C. macropetala* growing along a 6ft (2m) tall larch lap fence, in front of which was a large *Pieris* 'Forest Flame'. During late spring the fence would be completely covered in the delightful double blue bells of the clematis, while in front, the pieris was ablaze with its orangey-red shoots of young growth – a gorgeous combination.

For anyone with a yearning to use their garden as a palette on which to paint, the use of clematis with other plants presents endless opportunities.

8

GROWING IN CONTAINERS

Unfortunately not everyone has a garden with space in which to grow and enjoy a variety of trees, shrubs and clematis. However, many people will have a small area in which a pot could stand. Whether it is on a patio or terrace, a concreted backyard or a paved courtyard, a conservatory or a balcony, or even a roof garden, a clematis will brighten up a dull spot with its colourful display.

Many clematis will do well in containers if given the right growing conditions. Some clematis will look wonderful and do well in pots, others will do well but will not look so good, and a few simply will not flourish at all. You need to be aware of all the varying needs of container cultivation to achieve success. This success will not come without time and effort.

The choice of pot or container is vital, as is the compost used. The training, support and pruning all need to be carefully considered, as do feeding and watering. When growing clematis in containers in conservatories, glasshouses or 'garden rooms', it will also be necessary to keep a watch out for pests and disease. It is essential to deal with such problems as and when they occur.

Before considering which clematis to buy for your pot, give thought to all of these aspects in turn, as they will help you to select an appropriate clematis for your needs.

CHOOSING A POT OR CONTAINER

Nowadays there is an almost endless array of decorative pots and containers available in most garden centres. To select one suitable for a clematis will require careful thought. A major factor is whether or not the pot is frost-proof. If it is to stand out all winter, this will be essential, or else it will become a very costly error!

Pots and containers come in all shapes and sizes, and are made from a wide range of materials. They vary greatly in cost, from the elegant Grecian urn to the more humble plastic pot. They can all, however, be made to look equally beautiful once plants have been added.

Oak barrels, old chimney pots, terracotta, earthenware, concrete, plastic and wood – all can make good containers for clematis provided they are large enough and have adequate drainage.

The ideal size of container or pot will be one which is at least 18in (45cm) deep, as this will allow the clematis to be planted deep, which is so essential for success. The wider the pot is the better as it will hold more compost for the plant to root into, more nutrients, and more moisture, all of which are essential if the plant is to flourish.

Oak barrels, usually found cut in half, are excellent for clematis, and can be reasonably cheap to buy from a garden centre. Check before purchasing one that it has sufficient drainage holes in the bottom. Do not be tempted to buy one which has no holes in and make them yourself – it is a very tough job to do.

Old chimney pots can look charming planted with a clematis. Check to see if a local reclamation yard has one at a suitable price. They can be very expensive, but they are of course weather-proof and can be most attractive as visual 'full-stops' in garden design.

Terracotta is a favourite with many gardeners, and comes in all shapes and sizes. I would choose a fairly traditionally shaped pot rather than the 'Ali Baba' type, as the latter can be difficult to extract a plant from when it comes to re-potting. Remember when purchasing terracotta to ask if it is frost proof. Some pots can be left to over-winter out of doors, but with others it is necessary to move the pots under cover. Our terracotta pots stand outside for most of the year, but with the onset of winter they are carefully removed by sack-barrow into a polythene tunnel where they stay until spring.

Decorative earthenware pots are readily available and are usually quite reasonably priced; again, choose one of the larger ones and check that it is frost-proof.

Many decorative plant containers are made from concrete and come in various shapes and sizes. Avoid buying a shallow trough or bowl. Instead, choose one that is at least 18in (45cm) deep – a traditional urn shape would be more suitable for a clematis.

Plastic flower pots have gradually taken over from terracotta for nursery production, largely because of the vast difference in price. If it is intended to keep several clematis in pots, this makes sense. Decorative plastic pots can now be bought in a range of sizes and colours to suit most people's needs. However, plastic containers will provide no protection for your clematis against the elements, especially in extremes of temperature. I would not recommend using a plastic pot if it is to stand roasting in the sun all day during the summer, or if it is to be exposed to the worst of the cold during the winter. If it stands in a shaded position during summer and is then moved into a glasshouse or garden shed to over-winter, then this type of pot is adequate. In fact, plastic pots can be a bonus when moving clematis in and out during the various seasons. They are so much lighter, and are less liable to break than the more expensive pots.

There are also some very good wooden plant containers available now. Again, before purchasing, check on the drainage holes as some of these containers are designed only as decoration rather than actually to plant into. With wooden planters it is necessary every now and again to treat the wood with a preservative, checking first that it is 'plant friendly' and is not creosote.

With expensive decorative plant pots it is unnecessary to plant them up permanently. Why not have one or two of these good pots, but actually grow your clematis in large plastic flower pots, and then transfer them into the decorative pots when the clematis are in flower and ready to go out on display. This aspect of growing clematis is dealt with in greater detail later in this chapter.

DRAINAGE AND COMPOST

Having selected a suitable pot, you will then need to decide what compost to use. You may prefer to mix your own using good garden compost or leaf-mould and a loamy top soil, but for most people it is easier to buy a bag of compost which is already mixed. Almost any standard potting compost will be suitable and most garden centres offer a wide range. The compost I prefer to use when potting clematis is John Innes no. 3 – a loam- rather than peat-based compost, and the extra weight will help provide the pots with better stability. Because of this loam mix the compost will pack down quite firmly in the pot, so I would suggest mixing a small bag of peat (or cocoa-fibre if you prefer) into the compost beforehand. To one twenty-five litre bag of John Innes no. 3 I would mix one ten-litre bag of peat. You will find that the peat (or substitute) will help to 'lighten' the loam and will also help to retain moisture, which would otherwise drain through the compost quite quickly.

Before filling your pot or container with compost it is essential to put a layer of broken crocks or large, flat stones into the bottom of the pot to cover the drainage holes. Without this the compost will wash down and block the holes, thus preventing essential drainage. Obviously, the holes must not be blocked completely with the crocks or stones and must allow the water to seep through. To aid drainage it is worthwhile standing the pot onto 'feet', thereby raising it off the ground. Most places which sell pots and containers also sell ornamental feet. While these look very nice, you may well already have something else which will do the same job. We have used old house bricks, which work just as well.

Having completed this preparation you can now put a layer of compost into the pot, leaving enough room to allow the clematis to be planted deep. Check the depth before taking the clematis out of its pot, making sure it can be planted 4–6in (10–15cm) deeper than it was in its original pot. Add a good single handful of bonemeal to the compost in the bottom of the pot and mix this in lightly. Now you can remove the clematis from its pot and plant it firmly into its new compost. Do not forget to remove any ties which are around the plant and which would end up below soil level. Tease out some roots to encourage them to grow into the fresh compost. I would also recommend leaving a gap of at least a half to three-quarters of an inch (1–2cm) between the top of the compost and the rim of the pot. This will allow plenty of room when watering, and will avoid compost washing out over the top. You may like to leave the compost low enough below the rim to allow a layer of gravel or stones to be added. This helps to shade the roots as well as providing a surface to break the flow of water when watering. This ensures the surface compost is not washed away, and also discourages weeds. Gravel does look attractive on the surface of the compost. You need to choose the best colour of covering material to match your container and your clematis.

SUPPORTS

There are many different ways to support and train a clematis grown in a pot, depending where and how you wish it to grow. A pot standing close to a wall or fence could have the clematis trained on wires or trellis fixed directly onto the wall. If you do decide to use this method, as always, make sure the pot is frost-proof, as it will have to stand out all winter if the clematis is attached to the wall.

A free-standing method of support is probably far more appropriate. The pot can then be moved under cover for the winter if necessary. This also allows the plant's flowering position in the garden to be changed if desired. There are many decorative free-standing supports for clematis now available.

While purpose-made suppports look attractive, a similar effect can be made using bamboo canes, which are considerably cheaper to buy. Canes can be made into fans or wigwams very easily, and will last for many years.

CHOOSING A SUITABLE CLEMATIS

When growing a clematis in a pot as a specimen plant you obviously want the very best display possible from it, so you need to choose the best variety for the situation.

Many clematis will grow well in containers, but some will look far nicer than others. Those varieties with a compact, free-flowering habit

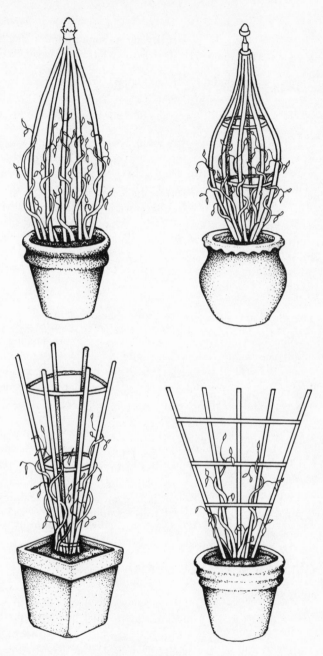

Decorative free-standing supports for pot-grown clematis.

will certainly be more pleasing to the eye than those which grow tall and 'leggy' and which would be better growing through a shrub rather than standing alone as a specimen. The clematis to avoid, which have this bare, leggy look are generally those that require hard pruning each year and make a substantial amount of growth before flowering. Varieties such as 'Ville de Lyon', 'Perle d'Azur' and 'Gipsy Queen', for instance, are lovely clematis, and would grow as well as any others in a pot, but will not look as pleasing because of their leggy habit.

The other clematis that I would avoid growing in containers because of their rampant nature are those which make an enormous amount of top growth and really do benefit from growing 'free' on the ground. Avoid therefore the *montana*s, the *armandii*s, the *orientalis* and *tanguticas*, *rehderiana*s and the *chrysocoma*s. If you are in any doubt at all when selecting a clematis to grow in a pot, ask a specialist grower who will advise you.

The ideal clematis to grow in a pot is one which has a naturally compact habit and which will flower very freely. I have selected a few of the very best clematis for containers and have listed them below, according to when they flower:

Winter to Spring-flowering   any of the *alpina*s. These will do well in almost any climate. In mild regions you could grow *C. afoliata* or any of the *cirrhosa*s outside.

Late Spring to Summer-flowering   'Anna-Louise', 'Arctic Queen', 'Asao', 'Capitaine Thuilleaux', 'Carnaby', 'Charissima', 'Corona', 'Dawn', 'Durandii', 'Elsa Späth', 'Fair Rosamond', 'Fairy Queen', 'General Sikorski', 'Gillian Blades', 'Guernsey Cream', 'Haku Ookan', 'H.F. Young', 'James Mason', 'Lady Londesborough', 'Lady Northcliffe', 'Louise Rowe', 'Maureen', 'Miss Bateman', 'Mrs P.B. Truax', 'Multi Blue', 'Peveril Pearl', 'Pink Champagne', 'Pink Fantasy', 'Proteus', 'Royalty', 'Royal Velvet', 'Snow Queen', 'Sunset', 'Twilight' and 'Veronica's Choice'.

Many of these varieties have two flowering periods and will benefit from dead-heading once the early flowers have finished. They will then give a second glorious display of blooms later in the summer. 'Durandii' will need regular tying in as it is non-clinging, but is well worth growing for its very long flowering season.

Flowering Midsummer Onwards   *C.* x *aromatica*, 'Ascotiensis', 'Comtesse de Bouchaud', 'Dorothy Walton', *C.* x *eriostemon* 'Hendersonii', 'Hagley Hybrid', 'John Huxtable', 'Madame Edouard André', 'Niobe', 'Pagoda', 'Pink Fantasy', 'Prince Charles', 'Rouge Cardinal' and 'Silver Moon'. Any of the *texensis* varieties would be suitable and almost all of the *viticella*s. However, *vit.* 'Mme Julia Correvon' is one of the best for pot cultivation. Both *C.* x *aromatica* and *C.* x *eriostemon* 'Hendersonii' will need regular tying in as they are non-clinging. 'Pink Fantasy' is ideal in a pot for both early and late flowering, depending on whether it has been lightly or hard pruned.

The little herbaceous integrifolias are super in pots. They will flower for most of the summer and will only need a relatively small pot. Following their hard prune during late winter or early spring, as they begin to grow, a few small pieces of twig can be pushed into the compost to hold the new growth upright. Otherwise you will find that once the plant is in full flower it may get top-heavy and collapse, draping over the edge of the pot. I grow integrifolia in a pot with no supports for its growth. The pot is then stood in front of the larger pots holding clematis and provides interest lower down.

Another way of growing clematis in pots is to grow two varieties together. It is essential then to have a large container. It is also advisable to select two clematis which have identical pruning requirements, for example, two hard prune or two light prune varieties. Some very pleasing colour combinations can be made, either by use of contrast, perhaps having a light with a dark colour or, alternatively, by blending two pastel shades. When selecting two clematis for a contrast in colour the effect will be less harsh if the colours complement one another. Some examples of effective combinations are given below.

'Pink Champagne' with 'Elsa Späth': the deep pink and mauve of 'Pink Champagne' contrasts with the dark blue of 'Elsa Späth', but they also complement one another with the dark, but slightly mauve blue of 'Elsa Späth' highlighting the mauve in 'Pink Champagne'.

'Gillian Blades' with 'Haku Ookan': these offer a startling contrast of white with dark purple. However, the flowers have similar star shapes. The mauve white of 'Gillian Blades' is enhanced by the dark purple sepals of 'Haku Ookan', whose crown of white stamens blends with the colour of 'Gillian Blades' sepals.

'Peveril Pearl' is a wonderful subtle mixture of pastel shades, and in different lights during the day many colours are revealed. It is a pale, silvery mauve-grey with a hint of pink in its make-up. Put 'Peveril Pearl' with a deep, rich purply-red such as 'Maureen' and the effect is beautiful.

If you prefer subtle, pastel shades together, try 'Pink Fantasy' with the light mauve-blue of 'Prince Charles', both hard pruned. Or perhaps the light pink of 'Comtesse de Bouchaud' with its seedling, the white 'John Huxtable'. These two clematis have flowers of an identical shape and size; only the colour varies.

Another interesting combination to try is the marrying of two completely different flower shapes. We grow, in two separate pots, *C.* x *eriostemon* 'Hendersonii' and 'Prince Charles' at the base of our wisteria.

Both clematis grow up through the foliage and stems of the wisteria and therefore need no separate support. As they grow their stems intertwine so that at flowering they are well mixed together. The combination of the dark blue, nodding, bell-shaped flowers of the *eriostemon*, with the open, flat, pale mauve-blue of 'Prince Charles' looks splendid.

A quite exotic look can be achieved by growing together a combination of clematis with colours that blend well, but which have flowers of different shapes. If you garden in a mild climate or can grow under cover, try pairing 'Venosa Violacea' with *C. florida* 'Sieboldii'. Their colouring is almost identical – 'Venosa Violacea' has a white centre with dark purple margins, whereas 'sieboldii' has a large crown of dark purple petaloid stamens, set off by creamy-white sepals. While their colours are the same they are displayed in reverse on the flowers. If you want to try this combination of clematis, but live in a cold climate and cannot move the pot under cover for the winter, try using several layers of garden fleece to protect the *florida* from the worst of the weather.

The joy and satisfaction derived from growing clematis in containers comes from the fascinating opportunities they offer in terms of colour, seasonal flowering performance, habit of growth and potential for companionable contrast. Selection and use is a matter of individual taste, as is always the case in gardening. It is fun, and often rewarding, to experiment.

CONSERVATORIES

Some clematis that are tender or semi-tender require the controlled cultivation of indoor protection in glasshouses, conservatories or garden rooms. These are a select band of beautiful varieties that flourish only when given the warmth and shelter from searing winds and frost that inside protection offters.

The varieties ideal for growing in pots under cover are: *C. afoliata*, *C. cirrhosa ssp. balearica*, *cirrhosa* 'Freckles' and *cirrhosa* 'Wisley Cream', *C. fasiculiflora*, *C. forsteri*, the *floridas* 'Plena' and 'Sieboldii' and the *marmoraria* types.

Pests and diseases can be a problem when growing clematis indoors. Regular watering and humidity control, foliar feeding and protection from the risk of scorching also need attention. Checking for pests and diseases can be carried out at the same time as regular watering. Flying pests can be controlled to a certain extent under glass by the use of yellow sticky fly traps. These can be bought quite cheaply from most garden centres and are simply hung up near the plants. Pests such as greenfly and whitefly are drawn to the yellow tapes and will be held fast by the glue.

Pest control is covered in detail in Chapter 10. Because the atmosphere needs to be kept humid, you may have problems with botrytis. Dispose of any leaves as they die off because, if left hanging in healthy foliage or on the compost, the botrytis spores will quickly multiply and cause the stems to rot. Botrytis can be recognised by remembering its common name – 'grey mould'.

A humid atmosphere will also help reduce the risk of infestation by red spider mite. Good ventilation is also a requirement, so windows need to be kept open as much as possible.

The need for regular liquid feeding is also greater when a clematis is confined to a pot. Using your liquid fertilizer as a foliar feed will ensure the whole plant remains in a healthy state and is therefore better able to fend off attack by pests and disease. A weak solution used once or twice a week through the spring, summer and early autumn is sufficient. Avoid the use of foliar feed when the sun is full on the plant, as this would cause severe scorching of the foliage. Spray the leaves early in the morning thus allowing them time to dry off before the sun gets too strong, or else wait until early evening when the sun is less powerful.

Strong sunlight is a problem for clematis grown under glass. Like many plants, clematis do not appreciate being baked in full sun, which is made worse by the effect of the glass. Where scorching becomes a problem pots are best stood in a sheltered position outside, or given shading inside.

Occasionally you may notice the new growing tips of the clematis dying back. The tip will go black and sometimes the top one or two sets of leaves will also be affected. This die-back is caused by stress, which in turn has been caused by extremes of climate or irregular watering. Early in the year the weather can be very hot during the day with the temperature under glass rocketing. At night the temperature plummets and can drop below freezing. The high daytime temperature encourages the clematis into lush, tender growth, which the freezing cold nights will damage. Allowing pots to dry out completely and then soaking the compost to rehydrate them, will also cause damage, particularly to the growing tip. Whilst regular watering is essential to maintain a healthy plant, do make sure the pot remains free-draining. If you are growing a potted clematis in a glasshouse, the pot will probably be standing on sand or gravel which will be free-draining. In a conservatory or garden room, however, the pot should stand in something waterproof to protect the flooring. Large plastic saucers are available, in which a layer of gravel can be placed; your clematis pot can then be stood on this and will drain freely when watered. A little water in the bottom of the saucer will help provide extra humidity, but to avoid waterlogging ensure that the bottom of the flower pot is not standing in water.

ACHIEVING A SUCCESSION OF FLOWERS

When clematis are grown in pots for a floral display, it is essential to get the longest, most spectacular display of blooms possible, both in colour and in quantity. The majority of clematis will flower for eight weeks, some for even longer, and in a relatively small display area such as a patio or terrace, the longer the flowers last, the better. There are two clematis that really do flower for many weeks, 'Durandii' and C. x *eriostemon* 'Hendersonii', both of which I grow in pots with great success. These varieties are non-clinging and also require hard pruning, so training has to be a top priority with these two each year, tying in the stems as they grow. The reward is weeks of glorious flowers throughout the summer months. Other clematis which give a long flowering season in pots are the early large-flowered hybrids which offer two periods of interest – late spring to mid-summer, and again from late summer to early autumn.

It is very satisfying to get a spectacular display of clematis blooms for as much of the year as possible within the confines of a patio. One way of achieving this is to buy just one or two expensive, large decorative pots. Instead of planting directly into these you could, as previously described, plant into cheap plastic flower pots which are almost the same size as their attractive counterparts. These planted pots can then be stood in the decorative pots when ready for display. The ideal situation would be to arrange a 'nursery area' where the clematis could be kept until almost ready to burst into bloom, whereupon they could be moved into their display position and inserted into the decorative containers. The plants could be potted, pruned, fed and trained out of sight, only to go out on view when in flower. They could then be returned to the nursery area when the blooms had finished.

By growing clematis in pots in this way, several plants can be grown, each flowering at different times of the year. The display can begin with one of the *alpina* varieties, flowering during the spring. This can be followed by one of the early large-flowered clematis which blooms in late spring to early summer. The pot can be changed again for one containing a clematis flowering in mid-summer. Finally, the early large-flowered clematis should be back in flower again for late summer and autumn when it can be put out on display again in the 'posh pot'.

So, with the help of three clematis and one decorative container, the floral display can last from early spring right through to autumn. We have tried this with great success. When a display of flowers is required in an important area of the garden, such as on a patio or terrace, it is advantageous only to see clematis which are in flower. As each finishes its display it can be changed for one about to bloom.

The changing-over of the pots is quite a simple procedure if the rim of the plastic pot is slightly higher than that of the decorative pot, as it can then be easily lifted out. We have an earthenware pot into which the plastic pot fits without leaving any rim to get hold of, causing us considerable problems when it comes to changing the plants over – it takes two of us to do the job. The plant and pots are very carefully placed on their sides on the ground. Then, with the aid of a cane pushed up into a drainage hole, the inner pot can be gently pushed out. The other person can take some of the weight by holding the plant and its framework, and can help to ease the two pots apart. This makes the task seem quite a problem, but it is really quite simple and well worth the effort.

To achieve a really spectacular display of potted clematis requires time, effort and dedication, but many people will find it an interesting challenge at least to try one pot of clematis.

If you are short on time, and have space for only one pot, for maximum colour and minimum effort use half an oak barrel and plant together three clematis with identical pruning, perhaps 'Carnaby', 'Durandii' and one of the *texensis* varieties. This should provide flowers from late spring through to autumn. Around the base of these clematis you could plant a few tulips, and as they finish flowering they could be removed to be replaced by a few summer bedding plants.

Plantings such as these will provide colour for many months, and yet will not require too much time other than that taken to prune, train, water and feed.

WATERING AND FEEDING

When keeping a clematis permanently confined to a pot, watering and feeding need to be kept up. It is wise to check your plant most days during the spring, summer and autumn to see if it needs water. In the spring your clematis will be growing rapidly, and attention needs to be paid most days to training and tying in the new growth, therefore, the need for water can also be assessed. During a really hot spell in summer, particularly if your pot or container stands in the sun, watering will need to be carried out every day. In the autumn, however, because the plant is not making fresh growth, the need for water will be reduced. It will still need to be checked regularly to prevent it from drying out.

During the winter, if the container is left outside, there will probably be no need to water, but if it is standing where it is sheltered from the rain, make certain it does not dry out.

Clematis need a great deal of water for most of the year, but resent standing saturated. When checking the need for water, if the top of the compost looks dry, and feels dry just below the surface, then water is urgently required. The amount needed will depend on the size of container, the type of clematis, the weather conditions, and when it was last watered. It is always safer to water little and often rather than allowing the pot to dry out completely and then flooding it. Once compost has been allowed to dry out it takes some time and effort before it will again retain moisture. During very hot weather it would be better to water a little every day, or even a twice a day.

Feeding a pot-grown clematis is essential to maintain the plant in a healthy, free-flowering state. Because its roots are confined to a relatively small area, they are unable to search for further nourishment as they would be able to if planted in open ground. Therefore, additional feed must be provided.

Early in the growing season start the feeding programme at pruning time, during late winter and early spring. This will consist of one good single handful of bonemeal lightly worked into the soil. When the clematis has been in the pot for about two years, I would suggest removing the top 1–2in (2.5–5cm) of compost from the pot. Bonemeal can then be added and worked into the soil around the roots and the pot can be topped up with fresh compost, which should then be watered in.

As soon as the weather has improved in the spring and the risk of severe late frost has passed, then liquid feeding can begin. Obviously, a clematis kept in a pot has to be watered, so the addition of liquid feed is quite simple. The liquid feeds I would recommend are Phostrogen or one of the tomato feeds – those which have a high potash content are best. (For further information on feeds refer to Chapter 4.) The feed can be diluted in the watering can and simply watered in. Avoid applying liquid feed if the pot has dried out, as this could damage the roots of the plant. Therefore, make sure the soil is slightly moist before applying liquid nutrients.

I would recommend using liquid feed once a fortnight if using it at full strength (as recommended on the packet or bottle.) Beware of overfeeding, which promotes lush foliage, but few flowers. Alternatively, the feed can be applied weekly at half the recommended dosage.

It is advisable not to use liquid feed at full strength once the buds have really fattened up ready to flower, or while the plant is in bloom. This is because the feed will continue to speed up performance and the flowers will be over and finished too quickly. However, a weak dose of liquid feed will cause no harm. Liquid feeding needs to be stopped early in the autumn to allow the plant a natural period of dormancy.

An alternative to liquid feeding container-grown clematis is to use a slow-release fertilizer. This can be bought in the form of thimble-sized plugs, using the recommended number for the volume of the container.

These are simple to use and can save time, and ensure that the plant receives the essential nutrients.

PRUNING AND TRAINING

Clematis grown in pots and containers require thoughtful pruning and training. This will allow the plants to grow and flower to their full potential, thus rewarding the gardener for his time and effort.

Clematis in containers are generally pruned as they would be if they were in the open garden (*see* Chapter 5). All clematis (including the spring-flowering *alpina*s, pruned after their first flowering) are hard pruned the first year after planting, to encourage a strong root system and a generous supply of shoots from below soil level. This treatment gets the plants off to a good start, with a sound network of vines low down. Subsequent pruning (from the second year) is done as recommended for the clematis group classification.

To recap on pruning: **Hard Prune** – starting at soil level, work up each stem checking for healthy, viable buds in the leaf joints. Leave at least two good sets of buds and prune off immediately above the second set. **Light Prune** – starting at the top of the plant, work down each stem, pruning off immediately above a good set of buds, then completely remove dead or weak stems.

With experience, however, this basic pruning can be modified so that you can dictate the time at which you wish your clematis to flower. The examples below explain how to achieve this:

The early-flowering large-flowered hybrids, such as 'H. F. Young' and 'Nelly Moser', normally have two periods of flowering: late spring to midsummer and again in late summer to early autumn. By altering the pruning of these you can change their flowering times. If you wish them to have a mass of flowers from midsummer through to early autumn, hard prune them during late winter or early spring. This will delay the flowering for some weeks. Instead of them having the early flush of flowers from the old wood, they will put all their vigour into providing one glorious display in late summer from the current season's growth.

If, however, you prefer to keep with the traditional double-flowering periods of these clematis, but find they are growing too tall for the support in the pot, then, when carrying out the spring pruning, cut them down lower than usual, to about 3ft (1m). This will allow the clematis to retain some old wood to produce an early display of flowers. Once these first flowers have died, it is worthwhile dead-heading the plant. This, with the addition of some liquid feed, will encourage the clematis to put on sufficient new growth to provide an equally good display of flowers later in summer.

With the varieties of clematis which require hard pruning, those that normally flower from midsummer onwards, the blooms can be delayed by a few weeks with additional pruning. Following their hard prune during late winter or early spring, they will begin to grow. Allow the young stems to make about 6–9in (15–22cm) of growth then nip out the tips just above a leaf joint, which will encourage the stem to branch out again. Do this once only during the spring, otherwise the clematis will not have time to make flowering wood, and bloom before the autumn frosts halt its progress. All our clematis which are pot-grown for display at flower shows are pruned in this way.

Following their initial hard prune in their first spring, the light prune varieties of clematis should be trained to build a good framework of stems. This is done by tying in the vines as they grow, in a horizontal manner, gradually training them in a spiral around their support. Garden twine or plastic-covered wires can be used as ties, although the metal split-rings designed for sweet peas are quick and easy to use. This early training is most important and its effect should last for many years.

The hard prune varieties will need training each year as they grow. When training these carefully, on a weekly basis in the spring, you will realise just how much new growth they can produce in a short time.

PREPARING POTS FOR OVER-WINTERING

Sometimes, having enjoyed a fine display from our flowering pots and containers during the summer, we neglect their care during the autumn and winter. It is worth giving them some attention at this time, in the hope they will repay you the following year.

To allow your clematis a period of dormancy, stop applying liquid feed early in the autumn. As the weeks progress and the weather deteriorates, necessary action will need to be taken to avoid disasters during inclement weather. If your container is exposed to severe wind and weather conditions, it would be advisable to secure it, to prevent it from blowing over, or to move it to a sheltered position. This could be by a window in a garage or garden shed or, best of all, in a cold glasshouse.

Where a pot has to be left out all winter, measures can be taken to protect it where it stands.

A small single handful of bonemeal worked into the soil and lightly watered in will give the clematis some slow-acting feed to sustain it throughout the winter. A mulch can then be applied to help insulate the plant from the worst of the cold – this could be peat, leaf-mould or garden compost. Or you could use bracken, or perhaps a few pieces of conifer, such as leylandii, with the stems pushed into the soil around the edge of the pot and the tops bent over towards the clematis to form a blanket. It is worth sprinkling a few slug pellets on to the soil prior to this, as slugs and snails might well find this an ideal spot to over-winter.

If, during the summer, your clematis has made a large amount of heavy top growth, cut some of this back to its support, thus pruning off the excess growth which could cause wind resistance. The pot will then be less likely to topple over if caught in a gale.

If you are growing one of the tender varieties of clematis in a pot, such as *C. afoliata*, or one of the floridas, and are unable to move it under cover for the winter, I recommend you use some form of effective protection for your plant, unless you enjoy a mild winter climate. Plastic bubble-wrap, used for packaging, is ideal for insulation and can be wrapped around the plant and fastened with string. In recent years garden fleece has become a popular method of giving plants winter protection. It is readily available and sold by the metre. Fleece reminds me of muslin, being a very fine, white material that can be wrapped around the plant, using two or three layers. The ends can then be fastened together with clothes pegs.

Whichever method you use to over-winter your pots, whether it is inside or out, do check the plants periodically to see if they need watering.

In the late winter or early spring the protective cover will have to be removed, to allow access for pruning, and then replaced until the weather has improved. As the days lengthen and warm up, the fleece or bubble plastic can be removed by day and replaced in the evenings if frost is forecast.

RE-POTTING

The need to re-pot a clematis is inevitable as, after a few years, the plant will become pot-bound. The frequency of re-potting will depend on the size of the pot being used. The larger the pot, the less often re-potting will be needed.

You will find that, given ideal conditions and treatment, your clematis will remain healthy for several years. There will, however, come a time when, despite all the care given to it, the plant will look sick and the vigour will be gone. The flowers too may be smaller than they once were and the whole plant will lack its former glory, thus signalling the need for re-potting.

Pruning time affords opportunity to check if the plant is pot-bound. When removing the top layer of soil, ready to top-dress with bonemeal and fresh compost, you can see whether the root growth has extended to the sides of the pot. If the roots are tightly packed against the sides, then the time has come to re-pot. This usually involves moving the plant into a larger container, but when a large pot is used in the first instance, it becomes difficult to re-pot into an even larger container. You therefore need to know how to use the same one again.

Pruning time is the best time to re-pot a clematis, as the plant will still be in a dormant state, ready to burst into growth as the weather improves. Unlike pruning, which can be carried out regardless of the weather, it would be better to re-pot a clematis during a milder spell. Avoid re-potting while the pot and compost are frozen.

This can be a tricky operation to perform and may require two pairs of hands. The first thing to do is to prune the clematis down to a manageable height. There is no need to check for viable buds in the leaf joints, as the final pruning will be done when the re-potting has been completed. Prune off all stems at approximately 2½–3ft (80–90cm) above the soil level and remove the old top growth. When removing the trellis or canes, remember to cut through any petioles (leaf stalks) attached to the lower part of your plant, and remove any ties that remain in place, because if the canes are pulled straight out, the stems in the pot may be damaged and may become a source of infection by the fungus which causes clematis wilt. The entire operation needs to be performed very carefully in order to avoid damage to the stems.

Having reduced the height of the plant, the next step is to remove it from its pot. This is a difficult process due to the size and weight of the pot, plant and compost. Prior to re-potting, the plant should be left unwatered and sheltered from any rain for about a month. This will not do the plant any harm at this time of year but will allow the compost and roots to dry out slightly, which should then allow it to be removed from the pot more easily. To ease the roots away from the sides of the pot, you will need to use an old carving knife, a stiff, metal rule or similar aid. This can be run around the inside edge of the pot to loosen the roots and compost.

Now comes the very tricky stage when the root-ball has to be removed from the pot. You will find it easier to lay the container on its side and, with the aid of a small hand fork, ease the plant out. If the pot cannot be laid down, slide a border fork down between the pot and the root-ball and prise the plant out of its container. Another pair of hands will come in useful to steady the pot, or to use a second fork. Do not be tempted to pull the plant out by its stems as irreparable damage could very easily be caused.

Having removed the plant from the pot, you need to prepare the root-ball for re-potting. This will involve cutting the roots down to allow room for extra compost to be added. Taking a sharp border spade, a small

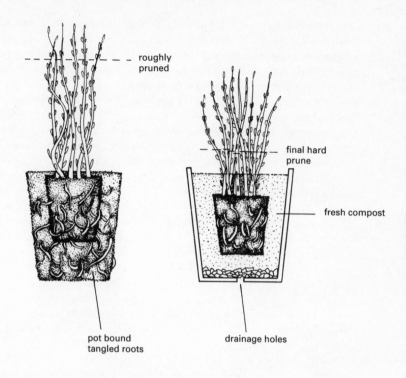

Reducing the root-ball to re-pot in the original container.

hand saw, or possibly an old carving knife, gradually slice down the sides of the root-ball, and cut off about 1–2in (2.5–5cm) of roots from the outer edges. Now lay the root ball on its side and cut off its bottom third. When performing this task for the first time, only remove a relatively small amount of root, just sufficient to add some fresh compost. Having satisfied yourself that this method works, on later occasions you can be more severe! Once you have reduced the mass of roots, the remaining root-ball can be re-potted into the original container as there will now be room to add fresh compost. Before doing so, clean out the container, replacing the crock or stones over the drainage holes. Fresh compost can be of a similar type to that used when first potting the plant, but this time add a double handful of bonemeal to the compost and mix well. Put a layer of compost into the bottom of the pot and test the depth using the plant, bearing in mind the plant needs re-potting 2–3in (5–7cm) deeper than it was originally. This should now be possible, because the root-ball has been reduced in depth. Having established the right depth, fill in with compost around the root-ball, firming it as you go. Allow a gap near the rim of the pot for watering and water well, thus allowing the compost to settle around the roots.

Having completed the task of re-potting, give the clematis a final prune. The initial prune was only a rough one, to make the clematis easier to handle. Now a good, hard prune is needed, leaving only two sets of leaf-joints with viable buds above the soil. The supports can then be replaced and within a few weeks the clematis will be back in full growth.

Growing clematis in containers can be very rewarding, especially if one does not have a garden in which to grow a large number of plants. We have one customer who lives in a tower block of flats and manages to grow clematis in pots on his balcony. This proves how little space you need to grow these lovely climbers.

9

PROPAGATION

Propagating clematis is, of course, a necessary task for the nurseryman to perform, but it can also be an enjoyable challenge for the keen gardener.

There are four ways to propagate clematis: by division, layering, cuttings and seed. The first three will provide you with a new plant identical in every respect to its parent. The fourth method will provide a new plant which has similar characteristics to its parent, but is not identical. Tissue culture has also been tried commercially, but so far it does not seem to have proved successful in the reproduction of clematis.

Cuttings are the only commercially viable means a nurseryman has to reproduce clematis in a large enough quantity for the market. Layering would take far too long, and a great deal of space would be needed, while division would not be viable due to the vast number of stock plants required. Because nurseries are generally reproducing hybrid clematis, the need to propagate them vegatatively is essential. The possibility of cross-pollination means that seed from hybrid clematis would not be identical to the parent plants. Therefore, calling young seedlings by their parents' hybrid names would be totally incorrect.

For the keen gardener, any of these methods of propagation would be suitable as only a relatively small number of plants are needed.

Hybridizing and growing clematis from seed provides a fascinating pastime. The excitement felt when one's offspring finally flowers far outweighs the disappointment of not always being able to produce a masterpiece. When one is eventually created, the thrill of having this reproduced by the thousand, and grown and loved by gardeners makes all the time and effort involved well worthwhile.

For most, though, the satisfaction of being able to produce just one new plant to pass on to a friend will be reward enough.

LAYERING

This method of propagation is simple and reliable, and when only a few new plants are needed it is the most satisfactory method of propagation. In fact, layering could not be simpler for, having prepared the vine, nature does the rest, apart from keeping it watered during a dry spell.

Layering is quite a slow process and can take about a year. Because of this and the amount of space needed to layer many stems, this method of propagation is not commercially viable for nurserymen to use.

The best time of year to attempt layering a clematis is during late spring and early summer, just as the weather and soil begin to warm up.

Method

First of all, select a good, strong stem at the side of your clematis plant which can be carefully untangled from the rest of the plant. This stem will be drawn down towards the ground very carefully, so as not to crack it. It can then be pegged down into the soil while remaining attached to the parent plant. If the clematis you wish to layer is normally hard pruned during late winter or early spring, when pruning, leave unpruned one or two stems which will be suitable for layering. Then, in the late spring these stems can be layered. Bear in mind that where the stem is going to come down, the soil will need preparing in readiness to accept it. This can be done in two ways: the stem can be pegged either direct into the ground or into a compost-filled flower pot which has been sunk into the ground.

When pegging directly into the ground, make a shallow trench about 3in (7cm) deep along where the stem will lie. Then fill this with cutting compost or, if your soil is in good condition, mix a little peat with the soil taken from the trench. Then add several handfuls of grit or sharp sand, mix well and replace in the trench. This open, gritty compost will be ideal for the layer to root into. If the trench is made long enough it will be possible to 'layer' as many as four or five joints.

You may however prefer to use flower pots for your layering. This method has the advantage that once the young plants are well rooted, they are already potted up. I would suggest using 4in (10cm) pots for this, and to use as many pots as you have good leaf joints available. To ensure success it is always worth doing two or three, even if only one plant is required. Fill each pot with cutting compost and then sink it into the ground where the leaf joint can be pegged into it.

Now the procedure will be the same whether pegging direct into the ground or into pots. Each leaf joint to be layered should have a ½in (1cm) cut made in it to aid rooting, as the stem will be quite woody and unlikely to produce roots without encouragement. With a very sharp knife, starting ½in (1cm) below the leaf joint, make an angled cut up towards the joint, on the underside of the stem. The cut and joint should then be dusted with hormone rooting powder. The prepared stem can then be buried, making sure that the prepared joint is about ¾–1in (2cm) below the surface of the compost and is pegged in place with a piece of stiff wire. If you wish to make more than one layer, repeat this procedure along the

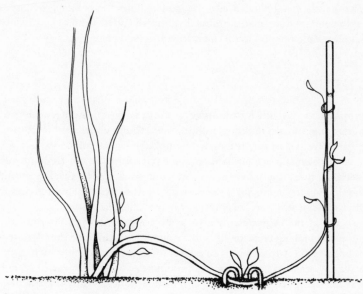

Layering.

stem at each leaf joint. The growing tip of the stem will be too soft to use and will not root, so at the last joint layered, insert a short cane or stick into the ground. The top 18in (45cm) or so of stem can then be tied up this, rather than being left lying on the soil.

The most important thing now is to water well and not let the 'layers' dry out – a regular check will ensure this does not happen. The layers will not require feeding while they are still attached to the parent plant. As always, the parent will provide food for its young!

Be aware that where the soil has been disturbed in the garden, might be considered an 'interesting spot' for a cat to dig. If this becomes a problem, the easy solution is to cover the area with a piece of chicken or livestock netting, bent over to form a small tunnel.

About a year later check to see if you have had success. Gently brush away the compost so that the wire peg can be removed and carefully give the stem a gentle tug. If the young plant stays firm it is well rooted. If, however, it yields but the leaf and joint remain healthy-looking, it is worth replacing the peg and compost leaving it in place for a few more weeks. When it is rooted, you can cut the old stem off the parent plant and insert each of the rooted stem sections, if they were layered direct into the ground, into 4in (10cm) pots.

Keep your young plants in their pots for a further year to eighteen months to allow them a chance to establish a strong root system of their own before being planted into the garden. The method for growing on and pruning young plants is described under *Potting Up Cuttings*, below. Use the same method to produce young layered plants.

CUTTINGS

Propagating clematis by means of cuttings is the method favoured by nurserymen. It is certainly the only commercially viable method to propagate hybrid clematis, as they would not come true from seed.

Many clematis cuttings strike quite easily, some within three to four weeks. Others are reluctant to send out roots and may take several months before doing so. There are a few varieties which seem almost impossible to strike and defy even wily nurserymen.

Some of the easiest clematis to strike are the montanas. If you have never tried taking clematis cuttings before, these would be the ideal ones to begin with. The best time to take cuttings from clematis grown in the garden is between late spring and midsummer when the growth is fresh and has not yet ripened into a woody state. Nurseries usually grow their stock plants under cover, which ensures that cutting material is ready earlier in the season. Once the first cuttings have been taken the plants will grow on quickly and will probably produce enough material for a second batch of cuttings to be taken. In England, nurseries usually take cuttings between April and August, a much longer season than would be possible from garden cutting material.

Preparation

Prepare the compost in pots or seed trays before removing the cutting material from the plant. Once the stem has been cut it is essential to prepare the cuttings, and get them into moist compost without delay. If there has to be a delay, the vines should be placed in a large, damp polythene bag which should then be sealed, avoiding damage to the stems! Alternatively, they can be laid in a tray and covered over with a damp cloth or newspaper. However, this is only a temporary measure and the cutting material will deteriorate quickly.

Ready-mixed cutting compost usually consists of equal proportions of peat and grit or sharp sand. If you are mixing your own compost you can change the proportions to whatever suits your needs best, but it is always better to have more grit and less peat, thus keeping the structure of the compost open.

The pots or seed trays should be filled level with compost and then firmed down and watered. It is then a good idea to put a thin layer of grit or sharp sand on top of the compost, bringing it level with the top of the pot or tray. This will prevent the risk of the leaf on the cutting touching the damp compost. The grit dries out more quickly than the compost underneath and thus prevents leaves rotting.

Having prepared the pots or trays in advance, you can now take the cuttings.

Softwood Cuttings

These are the most common type taken. The clematis stem should be in a strong state of growth and semi-ripe. It is better to avoid using the new soft growing tip, or the vine which is changing colour from green to brown, as this will be too ripe. This strong growth will feel firm to the touch, not soft nor woody. You must avoid using damaged stems as they will simply rot off very quickly and be wasted. Avoid too, using leaf joints which have sent out flowering stems, because they will have no viable buds in the leaf-joints from which the new plant can grow.

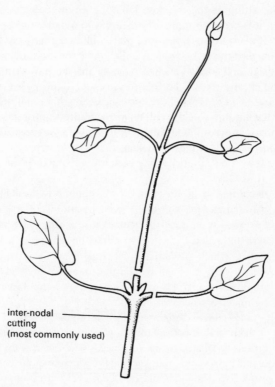

inter-nodal
cutting
(most commonly used)

Inter-nodal cuttings.

Having selected a good vine, cut it from the plant and take it to a bench which is out of the strong sunlight to prepare the cuttings. It is best to use a very sharp penknife, Stanley knife or razor blade to prepare the cuttings. Scissors should be avoided as they will not make a clean enough cut.

The majority of clematis cuttings are taken inter-nodal. This involves cutting through the stem immediately above a leaf joint (node), being careful not to damage the joint itself. The second cut is made approximately 1½in (3cm) below the leaf joint. One set of leaves should be removed from the leaf joint, and the other set reduced to one or two good leaflets. This will prevent the leaf losing too much moisture through transpiration. Only healthy leaves should be left on the cutting, as a damaged leaf could be the source of infection by Botrytis fungus, which will cause rotting. The bottom ½in (1cm) of the cutting can then be dipped into hormone rooting powder which will improve the chances of the cuttings striking. There are many hormone rooting powders available; we use one which is recommended for hardwood cuttings, which suits clematis cuttings very well. Gently shake off any excess powder and then place the cuttings in the compost. Do not push the stem directly into the compost; it is better to make a hole first with a narrow piece of cane or the like. If many cuttings are to be placed in a seed tray, put the stem of the cutting into the compost at an angle so that the leaf is held erect in the air (see diagram below). This will avoid having the leaves lying on top of one another, and air will be able to circulate. This in turn will help to avoid disease and the risk of the cuttings rotting. You will find it helpful to spray the cuttings weekly with fungicide to prevent rot. If you notice a leaf rotting, remove it immediately, again to avoid the spread of infection. When only a few cuttings are taken, they can be arranged around the edge of a flower pot, thus allowing each leaf to hang over the edge of the pot.

Once all cuttings are in the compost, the pot or tray should be carefully labelled, watered and placed on a bench or window sill out of full sun. The ideal condition for striking clematis is a warm, moist atmosphere.

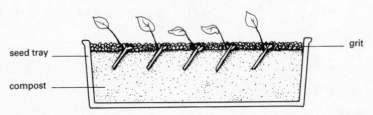

Placing cuttings in a seed tray.

A small plant propagator is therefore useful, or a glass-house bench with heating cables underneath. On an open glass-house bench conditions will probably not be humid enough, so try making a small polythene tunnel over the bench with stiff wire hoops and a sheet of polythene or bubble-wrap. Our propagating bench is designed like this: The bench itself has a layer of sand on it which is kept at about 20°C by heating cables. Every few hours during the day, the polythene cover is removed and the leaves of the cuttings are lightly sprayed with water. This, along with the bottom heat, keeps the cuttings warm and moist, while the polythene cover keeps the atmosphere humid. During very hot, sunny weather the cuttings may need damping several times a day. They should not be drenched in water from a watering can, but with a fine mist from a hand-held garden sprayer. On sunny days, when there is the risk of scorching, make sure the cuttings are provided with some shade.

After about three weeks test to see whether the cuttings have struck. Gently pull the cutting: if it moves easily it has not rooted, but if there is resistance the roots have begun forming. Leave for another week or two, after which if you hold up the pot or tray you may find roots beginning to grow through the drainage holes. The tray of cuttings should then be removed from the propagator and placed in the open, but shaded glass-

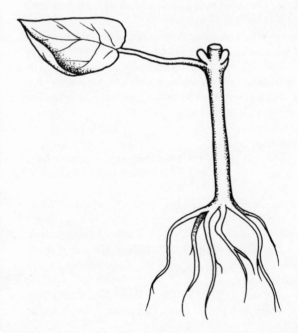

Rooted cutting.

house, to sit for about one month before potting. This period allows the roots to increase and become stronger to withstand the disturbance of potting-up.

Hardwood Cuttings

Hardwood cuttings are taken during the winter while the parent plant is in a dormant state. Not all clematis propagate successfully from hardwood cuttings, and certainly the hybrids are better taken from softwood.

Those which have proved successful are the montanas, evergreen armandiis, and the herbaceous jouinianas. Because the armandiis are evergreen they have no real dormant period and their cuttings, like the deciduous montanas, can be taken almost year round. *C. armandii* and its varieties can however be quite difficult to root. They will form a callus at the base of the cutting but will not send out any roots. With this particular clematis it is worth trying both hard, and softwood cuttings at different times of the year.

Hardwood cuttings will need to be taken inter-nodal, as described for softwoods, but, to encourage rooting, a small sliver of the bark about ½in (1cm) long should be taken off the stem at the base of the cutting. The compost, rooting powder and method of placing the cuttings into a pot or tray remains the same as for softwoods, although the cuttings can be placed into the compost vertically, rather than at an angle, if they have no leaves.

Heating a propagator bench in a glass-house during the winter can be expensive, and it is not essential to provide heat for hardwood cuttings, but they may take all winter to strike without any artificial heat. The cuttings should be kept damp rather than very wet, and there is no need to keep them misted as you would the softwood cuttings which were in full leaf.

Double-Noded Cuttings

These are used for a few varieties of clematis with hollow stems which, because of their structure, will not strike from the more normal inter-nodal cutting.

You will find when cutting through the stems of clematis such as *C. flammula, C. recta* and *C. heracleifolia* that the stems are hollow. Select a stem, and cut through it immediately above a leaf-joint (node), then, moving down the stem, cut immediately **below** the next joint. The cutting will then consist of a piece of stem perhaps 4–6in (10–15cm) long, with a node at the top and one at the bottom. Remove the leaves from the bottom node, dip the end of the cutting into hormone rooting powder and place it in a deep pot of compost as before.

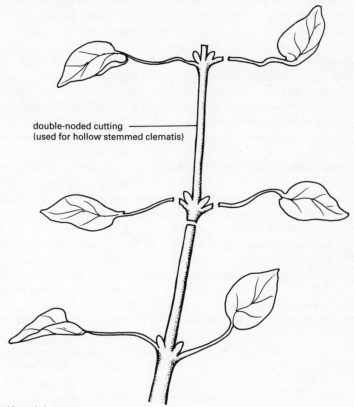

double-noded cutting
(used for hollow stemmed clematis)

Double-noded cuttings.

POTTING UP CUTTINGS

Potting up cuttings is a task which needs care. Loosen the compost in the cuttings tray so the roots can be eased out gently without having to pull them. The plants at this stage are quite fragile and all parts of the cuttings and roots can be easily damaged. They can be potted directly into two-litre pots, or into small, 3in (7cm) pots to grow on if preferred. Either way, use a good potting compost with slow-release fertilizer, and bury each cutting so that the leaf-joint (node) is about a ¼in (0.5cm) below the surface of the compost. This will encourage the young plant to shoot from the leaf-joint and grow on strongly.

As they grow the young plants will need pruning down at least twice to encourage a strong root system to form. When the plant has made about

12in (30cm) of growth, prune it down to just above the first set of leaves above the compost. This should make the leaf-joints break into growth and send out more fresh stems. Allow the plant to make another 12–18in (30–45cm) of growth, then prune again, this time to just above the second set of leaves. At this stage, if you originally potted into a 3in (7cm) pot, the young plant should be re-potted into a two-litre pot. When re-potting, place the young plant into its new pot so that the first leaf joint is covered with compost. This will encourage the buried joint to shoot out yet again whenever the plant is pruned.

QUICK CUTTINGS GUIDE

1   Cuttings compost equal proportions of peat and grit.
2   Level off compost in pot or tray, firm down and water.
3   Layer of grit on top of compost.
4   Internodal cuttings, remove one leaf. (Hardwoods – chip bark.)
5   Hormone powder.
6   Place cuttings in compost at an angle.
7   Water.
8   Bottom heat at 20°C.
9   Shade and keep humid (mist spray).

DIVISION

Division is a most successful way of propagating herbaceous clump-forming clematis where only a few new plants are required. *C. eriostemon* 'Hendersonii', and the varieties of heracleifolia, integrifolia, jouiniana and recta can all be divided, the best time being from late winter to mid-spring when the ground is frost-free.

After growing these herbaceous clematis for several years they will have made quite large clumps of growth and, if split up, each division will form another plant.

To prepare the plant for division prune the clematis in the normal way, and lift the plant out of the ground with a fork. The clump can then be divided using either a sharp spade or old carving knife to cut the plant into three or four pieces, or using two garden forks placed back to back, pushing down into the centre of the clump and prising it apart. The two resulting clumps can then each be divided once again.

Each divided piece will make a new plant provided it has some roots, and either new shoots or some old stems with viable buds, from which to grow.

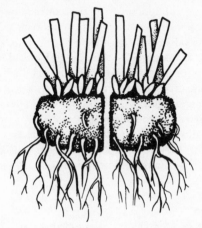

Division.

These new plants can then be re-planted straight into the garden, or potted up if required. Whichever you do, the young plants must be kept watered until re-established.

HYBRIDIZING

Clematis hybridizing has proved to be a fascinating challenge for professional nurserymen and amateur gardeners alike for the last 150 years.

George Jackman was among the first Englishmen to achieve success in hybridizing clematis, and it was largely due to him that we have so many varieties today. His book *The Clematis as a Garden Flower*, written jointly with Thomas Moore and published in 1872, spread the word about the genus, tempting others to grow and propagate these versatile plants.

Today's hybridizers have to meet the challenge of not only producing more and better flowers, but also of producing stronger, healthier, and more compact plants for modern, smaller gardens. This task has been undertaken by many nurserymen, and we are seeing some exceptional new clematis hybrids commercially available.

If you are a gardener who enjoys a horticultural challenge, and who has plenty of space together with abundant patience, then hybridizing can be rewarding. Remember, however, that you will have to produce hundreds of clematis plants before finding one worthy of naming and marketing! And these plants, as previously stated, demand much time and space to nurture effectively. This is no undertaking for the faint-hearted, since you must be prepared to abandon ruthlessly hundreds of your infant plants.

If you decide to go ahead with the challenge, have a specific target in mind. For instance, a good, double red clematis may be your aim, and with this intent you will need to select appropriate parents, perhaps 'Sylvia Denny', a good, strong, healthy, double white, crossed with a compact, floriferous red, such as 'Niobe'. Or perhaps a double light blue is to be sought, by crossing 'Sylvia Denny' with 'H. F. Young'. Always select as parents clematis that have the assets of strong, healthy growth, and which produce numerous, well-shaped flowers. These characteristics should then be passed on to the offspring.

Be prepared for disappointments, for few hybridizers actually achieve what they set out for, and the excitement of seeing your seedling flower can take what seems like eternity; in fact it is usually around three to four years.

Technique to Apply

Wait until the buds of your chosen parent clematis are almost ready to open into flower, and catch them before they do, otherwise nature may take over and pollination could be initiated by bees or insects. Having selected nice, fat flower buds, decide which variety is to be the 'seed' parent and which the 'pollen' parent. To prepare the 'seed' parent, carefully remove the sepals and then the anthers, which contain the pollen. By removing the anthers you will prevent the seed parent from pollinating itself. To do this use either a very sharp knife or fine-tipped sharp scissors. The central stigma of the pistil must be left to receive the pollen. A polythene bag should then be put over the prepared head and tied in place to prevent pollination from an unwanted source. The 'pollen' parent must also be prepared in advance to prevent insects from depositing unwanted pollen from another variety onto the anthers. For this it is only necessary to remove the sepals, then cover with a polythene bag tied below the flower head.

After a few days the stigma of the 'seed' parent will be ready to pollinate, having become shiny and covered with a sticky fluid. When the 'seed' parent is ready, the polythene bags can be removed and the 'pollen' parent flower cut from its plant. Gently brush the two heads together, so that the pollen is transferred from the anthers of one plant to the stigma of the other. Having completed this process, replace the polythene bag to prevent additional unwanted pollination. Tie it below the seedhead, not too tightly, but so as to allow a small breathing space between the stem and the polythene to prevent a build-up of condensation. Attach a label to the head with the names of the clematis parents and the date pollinated. Once the pollen is placed on the stigma, it moves down the style to the ovary where fertilization takes place and the seed is produced.

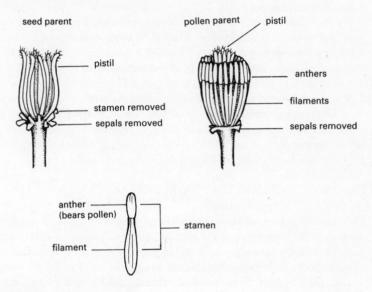

Hybridizing – preparing the blooms.

In order to be certain that the pollen and stigma are both at the right stage of development and ready for pollination, it is wise to repeat the procedure. The same 'pollen' parent flower can be used if it has been saved, or another flower from the same plant which has also been covered earlier as described above. The second pollination should be a few days after the first, with the 'seed' parent flower being covered between times.

Leave the bag in place for two to three weeks until the flower has died naturally and can then be removed without any concern that stray pollen from another clematis would cause further cross-pollination. Make sure the stem of the developing seedhead is labelled.

The seedhead can then be left to develop and ripen. This can take three to four months, or longer, before the seed can be collected. The seed is ripe when it turns brown, and when the individual seeds break away from the head if touched.

Late-flowering clematis will not set seed late in the year in the garden. Therefore, if you wish to hybridize any of these clematis it would be more successful to grow them in pots in a glass-house to encourage them to flower earlier. The seeds will then have a chance to ripen before the onset of winter.

When crossing clematis that have different flowering periods (one may be an early flowerer and one a late flowerer, for example), the pollen from the early flowerer can be kept in a labelled airtight container in the refrigerator until required.

If you decide to make several crosses, it is useful not only to label the 'seed' parent at the time of pollination, but also to keep a log of crossings, recording dates and other details. When the time comes to pot up the resulting seedlings, each one can be given a number so that a complete record of their history can be kept for future reference.

Whatever the modern hybridizers manage to achieve is often outclassed by nature, which by itself can produce masterpieces. Certainly, many new varieties nowadays have come not just from the hybridizers, but as chance seedlings.

GROWING CLEMATIS FROM SEED

This method of propagating clematis can be an interesting and rewarding pastime. It is more of a hobby than a profitable means of producing clematis. Usually the only time a nurseryman raises clematis from seed is when a specific hybridizing programme is underway.

Seed from species clematis will germinate quickly and easily when given ideal conditions, the offspring produced being similar but not necessarily identical to the parent plant. In the wild, literally thousands of seeds will fall to the ground from one clematis, but only a few will develop into plants. This natural method of reproduction will also happen in our gardens. It is worthwhile keeping a close watch when weeding around the base of your clematis, for seedlings may well be growing there. The seedlings that a hybrid clematis will produce in the garden could have been produced by self-pollination or pollen could have been transferred by insects from another clematis growing nearby. When this happens, the identity of the 'pollen' parent will not be known, unlike in controlled hybridization where both 'seed' and 'pollen' parents have been selected for their best attributes.

Seed from hybrid clematis is often sown in the hope of discovering a unique variety worthy of naming and marketing. Many hundreds of seedlings can be produced (each one will be unique), but unfortunately the chances of producing one of commercial interest is minimal. When the hybrid seedlings begin to flower, the producer, who has lovingly tended these plants for three or four years, must reluctantly discard the majority. Success comes from the one special plant found lurking among the seedlings.

Clematis seeds must be allowed to ripen on the plant. This ripening will take place during the summer and autumn, and the seedheads must be watched closely so that collection can take place before they drop

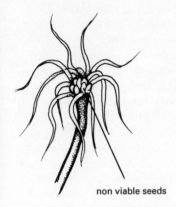

non viable seeds

viable seeds

Clematis seedheads.

naturally. As the seeds ripen the seedhead changes colour from green through to brown, and in the case of the species clematis, from silver to brown. The styles, or tails, of each seed of the species clematis will become feathery, while hybrid seeds will have a slightly hairy appearance. Not all the seeds on each seedhead will be viable; only those that have swollen achenes (bodies) have been pollinated and will germinate (see diagram above).

The seeds are best collected on a warm sunny day when they have dried off naturally. They can then be sown immediately, or stored in paper bags in a cool, dry place. If it is necessary to collect seeds on a damp day and they are not to be sown immediately, spread them out on a sheet of newspaper in a warm place, away from direct heat, to allow them to dry before storage. Avoid storing damp seeds as they will quickly go mouldy. Seeds should also be dried slowly so that they retain a certain amount of moisture to allow them to germinate.

When storing seeds, label the bag or container for it is only too easy to forget which plant they were from, and seeds look very similar. If seeds need to be stored long term they can be kept sealed in a polythene bag in a refrigerator for up to one year. Do not store seed longer than this, or freeze them, as they will be unlikely to germinate.

Before sowing or storage, the styles (tails) can be removed, although this is not absolutely necessary and can be fiddly. If you do wish to remove the style from a seed, cut it off, making sure you do not cut into the achene.

When sowing the seed, depending on the quantity to be sown, you could use either a flower pot or a half- or full-size seed tray. This should be filled with seed compost, which can be purchased ready-mixed, or you could mix your own. We use a compost containing 50 per cent peat and 50 per cent grit or sharp sand. The compost should be lightly firmed down and watered. Once it has drained the seeds can be sprinkled over it. They should then be covered with a fine layer of compost, or grit or sharp sand, which will prevent moss growing on top of the compost.

For successful germination ensure the compost never dries out; on the other hand it should not be regularly saturated. Place the tray or pot in a situation where it will be free-draining – the open nature of the gritty compost will then prevent waterlogging. Keeping the compost slightly moist is ideal.

Germination will take place more quickly if some form of heat is available; a propagator kept at 15–20°C is useful, although not essential. Seeds will germinate well if kept in a cold glass-house or cold-frame but they will simply take a little longer. The seeds will also germinate on a window sill in the house.

Do not cover the pot or tray with a sheet of glass or polythene, often mistakenly considered necessary, but allow air to circulate which stops mould growing and the seeds rotting. There is no need either to use any feed until the seedlings are growing on as the seed itself contains all the feed necessary for germination.

Once the seeds have germinated, keep direct sunlight off the seedlings, otherwise their tender growth will scorch. On the other hand, do not keep them completely shaded as this could cause the young plants to grow up weak and spindly. Ensure there is adequate ventilation.

You will find that many of the species clematis germinate in a few weeks. Seeds which germinate quickly have a very thin shell protecting the inner seed. The thicker and larger this casing is, the longer the seed will take to germinate, as is the case with many hybrid clematis. *C. campaniflora*, although a species, has relatively large seeds and takes about a year to germinate.

Seeds can germinate more quickly if they are collected and stored in a refrigerator over winter, and sown the following spring. These seeds will often germinate before those which were sown fresh the previous autumn.

Generally, seeds from the large-flowered hybrid clematis will take longer to germinate than those from the species. They can however sprout very erratically, perhaps only one or two in the first year but, if left alone, more seeds will germinate during the next year, or even the next two years. Never be too eager to throw away a tray of seed assuming it has failed; keep it for at least two years before giving up.

Transplant the seedlings when they are large enough to handle, but not before they have made at least one pair of leaves. They should ideally go into 3in (7.5cm) pots in a standard potting compost, and be kept shaded from direct sunlight for three or four days.

You will find that having been transplanted the seedlings will grow very quickly. They will need pruning down at least twice before allowing them to go on to flower. This encourages the young plant to produce a strong root system. At this stage fertilizer can be used, either a slow-release one mixed into the compost, or a half-strength liquid feed applied once a week.

Allow each seedling to make 12in (30cm) of growth and then prune it to just above the first set of leaves. This pruning should encourage the node to 'break' so that two stems will be produced. Allow the plant to grow another 12–18in (30–45cm), then prune it again above the second set of leaves. As the plant begins to make fresh growth this time it can be potted up into a two-litre pot where it can stay until it has flowered.

Overall, this is a long process, from hybridizing and collecting seed in the first year, sowing and germinating in the second, transplanting and growing on in the third year and, finally, flowering in the fourth year. Do not be too disappointed with the quality of the plants' first flowers, as they can sometimes take until their second or third flowering before producing their 'true' blooms.

When labelling your seedlings, particularly if they are to be passed on to others, it is important to label them correctly. For example, take the label 'Seedling from "Nelly Moser" ': it would be wrong to label it as 'Nelly Moser' if it was produced by cross-pollination. The only clematis entitled to be called by a specific hybrid name would be one that had been vegetatively propagated.

The excitement and anticipation this all creates, despite the work involved, is reward enough. But if you do produce a masterpiece, fame can be yours with the naming of the new variety!

When considering the naming of a new variety, it is important to ensure the name chosen will not be changed without the raiser's approval. To avoid this possibility there is an international register into which any new variety can be added. This is one of the areas where the British Clematis Society can be of help to the keen amateur. The address for the Society can be found at the back of this book.

Many gardeners find that they are able to propagate plants from their own gardens. Clematis are among the slightly more difficult category, but are by no means impossible to do this with. You may discover you have 'the knack' to produce more of your favourite varieties to pass on to your gardening friends.

10

PESTS AND DISEASES

CLEMATIS WILT

Wilt is probably the best known disease to affect clematis, which are generally fairly trouble-free plants, compared to many we struggle to grow. This problem began back in the late 1800s when hybridizers were using three large-flowered species in their hybridization programmes. These were *C. florida*, introduced from Japan by Thunberg during the late 1700s; *C. patens*, introduced in the early 1830s from Japan by Von Siebold; and *C. lanuginosa*, which was introduced from China by Robert Fortune in 1851. *C. lanuginosa* was considered by the early hybridizers as being probably the best large-flowered species, and was therefore widely used in their hybridization programmes. It is now thought, however, that *C.lanuginosa* was the 'rogue' of the three, being susceptible to attack by the wilt fungus.

By the late 1800s, clematis wilt had become such problem that hybridizing had virtually stopped. Wilt had so affected the stock of clematis around the world that research was being carried out to try and find the cause and, it was hoped, a cure for the condition.

There were various theories as to the cause of clematis wilt, such as bursting of the cells through excessive moisture, or injury from frost; too much water, nourishment or heat; and over-propagation. During the early part of this century, the majority of clematis were produced by grafting, and this was considered as a possible cause of the infection entering the plant. However, we still have clematis wilt as a thorn in our sides today, despite the fact that nurserymen very rarely, if ever, graft clematis as a method of propagation.

In America in 1915 the fungus *Ascochyta clematidina* was first recorded as being the cause of stem-rot and leaf-spot in clematis. These findings were not confirmed for fifty years but, in 1965, British researchers agreed that this same fungus was the one responsible for causing clematis wilt.

The small-flowered species clematis and the late-flowering hybrids we now grow are almost immune to clematis wilt and seem better able to defend themselves against attack by fungi. It is thought likely, though, that the same fungi can infect them, only without such devastating results. The varieties which seem rather more prone to wilt are the early large-flowered hybrids which take their characteristics from *C. lanuginosa*, some varieties appearing more susceptible to attack than others.

Modern research has identified a second fungus which can cause clematis wilt, *Coniothyrium clematidis-rectae*. Both this and the previously mentioned fungus *Ascochyta clematidina* are thought to be activated by particular conditions of temperature and humidity. This is possibly why, some years there seems to be hardly any clematis wilt, and other years the problem can be more of a nuisance. The rise in temperature and humidity in the British Isles is usually at its peak during May, and this is when we are most likely to witness a case of clematis wilt. Of course, this is also a time when the plant is bursting forth in the full surge of growth, preparing itself for flowering following its winter dormancy. This rush of sap puts the clematis in a very vulnerable position at a time when the weather conditions are especially favourable to the fungi.

How to Identify Clematis Wilt

As I have said, the most likely time of year for an attack of wilt will probably be during mid- to late spring. Unfortunately, this is the time of year when our early large-flowered hybrid clematis are budding up in preparation for their spectacular display of flowers. All will appear well until one day, quite suddenly, one or more of the clematis stems will droop, or you may notice the flower buds drooping their heads, or that the new growing tips are sadly hanging limp instead of being in their normal erect state. The whole plant will look as though it has been starved of water. Before immediately blaming the problem on clematis wilt, do check to see whether the problem might have been caused by something else. Severing of the stems by a quietly guilty 'strimmer driver', or possibly an attack by snails or mice, who occasionally enjoy a clematis stem to chew through, may be the cause. However, once these possibilities have been eliminated you can take appropriate action. It may be possible to detect a lesion, caused by the fungus, around the affected stems. This could be at a leaf joint or on the stem somewhere between two leaf joints. It can be above or below the soil. Each affected stem must be pruned out, below the lesion. If the whole plant is affected, or you cannot trace the point of infection, then the whole plant will need to be pruned down. It would then be advisable, if possible, to burn the resulting waste material as this will help to reduce the spread of infection. Having done this, I would strongly advise the use of a systemic fungicide to kill off the fungi. Mix the solution, as recommended by the manufacturer, in a hand sprayer or watering can and drench any remaining foliage and stems to a height of 18in (45cm) above the soil, plus the surrounding earth, to a diameter of approximately 18in (45cm). The spores of these fungi lurk in the soil, so drenching the soil is essential. I would suggest then that, having bought the fungicide, it would be a good idea to repeat this procedure at weekly intervals for at least two more drenchings. Being a systemic fungicide, the roots will take it up to the remaining stems and foliage.

Having done this, you can be quite confident that your plant will be well on the road to recovery. This is where deep planting comes in useful. When planting was discussed, above, I strongly advised that some of the leaf joints are buried below soil level when planting. An attack of wilt is one of those situations where, following the loss of all top growth, the clematis will almost always re-shoot from these buried nodes. After drenching the clematis, wait for several weeks before assuming it has died completely, as the buried nodes can take weeks, sometimes even months, before showing their new shoots above ground. If, having patiently waited for perhaps a year, the worst has happened and your clematis does not recover, and you decide to replant a clematis in that same position then, firstly, try to choose a clematis less susceptible to wilt, perhaps a viticella cultivar, or one of the species clematis.

Secondly, it would be advisable to change the soil. A cube 2ft (60cm) square and deep needs to be removed and replaced, either with topsoil from elsewhere in the garden, or with manure (as described in Chapter 3), or a sack of loam-based compost. Thirdly, having planted your new clematis, I would recommend watering it in with a solution of systemic fungicide. This is a real 'belt and braces' job, but one which is well worth trying. Clematis wilt usually only affects quite young plants; it seems that once a clematis has been in the ground for some years the stems become quite woody and less susceptible to attack. Clematis plants in nursery production very rarely suffer from wilt, possibly due to the necessary occasional use of fungicides.

Putting wilt into perspective, there are around 300 clematis in our garden and there is only one which has wilted in both the last two years. Early this spring we decided to try giving the offending plant a drench **before** it wilted and, sure enough, this year it has put on a huge display of early flowers, with no sign of wilt! Perhaps its stems have become woody enough to ward off the fungi, or perhaps it was the drench.

With a little forethought it may be possible to protect your clematis against wilt. For example, it is a good idea when purchasing a plant to check the stems, making sure there are no damaged areas above the soil where the fungi could enter. Another point to bear in mind is that if you leave a lot of heavy top growth on your clematis over the winter this will catch the wind and, in rocking back and forth, will cause damage to the stems lower down, thus providing another possible site of entry for the fungus. It would therefore be advisable to check your clematis before the onset of any autumnal gales and carry out a quick, light pruning to tidy the growth back to its support. Further pruning should wait until early spring.

With the help of modern fungicides and specialist nurseries offering advice on planting and after-care, clematis are once again a popular garden plant, with today's gardeners not needing to worry about 'the dreaded wilt'.

SNAILS

Slugs and snails can also cause damage to your plants' stems. These pests can cause tremendous problems if their numbers are not kept under control. Following a very wet winter and spring there is often a population explosion of snails, not just the little ones, but the really enormous snails which wreak havoc in the garden. Here, in the Eastern Counties of Britain, which are quite dry, we are normally fortunate not to suffer too badly from problems with snails. However, when we do have a wet winter, our clematis suffer from attack by snails during the following spring. After their winter hibernation they emerge hungry and go into the attack. We have a sunken garden laid out with clipped box hedging. In the centre of each 'knot' is an obelisk with a climbing rose and clematis growing together. Unfortunately, snails seem to adore living in box hedging and when they come out at night they do their best to annihilate our clematis. I first noticed the problem in late spring when, at a quick glance, the symptoms were identical to clematis wilt. The plants, which were full in bud and had been growing vigorously, were hanging their heads down and all the foliage was limp. Not every stem was affected; just the odd one or two on each plant, which led me to think the problem may be caused by wilt. When I came to prune down the affected stems, as part of my wilt treatment, I noticed the telltale signs that snails had been the cause of our problem. The bark on each of the affected stems had been stripped off up to a height of about 18in (45cm) above soil level. Instead of the stems being their normal dark brown, you could see the paler, beige inner wood of the stems. This stripping of the bark was enough to cause the stems to collapse. Snails are partial to any part of a clematis!

SLUGS

Slugs in a clematis garden can be as big a menace as snails. They are as partial to a diet of clematis as their close relative, the snail, but seem much to prefer the tender young shoots of the hard prune varieties as these begin to sprout forth during the spring.

If you have problems with either slugs or snails in your garden there are one or two different courses of action you can take. First of all, prune out the damaged stems, the damage will usually go right down to soil level. Next you will have to take measures to control the pests. Being a somewhat squeamish gardener I have never readily taken to squashing pests – until this year. If you cannot bear to do this, then slug pellets may be the answer. These will kill both slugs and snails, and should be sprinkled around the base of your clematis. It is best that the site is then regularly checked first thing each morning so that the dead slugs and snails can be collected up and disposed of carefully, thus preventing them from being eaten by birds and hedgehogs as, of course, they will be poisonous.

The suggested use of concrete slabs or roof tiles to shade the root systems of clematis will provide a perfect refuge for slugs and snails, so these should be checked regularly, and the offending beasts removed, and slug pellets should be sprinkled underneath them.

Biological control has been a fairly recent introduction regarding the destruction of slugs, and involves introducing a microscopic nematode, by mixing it in water and watering it onto the soil. Probably because it is relatively new, the price for this method of control is rather high, although a single application is meant to last for six weeks.

There are one or two cheaper methods of controlling slugs and snails, without the use of chemicals, which have been adopted over the years by some people. They often involve a night raid, armed with torch and bucket.

I do feel strongly that we should all make an effort to use less chemicals where possible. We should be looking more to encouraging natural predators into our gardens, which will help to alleviate the worst of our problems.

Birds adore slugs and snails; thrushes particularly enjoy cracking open snail shells on large stones. Hedgehogs are another 'garden friendly' animal to have around, as they, too, enjoy feasting on slugs and snails.

Despite being absolutely terrified of frogs and toads, I must admit that these are some of the most useful pest controllers around. Many people have a pond in their garden, and to introduce some frog or toad spawn from a friend's pond could be one of the best moves ever made. It will be only a short while before your slug population has decreased noticeably.

Another slug and snail deterrent which I have heard is successful, but have not tried myself, is the use of very sharp sand or grit placed around the base of each clematis. Apparently, these pests do not enjoy sliding over something sharp and will move off elsewhere. This means, however, that the other plants in your garden will be more vulnerable as a result.

EARWIGS

These are creatures of the night; they prefer to sleep hidden in cracks and crevices by day, to emerge with a voracious appetite as dusk falls.

The damage they cause is similar to that of slugs and snails, in that they will attack the leaves and new shoots of clematis. They also enjoy flowers and flower buds.

Earwigs tend not to be a big problem early in the year but, as summer progresses, especially if we have a very dry summer, their numbers seem to increase tenfold. Dahlia growers will sympathize with clematarians as earwigs are equally fond of these wonderful border plants. So, later in the summer, if you discover holes in the leaves and flowers of your clematis but can find no pest munching happily, I would be almost certain the culprits were earwigs. You may also find that the fat flower buds have had their tips and centres completely eaten away, even down to their stamens, which the earwigs find delicious.

Again you have two choices of pest control: the use of chemicals, or a 'green', environmentally friendly method. If you decide to try the 'green' method, one which has been favoured by dahlia growers for many a year is the 'up-turned flower pot'. This will require a bamboo cane or stick, a flower pot and some hay or straw. The idea is to stuff the hay or straw into the flower pot. (If you cannot get hold of hay or straw, newspaper will do just as well.) Up-turn the filled pot on top of the cane and stick this in the ground close to your clematis. This needs to be checked every morning by carefully removing the 'stuffing' which should contain some earwigs. Then all you need to do is dispose of the earwigs and the stuffing material. Of course, this procedure will need to be repeated each day. I must add that it really does work.

Another environmentally friendly method to try is one which involves soaking mint in just enough boiling water to cover it, in a large container. Allow this to ferment for a few days and then add two gallons of cold water, strain off the liquid and spray this over your plants. Try this during midsummer; one dose should be enough.

If you decide that all this is too much trouble and you resort to using insecticides, to be really effective they need applying during the evening. Your local garden centre should be able to suggest a suitable insecticide to kill earwigs; most of these come ready to use, thus avoiding the need to handle chemicals.

RED SPIDER MITE

Some slightly tender varieties of clematis are grown in conservatories and these, like greenhouses, provide a near perfect environment for pests to establish themselves. While greenfly and whitefly are easily detected, red spider mite is not. A check must be kept on the condition of the leaves of your plant, and any changes investigated. When infested with red spider mite, the leaves have a mottled, rather rusty appearance. If the leaf is then turned over so that the under-side can be seen, a *very* fine cobweb may be visible. The minute mites, which are sometimes only visible through a magnifying glass, can be seen crawling all over the under-side of the leaf. They are not red as their name suggests, being more a rusty beige colour. They are not actually spiders, but very tiny mites.

There are insecticidal sprays available to tackle this pest, but the biological controls are equally as effective. These mites thrive when conditions are dry and warm, so if adequate humidity is maintained the problem is less likely to occur. A daily spray with clean water to keep up the humidity must be the cheapest and most environmentally friendly pest control available.

GREENFLY AND WHITEFLY

These, again, are not as much of a problem in our gardens as they can be in conservatories and greenhouses. Usually greenfly cluster along the new growing tips of the clematis, while whitefly more often confine themselves to the under-sides of the leaves. There are both insecticides and biological controls for use under glass against these pests. In the garden, however, if you are unfortunate enough to have a sudden infestation by either of these, a quick spray with insecticide is a simple solution to the problem. These pests can also be controlled to a certain extent by the use of foliar feed. This will keep the plants in a healthy state, seemingly making them better able to fight off infestation. I am not certain of the scientific explanation behind this, but suffice it to say that for many years my father has used a seaweed foliar feed with excellent results. This helps to keep down the number of insect pests, thus reducing the need for regular spraying with insecticides.

MILDEW

Mildew tends only to be a problem in the garden from mid- to late summer onwards. It is quite noticeable, and appears as a fine, white powder covering the leaves, stems, buds and flowers. The flowers, on opening, are misshapen and the whole plant looks very poorly. Some varieties of clematis seem more prone to mildew than others, the texensis cultivars being one. It is thought by some that if the garden is open to the wind and weather, mildew may not be a problem, but where a garden is very sheltered the risk of mildew is much greater. Our garden is both open and windy, yet we still have the odd plants getting mildew. The problem can be controlled successfully by using the occasional spray with fungicide from midsummer onwards, but this may not be necessary at all in some years, unless your garden is particularly prone to mildew.

SLIME FLUX

I first came across this problem several years ago at our local agricultural show where we were displaying our clematis, along with other trade exhibits, in the flower marquees. During the show a very pleasant lady came up to me and asked if I could identify the problem she had with her *C. montana*. She explained to me how the growth had suddenly all gone limp a few weeks before and, upon examining it, she had discovered this 'smelly stuff' oozing out of the stem. The cause was 'slime flux'.

This problem very rarely happens, but late one spring, a *C. montana* 'Marjorie' and a *C. flammula* in our garden were both struck down by slime flux. There had been some unusually late hard frosts coinciding with a spell of rather mild days. At this time of year sap is rising very quickly through the clematis stems, allowing them to become vulnerable to damage by these hard frosts. The frost damage opens the stems, and out leaks the sap. On this grow fungi, yeast and bacteria, which cause the awful smell. As soon as the problem is discovered, the affected stems should be pruned out below the diseased area. The clematis will soon re-shoot, grow on and may never have the problem again.

I have not known this problem to occur on the finer-stemmed clematis; slime flux seems to confine itself to types of clematis which over the years make very thick, woody trunks.

RABBITS AND MICE

I will consider these two pests together, as they are similar in many ways. If you live in a built-up area, you may never suffer from the effects these can create in a garden. Both rabbits and mice are very fond of clematis, especially in spring, when new clematis shoots are particularly tempting. During the winter, mice will chew through clematis stems and take these away with a few dead leaves to make a nest.

The mouse problem can be controlled two ways, either with the aid of traps, or by using rat bait. Both methods need shielding from unwary birds, cats and dogs. The traps can be baited with one of a number of tasty morsels: mice not only like cheese, they will also eat chocolate and runner bean seeds. The prepared trap can then be placed near the base of the clematis and shielded with a roof tile. This method can also be used to shield rat bait.

Rabbits are even more of a problem to those of us living out in the country. If rabbits are a real problem to you, the only effective deterrent is to 'rabbit-proof' your whole garden using mesh netting. The galvanised netting can be obtained from an agricultural supplier, whose whereabouts can usually be traced through *Yellow Pages*. I would suggest buying fine mesh netting, because baby rabbits are extremely agile and can squeeze themselves through very small holes. The netting needs to be at least 3ft (1m) tall, so that about 9in–1ft (20–30cm) can be buried below soil level to prevent rabbits from burrowing underneath it. This is an expensive exercise, but if it is done well, using galvanised netting which will not rust, then it should last for many years. It should relieve you of much anxiety and all the expense of replacing costly plants. A cheaper course to take would be to net each individual clematis, but then the rabbits could chew other equally treasured plants instead. When all is said and done, it may be simpler to net the whole garden. I have been told that crushed moth-balls placed around the base of clematis will also deter rabbits.

MOLES

These deceptively delightful little creatures are, again, usually only a pest to those living in the country. Unfortunately, moles usually seem to root around right underneath our favourite plants, causing enormous damage to the root systems. Again, trapping is one course of action to take, although it may be worth employing a professional 'mole trapper' as moles are quite devious creatures and difficult to catch. A deterrent is worth a try; you will find various mole scarers in garden centres nowadays.

USING CHEMICALS

There are a few important points to consider when using chemicals in our gardens and greenhouses and, as responsible gardeners, we must all bear these in mind.

Firstly, it is wise to wear rubber gloves when handling and using any chemicals. Even so, your hands should **always** be washed thoroughly afterwards. The gloves can then be stored along with the chemicals, to avoid them being used for other purposes.

Secondly, make absolutely sure that your garden chemicals are stored safely between use. A small, lockable cabinet in your garden shed or

'Haku Ookan'.

'John Warren'.

Clematis *'Prince Charles'*, with roses *'Alberic Barbier'* and *'Blairi No. 1'*.

Clematis integrifolia.

Viticella 'Venosa Violacea'.

Viticella 'Betty Corning'.

'Henryi'.

Clematis florida.

Montana 'Marjorie'.

Alpina *'Willy'*.

'Dawn'.

Montana *'Rubens'*.

'Ville de Lyon'.

Montana 'Tetrarose'.

'Bees Jubilee'.

Clematis × jouiniana *'Praecox'*.

'Royalty'.

'Hagley Hybrid'.

Texensis *'Gravetye Beauty'*.

'Bill Mackenzie'.

'Miss Bateman'.

'Warsaw Nike'.

Macropetala 'Markham's Pink'.

'Duchess of Edinburgh'.

'Asao'.

garage could be a sensible precaution to take against possible disaster, especially if you have children or grandchildren around.

Thirdly, *always*, with *no* exceptions, follow the manufacturer's instructions.

CONCLUSIONS

Nurserymen, as well as gardeners, are becoming increasingly aware of the need to reduce the amount of chemicals used. One way of achieving this is through biological control, which can be very satisfactory in a greenhouse environment, where serious infestations can build up if not controlled in some way. There are now effective biological controls for red spider mite, whitefly and greenfly, all of which can be a real problem to the amateur and professional alike. For those situations where nurserymen find the use of chemicals unavoidable, a product has been developed in recent years which reduces the quantity of chemical used by around 50 per cent. The product is an additive, based on rape seed oil, and is designed to ensure the chemical is absorbed more readily.

Not only have the gardening public become much more aware of the need to reduce the use of chemicals to safeguard the environment, but nurserymen too are becoming conscious of the need to help. The less we use sprays, the more we will give our beneficial insects and animals, such as ladybirds, frogs and toads, a better chance to reproduce and therefore continue the battle against pests on our behalf.

11

CLEMATIS PROFILES

The colour of flowers on one plant can vary from very deep, rich shades on opening, to more subtle shades, fading as the flowers age. The aspect, soil, climate and feeding will all affect the colour of the flowers, and everybody sees colours differently. For instance, I might suggest that a pink flower is on the mauve side of pink (mauvy-pink), whereas you may look at the same bloom and suggest it is a bluey-pink. Whichever, allowance needs to be made as far as colour descriptions go, not just in this book, but in the growers' catalogues as well.

The aspect suggested for each variety should, again, be used purely as a flexible guide; some gardens are open and exposed to the elements, while others are sheltered and several degrees warmer. A few clematis will fade, losing their colour quite badly, if grown in full sun, and I have indicated that these should be grown in full- or semi-shade, which will preserve their delicate colouring. Other clematis will actually benefit from being grown in a sunny position, which can help some varieties to improve their colour and encourage the very late-flowering varieties to bloom a little earlier.

The approximate height given for each clematis is also intended as a guide. There is a big difference between 8ft and 12ft (2.7m and 4m) and the aspect, climate, feeding and pruning will all affect the overall height to which a clematis will grow. These factors will also affect the flowering period which I have indicated in general terms as spring, summer, autumn and winter. The difference in flowering times, even across the British Isles, can be several weeks, and for me to suggest that a particular clematis begins flowering during the second half of May for six weeks would not necessarily be accurate.

Like height and flowering times, the size of flowers may also vary from one garden to another. Clematis which have two periods of bloom in a year will usually produce large flowers from the old wood early in summer, with slightly smaller blooms later in the season from the growth made in the current year. It is often found that clematis flowering twice in the year will produce flowers of a different shade in the second flush (this is particularly noticeable in 'Dr Ruppel').

Despite these limitations, the following descriptions are intended to give a helpful indication of what you can expect from a named variety, where it can be grown and any particular points of interest.

The spellings and nomenclature are based on the reference book *Clematis Index* by Wim Snoeijer.

The Award of Garden Merit of the Royal Horticultural Society (AGM) is given to plants of 'outstanding excellence'. Those listed within this chapter were awarded when the AGM was reinstituted in 1992.

C. aethusifolia

Introduced in 1875 from Northern China. Has a delicate clove-like scent, reminiscent of carnations. APPROX. HEIGHT: 6–7ft (2–2.5m). FLOWERS: late summer to mid-autumn; tiny, nodding bells; pale, slightly greeny-yellow sepals about ¾in (2cm) long and deeply ribbed on the outside, roll back to reveal beige anthers, making a very dainty flower; flowers borne singly, usually with groups of nine flowers on short branches. FOLIAGE: most attractive, pale green, almost fern-like owing to the deeply dissected leaflets. ASPECT: in view of its late flowering habit it is better grown in some sunlight. PRUNING: Group 3 (hard).

Each winter, the specimen in our garden dies right down, disappearing completely, and emerges from below the soil only when the worst of the winter has passed. Unfortunately difficult to propagate, but once established it grows strongly.

C. afoliata

A native of New Zealand, often called the 'Rush Stemmed Clematis' owing to its very tangled, branching stems, which are particularly visible because of the lack of leaves. APPROX. HEIGHT: 6–8ft (2–2.6m). FLOWERS: late spring to early summer; greenish-yellow, covering the plant in masses; sepals, usually four, open out ½–¾in (1–2cm) across, dioecious, the male bearing slightly larger flowers of a brighter yellow. FOLIAGE: small leaflets which are hardly more than leaf-stalks. ASPECT: this variety is not fully hardy in all districts and benefits from a south-facing, sunny, or at least, sheltered site. PRUNING: Group 1 (tidy after flowering).

The stems often look an unhealthy yellow or brown over the autumn and winter. Despite this unappealing description, it is well worth growing for the flowers.

'Aljonushka'

Semi-herbaceous, non-clinging. From the State Nikita Botanical Garden in Yalta, Crimea, 1963, one of many new varieties to come from the countries of the former Soviet Union. This beautiful herbaceous clematis is a cross between 'Jackmanii' and *C. integrifolia*. APPROX. HEIGHT: 4–6ft (1.3–2m). FLOWERS: mid-summer to early autumn; rich, slightly mauve pink; sepals about 2½in (6cm) long, with heavily textured surface, deep grooves on the reverse, deeper pink along the mid-ribs, and with crimped edges which recurve as the flower opens; at the same time the tips of the sepals twist; each flower does not open fully and remains a hanging bell shape with the bright yellow stamens deep inside. ASPECT: any. PRUNING: Group 3 (hard).

A most distinctive, hardy and free-flowering introduction.

'Allanah'

A very pretty clematis of unknown parentage, introduced by Jim Fisk in 1984 from Alister Keay in New Zealand. APPROX. HEIGHT: 8–12ft (2.6–4m). FLOWERS: mid or late summer, to late autumn; 5–5½in (12–13cm); deep crimson – rich velvety red on first opening, then fading slightly towards the margins but retaining a deeper red bar; six sepals, each tapering at both ends making the flowers appear rather gappy (but not to their detriment); blunt tips give the flower a very round appearance; stamens have white filaments with very dark red, almost black, anthers. ASPECT: sunny. PRUNING: optional Group 2 (light) or Group 3 (hard).

A late-flowering variety which, we have found, benefits from light pruning, rather than the normally recommended hard pruning.

THE *ALPINA* GROUP

The species *C. alpina* is native to parts of Europe and north-east Asia and was introduced to Britain in 1792. The natural colour is violet-blue, although the species *C. alpina ssp. sibirica* is white. During this century hybridists have produced a wonderful selection of colours varying from white, through shades of blue and pink, to purple. It produces bell-shaped flowers, singly, from the leaf axils of the old wood during the spring, the bells being around 1½–2in (4–5cm) long, and each flower having four sepals tapering to a point. With some varieties the 'bells' open out almost flat and then turn on their sides so that the flower appears to look at you.

The charm of the alpina's bell flowers is enhanced by the significant petaloid stamens inside the four main sepals. These petal-like stamens make an inner skirt, usually of a complementary colour – often a creamy-white. Although flowering is mainly from the old ripened wood during mid- to late spring, you will find that during the late summer and early autumn a few more flowers will appear as a bonus. A fine array of seedheads will keep the plant interesting for many months.

This group of clematis is especially useful if space is limited and you want early colour in the garden. They are deciduous climbers, and will grow to a height of around 6–8ft (2–2.6m). Their compactness makes them an excellent choice for growing in containers.

Alpinas are extremely hardy. They will cope with the harshest weather conditions, and will do well even on relatively poor soil. The only thing they dislike is to stand wet through the winter. This goes for all clematis, but is worth paying particular attention to with alpinas and other species that have very fine roots. Despite their delicate appearance, the flowers are remarkably resilient to the most inclement weather.

The foliage is lightly structured, the leaflets being in groups of three, with each having a toothed edge, their soft green colour adding to the delicate aura of these plants. Pruning is usually a 'tidy' after flowering has finished, but it is worthwhile hard pruning one or two stems out at this time. This will encourage new growth from the base of the plant which can be trained into position during the summer, enabling bare patches to be filled, thus avoiding a 'leggy' base.

Despite the short season of flowers, the attractiveness of hundreds of these little bells so early in the year makes the alpinas a welcome part of the garden. They can also bring colour into the home in spring as their blooms last well in water.

All varieties of alpina are between 6 and 8ft (2 and 2.6m) in height. They flower in mid- to late spring, and can be sited anywhere in the garden. They require Group 1 pruning (tidy after flowering). Since these details are appropriate for all alpina varieties, they will not be repeated in the following profiles.

C. alpina 'Burford White'
Introduced by the late John Treasure of Tenbury Wells. FLOWERS: four sepals, 1¾–2in (4.5–5cm) long, white, with the appearance of tissue paper, wider and more blunt than the other alpinas, giving a more rounded look to the flower; the blooms remain bell shaped, rather than opening out as other varieties do. FOLIAGE: pale green.

C. alpina 'Columbine'
Raised by Ernest Markham and exhibited by him in 1937. FLOWERS: clear light to mid-blue, the colour paling to a powder blue as the flower matures; sepals are 1¾in (4.5cm) long, tapering to a point and opening to reveal the creamy-white petaloid stamens.

C. alpina 'Constance'
FLOWERS: very deep reddish-pink; sepals of 1½–1¾in (4–4.5cm) long and, although similar in colouring to alpina 'Ruby', the flowers of 'Constance' are shorter, wider and not so pointed; outer layer of petaloid stamens the same deep pink as the sepals and equally as long, which make the flower look almost semi-double; inner layers creamy-white and easily visible as the bell opens wide.

C. alpina 'Frances Rives' (Dutch Form)

Originally raised from seedling by Sir Cedric Morris and sometimes seen incorrectly named *C. alpina* 'Blue Giant'. Although listed in the Clematis Index as 'Frances Rives', it is commonly sold as 'Francis Rivis'. The deepest and richest blue of all the alpinas, it also has the largest flowers. FLOWERS: deep blue; sepals about 2½in (6cm) long, opening to reveal the white skirt of petaloid stamens; flowers are an irregular shape with the sepals sometimes twisting and blunt in appearance, which adds to their charm.

C. alpina 'Frankie'

A relatively new and extremely good addition to the range of alpinas. FLOWERS: deep mauve-blue, paling slightly as the flower matures and at the same time opening to show the petaloid stamens which are creamy white with blue shadings on the outer ring; sepals are 2in (5cm) long, tapering to a point. A well-shaped, balanced flower produced in abundance in the spring, and which the plant continues to produce in lesser numbers throughout the summer.

'Helsingborg' AGM

An elegant rather than pretty alpina type. As a cross it is not a true alpina, but it is regularly listed with this group, whose characteristics it matches so closely. FLOWERS: bell-shaped; four bluey-purple sepals, slightly twisted, 2in (5cm) long, with paler margins; petaloid stamens pale purple, the same shade as the inside of the sepals; before opening the flower buds are a deep rosy purple. FOLIAGE: light green.

C. alpina 'Ruby'

Raised by Ernest Markham in the 1930s. FLOWERS: sepals very deep, almost purply-pink, 2in (5cm) long, narrow and tapering to a point; open to reveal yellowy-cream petaloid stamens with pink shadings on the outer skirt. FOLIAGE: pale green. Best displayed in full sun, where its colour is so much more vibrant than if it is grown in the shade.

C. alpina ssp. sibirica

Native to Norway and Finland and parts of Europe through to Siberia. Introduced to Britain during the mid-1700s. FLOWERS: small, pure white, pointed, bell-shaped. Four sepals conceal white petaloid stamens. Looks extremely delicate but copes with severe winters, even temperatures as low as −30°C.

C. alpina ssp. sibirica 'White Moth'

Produces double flowers similar to those of the macropetalas. Sometimes incorrectly labelled as *C. macropetala* 'White Moth'.

C. alpina 'White Columbine' AGM

Identical to the blue alpina 'Columbine' in every way except colour. FLOWERS: creamy-white on first opening, clearing to pure white and remaining white even in the worst weather; white petaloid stamens with greenish-yellow tips.

C. alpina 'Willy'

FLOWERS: four pointed, very pale mauve-pink sepals 2in (5cm) long, with deep rose pink shadings where they join the flower stalk and the same rose pink running through the veins on the reverse; open out almost flat to show creamy-white petaloid stamens. An ideal candidate for a shady corner where spring colour is needed.

'Anna-Louise' (PBR – propagation by licence only)

Introduced by Raymond Evison. Colouring very similar to 'Mrs N. Thompson', but flowers are larger and growth is much more substantial. APPROX. HEIGHT: 6–8ft (2–2.6m). FLOWERS: late spring to early summer and again, late summer to early autumn; flowers are 7.5in (18cm) across with blunt-ended, very deep purply-blue sepals, slightly gappy as the flower matures, with a bar of rich, velvety cerise and an almost satin sheen; wide white bar on reverse, gradually merging towards mauve margins. Stamens have white filaments with deep pink anthers. ASPECT: any. PRUNING: Group 2 (light).

Ideal for containers owing to its compact, free-flowering habit.

'Arctic Queen' (PBR – propagation by licence only)

Introduced by Raymond Evison. APPROX. HEIGHT: 6ft (2m). FLOWERS: 4½in (11cm), double in late spring to early summer, and again in late summer to early autumn, on both old and new wood; eight pure white outer sepals taper to a point, each has a deep groove running down the centre from which radiate a myriad of fine grooves at an angle towards the margins, making each sepal look like a feather; a pale green rib runs down the reverse of each sepal; inner layers of sepals between half and three-quarters the length of outer sepals; stamens have white filaments with cream anthers. ASPECT: any. PRUNING: Group 2 (light).

Compact and very free flowering, well suited for use in containers.

C. armandii

Evergreen and vanilla-scented. Introduced from China by E. H. Wilson in 1900. APPROX. HEIGHT: 15–20ft (5–6m). FLOWERS: early to late spring; borne in clusters from the leaf axils; 1½–2in (3.5–5cm) across, with creamy-white stamens and usually five or six sepals. FOLIAGE: long, oval, leathery-looking; dark, glossy green, about 6in (15cm) long and 2in (5cm) wide; young leaves have a bronze tinge; ASPECT: sheltered, as leaves can be badly damaged if grown in an open site exposed to harsh winds. PRUNING: Group 1 (tidy after flowering). If it becomes necessary to prune an established armandii, do so when it has finished flowering, trying to avoid cutting down into the old woody trunks. It is a good idea to do a little pruning each year to avoid a build-up of tangled stems, as these will hide a multitude of dead leaves and the problem will be much worse to sort out.

C. armandii 'Apple Blossom'
(Pinky-White.)

C. armandii 'Jeffries'
(Pure white flower with long, pointed leaves.)

C. armandii 'Snowdrift'
(Pure white.)

All of these cultivars are selected forms of *armandii*. They have slightly larger flowers than the species, but in other respects (growth, habit, and so on) they are identical.

C. x *aromatica*
Semi-herbaceous, non-clinging, with very little scent other than that of a sweet, spicy pollen. Assumed to be a cross between *C. integrifolia* and *C. flammula*. First recorded during the mid-1800s. APPROX. HEIGHT: 4–6ft (1.3–2m). FLOWERS: mid-summer to early autumn; dainty, deep reddish-blue, 2in (5cm) across; four narrow sepals open out flat to form a cross; ½ in (1cm)-long stamens have cream filaments, merging to primrose-yellow anthers, and stand up in a crown. ASPECT: any. PRUNING: Group 3 (hard); growth dies back completely each winter, so prune off previous season's wood during late winter or early spring.

'Asao'
Originated in Japan. APPROX. HEIGHT: 6–8ft (2–2.6m). FLOWERS: late spring to early summer and again late summer to early autumn; open, star-shaped flowers are 6–8in (15–20cm) across; sepals, usually seven, have a broad, rich, deep pink margin, the same deep pink running through veins across a white bar; bright golden anthers make this flower a stunning sight early in the summer. ASPECT: any. PRUNING: Group 2 (light).

This is a compact, free-flowering plant which is well suited to being grown in a container.

'Ascotiensis' AGM

This clematis, of unknown parentage, was introduced in 1871. APPROX. HEIGHT: 8–10ft (2.6–3.3m). FLOWERS: profuse, from mid-summer to early autumn; 5in (12cm) across; often has four, but occasionally five or six, deep mid-blue sepals, broad and tapering to a point with darker blue in the veins; a broad white bar on the reverse merges towards light blue margins; sepals recurve and twist as the flowers open, reminiscent of children's beach windmills; stamens have greenish-cream filaments with beige anthers. ASPECT: any. PRUNING: Group 3 (hard).

Excellent for late summer colour and ideal in a pot.

'Barbara Jackman'

Hybridized by Jackman's of Woking. APPROX. HEIGHT: 6–8ft (2–2.6m). FLOWERS: late spring to early summer, and again in late summer to early autumn; flowers are 4–5in (10–12cm) across and have seven or eight overlapping, rounded sepals with pointed tips; light mauve-blue with central bar of very deep, rich purply-pink; stamens have white filaments with primrose yellow anthers, and have a pale green bar on reverse. ASPECT: any. PRUNING: Group 2 (light).

This is one of the varieties whose flowers keep well in water.

'Beauty of Worcester'

A compact variety, hybridized by Messrs Smith of Worcester in about 1890. APPROX. HEIGHT: 6–8ft (2–2.6m). FLOWERS: double, late spring to early summer, and single, late summer to early autumn; some flowers are very double, others semi-double, all about 6½in (16cm) across; outer ring of six reddish-purple sepals have rounded edges and pointed tips; six or seven further layers of sepals are the same shape, each ring is slightly smaller than the previous, but are deep mid-blue with a hint of pink, and have a white bar on reverse; stamens have white filaments with yellow anthers. ASPECT: best grown in some sun. PRUNING: Group 2 (light).

'Bees Jubilee' AGM

Introduced by Bees of Chester in about 1950, this clematis looks almost as if it is a pink version of 'Nelly Moser'. APPROX. HEIGHT: 8–12ft (2.6–4m). FLOWERS: late spring to early summer, and again in late summer to early autumn; flowers are 6–7in (15–17cm) across, with seven or eight broad, overlapping sepals, each tapering to a blunt tip; sepals have deep carmine bars radiating out towards the margins which are a pale mauvy-pink; stamens have white filaments with beige anthers. ASPECT: best out of direct sunlight. PRUNING: Group 2 (light).

Occasionally slow to establish, but flowers profusely when it is settled.

'Belle Nantaise'
Introduced by Boisselot in 1887. APPROX. HEIGHT: 8–12ft (2.6–4m). FLOWERS: late spring to mid-summer; star-shaped flower 7½–8in (18–20cm) across; six sepals with a textured surface and a satin sheen, and crimped edges tapering to a point, open slightly mauve mid-blue with an almost white base, and greenish-white bars on the reverse; as the flower matures the sepals fade to pale mauve-blue and reflex slightly along the margins, and the bars lose greenness; stamens are greenish-cream, with primrose yellow anthers; ASPECT: any. PRUNING: Group 2 (light).

'Belle of Woking'
One of the first double clematis to be introduced and still available today, this was hybridized by Jackman's of Woking in 1875. APPROX. HEIGHT: 6–8ft (2–2.6m). FLOWERS: double, early to mid-summer; open a silvery-mauve but quickly lose the mauve tint, turning silvery-grey; only 4in (10cm) across, but very double, with many layers of broad sepals each tapering to a point; stamens have white filaments with cream anthers. ASPECT: avoid exposed, north-facing situation. PRUNING: Group 2 (light).

I do not find this a strong grower, but it is one worth trying as the flowers are beautiful.

'Bill Mackenzie' AGM
Discovered as a seedling by Bill Mackenzie when visiting Water Perry Gardens in the Cotswolds. Often sold as *C. orientalis* 'Bill Mackenzie', and probably a cross between *C. tibetana* ssp. *vernayi* 'L & S 13342' and *C. tangutica*. APPROX. HEIGHT: 10ft (3m) or more. FLOWERS: late summer to late autumn; brilliant yellow, nodding, open, lantern-shaped flowers 3in (7cm) across; four sepals taper to a point, recurving at the tip and margins to reveal the reddish-brown filaments and beige anthers; surface texture of the sepals is reminiscent of slivers of lemon peel; when the flowers die the display continues with the charming, silky seedheads. ASPECT: any. PRUNING: Group 3 (hard); our 'Bill Mackenzie' is severely hard pruned each spring to keep it under control – it is a very rampant grower.

If garden space is unlimited 'Bill Mackenzie' could be allowed the freedom to grow 'wild'. Leaving the plant unpruned, or simply tidying it up will result in the flowers beginning during early to mid-summer. When buying 'Bill Mackenzie', check to make sure the young plants were produced from cuttings, not from seed, as those from seed will not come true to type.

C. campaniflora
Native to Portugal, this species was introduced to Britain in 1820. APPROX. HEIGHT: 12–15ft (4–5m). FLOWERS: mid-summer to early

autumn; dainty little nodding, bell-shaped, ¾–1in (2–2.5cm)-long flowers; four bluey-white, slightly twisted sepals with jagged, recurved tips; greenish cream stamens; the insides of the sepals are pure white and glisten like sugar icing, feeling waxy to the touch. ASPECT: any. PRUNING: Group 3 (hard); this is a vigorous climber, growing strongly after its annual hard prune.

C. campaniflora 'Lisboa'

Raised in the Lisbon Botanical Garden, this is a cross between C. campaniflora and C. viticella. APPROX. HEIGHT: 12–15ft (4–5m). FLOWERS: mid-summer to early autumn; flowers are 2in (5cm) across; four deep, purply-blue sepals, 1in (2.5cm) long and approximately ⅓in (8mm) wide, taper to a point; sepals do not open out flat but remain cup-shaped at the base, while the tips curve back; where the sepals join the greenish-yellow stamens, there is a splash of yellowy-white. ASPECT: any. PRUNING: Group 3 (hard).

A very dainty flower which keeps well in water.

'Capitaine Thuilleaux'

Hybridized by a French nurseryman and named after his son who was killed in the First World War. Also sold as 'Souvenir de Capitaine Thuilleaux'. Introduced to Britain by Jim Fisk in 1969. APPROX. HEIGHT: 6–8ft (2–2.6m). FLOWERS: late spring to early summer, and again late summer to early autumn; star-like flowers, 5–6in (12–15cm) across; seven (sometimes six or eight) pointed, overlapping sepals; pale pink sepals, almost white at the margins, have a central bar of raspberry pink sprinkled with pale pink; stamens have white filaments with dark red anthers. ASPECT: any. PRUNING: Group 2 (light).

A compact plant which flowers well low down. Another excellent variety for container use.

'Carnaby'

Introduced from America in 1983 by Treasures. APPROX. HEIGHT: 6–8ft (2–2.6m); FLOWERS: late spring to early summer; rounded-looking flowers, 6–8in (15–20cm) across; six to eight very deep reddish-pink, pointed, overlapping, reflexed sepals; colour pales towards pale mauve-pink at the margins, which are crimped; greenish-yellow bar on reverse; stamens have white filaments with dark red anthers. ASPECT: avoid direct sun, as the colour fades; in partial shade it keeps a colour reminiscent of raspberries and cream. PRUNING: optional, Group 2 (light) or Group 3 (hard).

An excellent compact and free-flowering plant ideal for container cultivation.

'Caroline'

APPROX. HEIGHT: 6–8ft (2–2.6m). FLOWERS: mid-summer to early autumn; pretty, 4in (10cm) across; six sepals, each recurves sightly and tapers to a point; base colour is pinky-white, lightly overlaid with deep satin pink along the bar and margins; very pale pink on reverse, with deep pink along the mid-ribs and margins; stamens have white filaments with pale yellow anthers. ASPECT: on account of its pale colouring, I feel it would be better grown out of direct sunlight. PRUNING: Group 3 (hard).

C. x cartmanii 'Joe'

Raised from seed sown in 1983 and sent to H. and M. Taylor of Invergowrie, Dundee, by J. Cartman of Christchurch, New Zealand. Evergreen, the result of a cross between C. marmoraria and C. paniculata (both endemic in New Zealand). APPROX. HEIGHT: low, forms clumps. FLOWERS: mid- to late spring; male flowers, 1–1½in (2–3cm) across; six (occasionally five, seven or eight) white sepals which recurve as the flowers mature; stamens are yellow with beige anthers. FOLIAGE: finely dissected leaves, almost fern-like. ASPECT: well drained, sunny situation or alpine trough. PRUNING: none necessary.

This may prefer an acid compost in alpine conditions.

'Charissima'

Hybridized by Walter Pennell in 1974. APPROX. HEIGHT: 6–8ft (2–2.6m). FLOWERS: late spring to early summer and again, late summer to early autumn; star-shaped flower, 6–8in (15–20cm) across; six to eight overlapping sepals, each tapering to a blunt point, and with a delicately textured surface and lightly crimped edges; very pale pink, heavily overlaid with deep, cherry pink which is even darker along the extreme margins, making the sepals look as though they have been outlined; white bars on the reverse with deep pink ribs along the centre-line and wide margins of mid-pink, again with the dark red outline to the edges; stamens have white filaments, passing through shades of pink to wine-red anthers. ASPECT: any. PRUNING: Group 2 (light).

C. chrysocoma 'Continuity'

Given to John Treasure by Rowland Jackman. Resembles the montanas in growth and habit. APPROX. HEIGHT: 15–20ft (5–6m). FLOWERS: late spring to late summer; though not as profuse as those of the montanas, flowers are held over a much longer period; four mid-pink sepals with a satiny, textured surface, that taper to a blunt tip and have crimped edges; very deep cherry-pink reverse, paling towards the margins; stamens have white filaments with very long, bright yellow anthers – almost half the length of the sepals; unusually long flower stem of about 8in (20cm). FOLIAGE: leaves are similar in shape to those of the montanas, but they appear 'coarser' and have a bronze tint. ASPECT: southern or western – not exposed. PRUNING: Group 1 (tidy after flowering).

Not thought to be quite as hardy as the montanas but is an interesting variety to try.

C. chrysocoma 'Hybrid'

APPROX. HEIGHT: 15–20ft (5–6m). FLOWERS: late spring to early summer; flowers are 3in (7cm) across; four rounded sepals, white at base with pale pink shadings towards outer margins, giving the appearance of a pale pink flower; stamens have white filaments with bright yellow anthers. FOLIAGE: similar in shape to that of the montanas, but hairy along the outer margins of leaflets, the reverse being quite hairy. FOLIAGE: new foliage is tinted bronze. ASPECT: not exposed. PRUNING: Group 1 (tidy after flowering).

THE CIRRHOSA GROUP

The clematis in this group are native to Southern Europe and the Mediterranean. All are evergreen and must have the protection of a warm, sheltering wall and soil, which does not stand waterlogged through the winter, in order to grow really well. Given ideal growing conditions they are quite vigorous, making a height of 15–20ft (5–6m).

Winter-flowering, they are generally in bloom from mid-winter to early spring, although C. cirrhosa 'Freckles' flowers a little earlier – from mid-autumn to mid-winter.

None will make a 'traffic stopping' display of flowers, so plant them where they can be appreciated at close range. For all members of the group, pruning consists of a good tidy after flowering has finished.

They are ideal candidates for a conservatory, but watch out for pests! If space is confined, prune back hard after flowering each year, to around 3ft (1m).

There are many different forms of all these plants and some sources of supply may stock them under alternative names, including C. calycina.

C. cirrhosa

Introduced from southern Europe in 1590. FLOWERS: 1½in (4cm) long; creamy white, hanging like bells from the leaf axils; four 1½in (4cm)-long sepals which sometimes have light maroon freckles on the inside.

C. cirrhosa ssp. balearica AGM

Brought from the Balearic Isles in 1783. FLOWERS: four creamy-white sepals dotted with maroon freckles form bells of 1½in (4cm) long, hanging down from the leaf axils; FOLIAGE: more finely cut than that of C. cirrhosa; tips of the new growth have a bronze tinge.

C. cirrhosa 'Freckles' AGM

Introduced by Raymond Evison. FLOWERS: bell-shaped; four translucent pale cream sepals, 1½–2in (4–5cm) long, broad and tapering to a point, hang from the leaf axils; inside colouring of pale cream, heavily overlaid with dark red freckles, can be seen through the sepals; stamens are pale greenish-yellow.

In cold climates 'Freckles' is best grown in a conservatory or cold glass-house.

C. cirrhosa 'Wisley Cream'

Very similar to C. cirrhosa, but flowers are slightly larger and a good cream colour, with no freckles.

'Colette Deville'

Re-introduced to England in 1990 by Caddick's Clematis at Thelwall, near Warrington, who describe it as 'An old French variety'. APPROX. HEIGHT: 8–12ft (2.6–4m). FLOWERS: late spring to early summer, and again late summer to early autumn; flowers are 6in (15cm) across and very beautiful; early flowers have eight deep mauve sepals, which pale to a central bar of light mauve with deep mauve veins; appear pinky-mauve in sunlight, and deep, grey-mauve in the shade; later flowers have a 'maroon hue', described by Ernest Markham in his book of 1935, as 'violet-red'; sepals have a satin sheen; stamens have cream filaments with red anthers. ASPECT: any. PRUNING: Group 2 (light).

'Comtesse de Bouchaud' AGM

Hybridized by Morel in about 1900. APPROX. HEIGHT: 6–8ft (2–2.6m). FLOWERS: early to late summer; 4–5in (10–12cm) across; deeply textured sepals have a satin sheen, rounded, crimped edges and blunt, slightly recurved tips, and twist slightly as the flower ages; mid-pink, deepening towards the margins; stamens have white filaments with pale yellow anthers. ASPECT: any. PRUNING: Group 3 (hard).

Ideal in a pot.

'Corona'

Hybridized by Lundell in Sweden in 1972. APPROX. HEIGHT: 6–8ft (2–2.6m). FLOWERS: late spring to early summer and again, late summer; flowers 6in (15cm) across; eight overlapping, round-tipped sepals are rich purply-cerise paling to mauve at the margins; white central bar, radiating out into purply-pink, on reverse; white filaments with dark red anthers. ASPECT: avoid exposed, north-facing situation; attractively coloured flowers, best grown out of strong sunlight as it can cause them to fade. PRUNING: Group 2 (light).

Compact and free-flowering, and ideal for a container.

'Countess of Lovelace'

Hybridized by Jackman in 1871. Today, over 120 years later, it is still one of the most sought-after clematis. In his book of 1872 Jackman describes it as being a cross between *C. Sophia plena* (no longer seen) and hybrids of the Jackmanii type. APPROX. HEIGHT: 6–8ft (2–2.6m). FLOWERS: double, late spring to early summer, and single in early autumn; 6–7in (15–17cm) across; outer layers of six to eight very pointed, reflexed sepals which are pale mauve with a hint of green; further layers of pointed, deep bluey-mauve sepals that get progressively shorter; reverse of each sepal has a white bar; early flowers in May occasionally have a pale green tint if the spring has been cold and dull; single flowers in autumn, at least as large as the early flowers, have six open, gappy sepals; stamens have white filaments with yellow anthers. ASPECT: any. PRUNING: Group 2 (light).

C. crispa

'The Marsh Clematis'. Native of south-eastern USA, and introduced to Britain in 1726. APPROX. HEIGHT: 6ft (2m). FLOWERS: early to late summer; 1½–2in (4–5cm)-long, nodding, bell-shaped flowers; four pale mauve sepals, whose tips recurve to reveal the bluish-purple to light blue colouring inside, have serrated edges and a white bar deep in the throat of the flower; ASPECT: sheltered. PRUNING: Group 3 (hard).

Ernest Markham suggested that this clematis was 'rather delicate'. As it is often reduced to ground level each winter, it is advisable to protect the crowns with a mulch in early winter. I would also suggest growing this slender climber through a small shrub, which would help to insulate it.

C. x *cylindrica*

APPROX. HEIGHT: 3–4ft (1–1.3m). FLOWERS: mid-summer to early autumn; 1½in (4cm)-long, nodding, bell-shaped, deep purply-blue with four narrow, twisted sepals. ASPECT: any. PRUNING: Group 3 (hard).

This herbaceous clematis is best scrambling over other low-growing plants. We grow ours amongst heathers at the base of a sundial, where it is shown off to its best advantage.

'Daniel Deronda' AGM

Hybridized by Noble – *Daniel Deronda* was the last book written by George Eliot (1819–80). APPROX. HEIGHT: 8–10ft (2.6–3.3m). FLOWERS: late spring to late summer, sometimes producing semi-double flowers early in the season; large, star-shaped blooms, 7–8in (17–20cm) across; usually eight pointed sepals, that recurve slightly along the margins; deep bluey-purple; merest hint of an off-white bar along the centre of each sepal, showing off the cream stamens perfectly. ASPECT: avoid exposed, north-facing situation. PRUNING: Group 2 (light).

'Dawn'

This hybrid was introduced by Treasures in 1969. APPROX. HEIGHT: 6–8ft (2–2.6m). FLOWERS: late spring to early summer, and occasionally in late summer; flowers are 6in (15cm) across; eight broad, overlapping sepals, each tapering to a blunt tip; very pale pearly-pink, the colour deepening through the veins and towards the slightly deeper pearly-pink margins; stamens have white filaments with deep wine-red anthers. ASPECT: avoid full sun, as it will cause this clematis to fade horribly; grown in partial shade, it is a sight to remember, and grown in full shade the early flowers will probably have a pale green bar. PRUNING: Group 2 (light).

Well suited to container cultivation.

'Dorothy Tolver'

Hybridized by my husband Jonathan and introduced by us in 1993. Named after my mother, it is a cross between 'Vyvyan Pennell' and 'Niobe'. APPROX. HEIGHT: 8–12ft (2.6–4m). FLOWERS: late spring to early summer, and again early to mid autumn; 6in (15cm) across; six overlapping sepals with textured, satiny surface and rounded, lightly crimped edges, tapering to a point; sepals are vibrant deep mauve-pink with a satin sheen, and on closer inspection are mauve at the base, heavily overlaid with deep mauve-pink; stamens have white filaments with a hint of pink and bright, buttercup-yellow anthers. ASPECT: any. PRUNING: Group 2 (light).

'Dorothy Walton'

A lovely plant which deserves to be grown more widely. APPROX. HEIGHT: 8–12ft (2.6–4m). FLOWERS: early summer to early autumn; open, star-shaped flower, 4–6in (10–15cm) across; pointed sepals are mid-blue with a strong hint of mauve and pink, which is more pronounced along the bar and down the margins, and have white mottling; same colouring on reverse, but paler; stamens have white filaments with coffee-coloured anthers. ASPECT: avoid exposed, north-facing situation. PRUNING: Group 3 (hard).

Well suited for container display.

'Dr. Ruppel' AGM

Introduced by Jim Fisk in 1975 from Argentina. This wonderful flower has become even more popular than 'Nelly Moser', probably because it holds its colour better. APPROX. HEIGHT: 8–10ft (2.6–3.3m). FLOWERS: late spring to mid-summer, and again in early autumn; 6–8in (15–20cm) across; early flowers, usually larger than the later ones, can be up to 8in (20cm) across; eight overlapping sepals; early flowers have deep pinky-mauve sepals with pale mauve margins and a central bar of rich cerise pink; mauve on the reverse, with a white bar; crown of stamens with white filaments and coffee-coloured anthers; later flowers have a more intense colouring and lack the paler margins. ASPECT: any. PRUNING: Group 2 (light).

'Duchess of Edinburgh'
This very old and very unusual double white clematis was hybridized by Jackman in 1875. APPROX. HEIGHT: 6–8ft (2–2.6m). FLOWERS: early to late summer; flowers are 4–4½in (10–11cm) across, and have been likened to dahlias; flower heads are made up of layer upon layer of white sepals, in the centre of which is a boss of cream stamens; a few inches below the bloom is a ring of leaflets on long stalks and above this, just underneath the white sepals there is a ring of what appear to be half leaf and half sepal, being a mixture of green and white. ASPECT: avoid exposed situation. PRUNING: Group 2 (light).

The growth tends to be on the weak side and is therefore best grown through another plant, perhaps a climbing rose such as Zéphirine Drouhin, to give the clematis some support.

'Durandii' AGM
My favourite herbaceous variety, this non-clinging, semi-herbaceous clematis was hybridized by Durand Frères of Lyon, France in 1870 and is a cross between C. integrifolia and C. 'Jackmanii'. APPROX. HEIGHT: 5–6ft (1.6–2m). FLOWERS: early summer to early autumn; 3–4in (7–10cm) across; four (sometimes five or six) deep indigo-blue sepals; deeply ribbed and tapering to a point; as the flowers mature, the margins near the tips recurve; reverse of each sepal is dusky mid-blue with dark satiny-blue along the mid-ribs; stamens have white filaments flushed blue at base with golden anthers. ASPECT: any. PRUNING: Group 3 (hard).

Owing to its free-flowering nature, 'Durandii' is ideal for growing in a container, although it will need regularly tying to its support as it grows. Ours is displayed to perfection growing over a curry plant (*Helichrysum italicum*), which has silver foliage and yellow flowers.

'Edith' AGM
A chance white seedling from 'Mrs. Cholmondeley', this very free-flowering clematis was introduced in 1974 by Treasures. APPROX. HEIGHT: 8–10ft (2.6–3.3m). FLOWERS: late spring to early summer, and again in late summer; 5–6in (12–15cm) across; rather gappy where the six white, textured, satiny sepals join the flower stalk; sepals recurve along the margins, and are very rounded with blunt tips; pure white on reverse; huge crown of stamens, each having a white filament and dark, burgundy-red anther. ASPECT: any. PRUNING: Group 2 (light).

'Elsa Späth' AGM

Occasionally seen mislabelled as 'Xerxes'. APPROX. HEIGHT: 6–8ft (2–2.6m). FLOWERS: early to mid-summer and early autumn; 6–7in (15–17cm) across; eight overlapping and very rounded dark blue sepals, which pale to a more mauve-mid-blue as the flower matures, and appear pinky-blue in the sun; sepals have a hint of rose-pink, especially at the tips; mid-blue on reverse with greenish-cream bars; stamens have white filaments with very dark, dusky red anthers. ASPECT: any. PRUNING: Group 2 (light).

C. x eriostemon 'Hendersonii'

A cross between C. integrifolia and C. viticella, this semi-herbaceous, non-clinging clematis was hybridized by Henderson in about 1835, making it one of the very earliest clematis hybrids. APPROX. HEIGHT: 6–8ft (2–2.6m). FLOWERS: profuse, from early summer to early autumn; very dainty 3in (7cm)-long bells, reminiscent of fairies' hats in children's books; four sepals which reflex as the flower opens; appear very dark blue to deep purple, depending on the light; reverse is the same deep colour along the mid-ribs, fading to a more dusky purply-blue at the margins; pale yellow stamens. ASPECT: any; the colour is rich and is held very well, even if grown in full sun. PRUNING: Group 3 (hard).

Ideal for pot cultivation, provided it is regularly tied in to its support.

'Empress of India'

Hybridized by Jackman, this grand old variety was seemingly 'lost', until re-introduced from America a few years ago. APPROX. HEIGHT: 8–10ft (2.6–3.3m). FLOWERS: mid- to late summer; elegant, 7–8in (17–20cm) across; usually six sepals, their light violet-purple colour deepening to form a bar along the centre of each sepal; stamens pale with coffee-coloured anthers. ASPECT: any. PRUNING: Group 2 (light).

'Ernest Markham' AGM

Named after Ernest Markham, head gardener for William Robinson at Gravetye Manor in East Sussex, the original plant was one of a batch of seedlings given to Jackmans of Woking. Following Markham's death in 1937, Jackmans introduced the red-flowered seedling, naming it after him in recognition of his work with clematis. APPROX. HEIGHT: 16ft (5m) or 8–10ft (2.6–3.3m). FLOWERS: early to late summer, or mid-summer to early autumn; size depends on pruning; hard pruning results in a mass of flowers about 4in (10cm) across, while light pruning produces slightly fewer flowers of about 6in (15cm) in diameter; six broad, overlapping, light magenta sepals, each tapering to a point, and having a deeply textured surface and crimped margins; sepals reflex slightly as the flower opens, making it appear very round; stamens are a rather dull beige, and quite insignificant. ASPECT:

flowers better in a sunny position. PRUNING: optional: Group 2 (light) or Group 3 (hard); to encourage a better display of flowers, adapt pruning to suit growing conditions: in a mild climate, hard pruning will be necessary, but in colder districts, light pruning and a sunny position will improve performance.

'Etoile de Malicorne'

Of unknown origin. APPROX. HEIGHT: 8–10ft (2.6–3.3m). FLOWERS: late spring to early summer, and again in early autumn; 6–7in (15–17cm) across; very rounded and full; eight overlapping, slightly pointed sepals, which remain cupped for some time after opening; very rich, purply-blue which fades as the flower matures; narrow central bar of purply-red; mid-blue reverse with white bar; stamens have white filaments with dark red anthers. ASPECT: any. PRUNING: Group 2 (light).

'Etoile de Paris'

APPROX. HEIGHT: 6–8ft (2–2.6m). FLOWERS: late spring to early summer; star-shaped; 6–7in (15–17cm) across; slightly gappy where the eight sepals join the stem; sepals are deep mid-blue with dark blue veins and have a light blue reverse with a white bar; sepals widen out, then taper off again to a fine point at the tips; stamens have white filaments with dusky red anthers. ASPECT: any. PRUNING: Group 2 (light).

'Fair Rosamond'

Hybridized by Jackman in 1871 and awarded a First Class Certificate in 1873. APPROX. HEIGHT: 6–8ft (2–2.6m). FLOWERS: late spring to early summer; star-shaped; 5–6in (12–15cm) across; six to eight very pointed, overlapping sepals; white with a textured satin surface, overlaid with a hint of deep pink shading down the centre of each sepal, which soon fades away if the plant is grown in full sunlight; stamens, which form a huge crown in the centre of the flower, have white filaments, merging into very dark purply-red anthers. ASPECT: avoid exposed, north-facing situation. PRUNING: Group 2 (light).

Its compact, free-flowering habit makes it ideal for growing in a pot.

'Fireworks' AGM

Introduced by Treasures in early 1980s. APPROX. HEIGHT: 8–10ft (2.6–3m). FLOWERS: late spring to early summer, and again in early autumn; twisted star, 6–8in (15–20cm) across; as the flower opens, the six or seven pointed, satiny sepals twist and their tips recurve slightly; each sepal has deep mauve, almost lavender margins and a rich cerise bar, darkest at the base and fading out at the tips; reverse has a green bar and mauve margins; stamens have white filaments with wine red anthers. ASPECT: any. PRUNING: Group 2 (light).

C. flammula

Known as 'The Fragrant Virgin's Bower', this clematis was introduced from Southern Europe in 1590 and has a sweet, hawthorn-like scent, reminiscent of country hedgerows in the spring. APPROX. HEIGHT: up to 15ft (5m). FLOWERS: there are literally thousands on a mature plant from late summer to mid-autumn; clusters of dozens of tiny, creamy-white flowers ¾–1in (2–2.5cm) across, with four narrow, blunt-tipped sepals. ASPECT: any. PRUNING: optional: Group 2 (light) or Group 3 (hard); if more height is required, lighter pruning may be adequate, but do remove the previous season's flowering wood.

Certainly one of the most strongly perfumed clematis, which fills its corner of the garden with scent on a late summer's evening. Gertrude Jekyll described flammula as one of the chief beauties of September. I would certainly agree with her.

THE FLORIDA GROUP

C. florida, C. florida 'Plena' ('Alba Plena') and C. florida 'Sieboldii' ('Sieboldiana', 'Bicolor').

This is a small group of very attractive clematis which all have the same general habit and requirements. APPROX. HEIGHT: 6–8ft (2–2.6m). FLOWERS: early summer to early autumn; borne singly from the leaf axils on stems about 6in (15cm) long. ASPECT: sheltered, or conservatory, as these clematis are not totally hardy, except perhaps in milder conditions. PRUNING: Group 3 (hard).

It is advisable to use some form of protection during the winter – garden fleece draped around and fixed with clothes pegs works extremely well. When planting, ensure adequate drainage, as this group does not do well in ground that stands wet during the winter.

If in any doubt, it is better to keep floridas in large pots which can be stood out in a sheltered position late in the spring, for the summer and early autumn. When the weather breaks for the winter, move them into a cold glass-house or conservatory. Under cover and without artificial heat, they will often remain semi-evergreen. With a little extra warmth, they can flower right through until Christmas.

Floridas are very difficult for the nurseryman to propagate, which means they are often only to be found at specialist clematis nurseries or the larger garden centres.

They are not the easiest varieties to grow, and will definitely not thrive if simply planted in the garden and left to their own devices. If you like a challenge, however, do give one a try. Take good care of it and it will more than repay you with a wonderful display of quite exotic flowers.

C. florida

There is some confusion over the introduction of C. florida to Europe. It was most certainly a native of Western China, being found by Augustine Henry (1857–1930), in about 1885 near Ichang, in the province of Hupeh, and later by E. H. Wilson in the same area. There is also reference to Thunberg finding it growing in gardens in Japan and introducing it to Europe in 1776. It seems quite likely that the plant introduced by Thunberg could have been C. florida 'Plena'. C. florida is a very rare plant, in fact it is on the NCCPG 'pink sheet' of rare or endangered plants. FLOWERS: mid-summer to early autumn; borne singly; 3–4in (7–10cm) across; six (or occasionally four) wide, textured, overlapping sepals, each tapering to a point; sepals are creamy-white on both sides but sometimes have a pale green bar on the reverse; stamens form a striking crown, having white filaments which merge to dark purple, and purply-black anthers; pollen makes a fine purple dusting on sepals, adding to the flower's delicate charm; about half way along the flower stalk are a pair of heart-shaped bracts with no leaf stalk of their own. PRUNING: our plants grown under cover with no heat are hard pruned during February or March.

Unlike the better known C. florida 'Sieboldii' and C. florida 'Plena', which do not set seed, C. florida makes very attractive whorls of seeds.

C. florida 'Plena'

Introduced from Japan in about 1776. FLOWERS: about 4in (10cm) across; the most double clematis I know of, looking like a rosette; outer layer has six overlapping, pale greenish-cream sepals, each tapering to a point; distinctive green bar on reverse; each flower can take two to three weeks to open fully, as each layer gradually unfurls; it takes equally long to die: losing the outer layer of sepals first, the flower gradually diminishes in size. Because of this slow process, each flower is displayed for many weeks.

This variety can occasionally revert to 'Sieboldii', although reversion is usually the other way round.

C. florida 'Sieboldii'

Also known as 'Bicolor' and 'Sieboldiana', this variety was introduced from Japan in about 1835 by Philipp F. von Siebold (1796–1866). FLOWERS: very full, star-shaped; about 4in (10cm) across; six creamy-white sepals which overlap and taper to points; reverse of sepals are light green towards the tips; in the centre of each flower is a huge crown, about 2–2½in (5–6cm) across, made of many layers of rich purple petaloid stamens; as the flowers die, they lose their outer sepals first, leaving their purple crowns on the stems for several more days; stamens are virtually non-existent and these flowers are sterile.

The eye-catching appearance of this variety has earned it the name of the 'passion flower' clematis. This popular variety has a tendency to revert to *C. florida* 'Plena'. I have seen plants with a stem of each variety, and even, on one occasion, a bloom of which half was 'Plena', and the other half 'Sieboldii'.

C. fusca

Introduced from north-east Asia in 1860. APPROX. HEIGHT: 6–8ft (2–2.6m). FLOWERS: early to late summer; bell-shaped; ¾–1in (2–2.5cm) long; hang down singly from the leaf axils; four thick, ribbed sepals of dusky purple, the colour disguised by a covering of reddish-brown hairs; sepals recurve slightly to reveal the pale greenish-cream inside. ASPECT: any. PRUNING: Group 3 (hard).

This is a delightful and unusual clematis, though not one to grow if you are wanting a stunning visual impact. I was pleasantly surprised when I saw it in flower last summer.

C. fusca var. violacea

APPROX. HEIGHT: 6ft (2m). FLOWERS: mid- to late summer; usually borne in threes at the top of the current season's growth; 1in (2.5cm)-long, bell-shaped flowers; four dusky, purply-brown sepals, ¹⁄₁₀in (0.25cm) thick; tips of sepals turn out only slightly to reveal the tips of the furry beige anthers. ASPECT: any. PRUNING: Group 3 (hard).

An unusual, interesting plant.

'General Sikorski' AGM

Introduced from Poland by Jim Fisk in 1980. APPROX. HEIGHT: 6–8ft (2–2.6m). FLOWERS: profuse, from early summer to early autumn; 5–6in (12–15cm) across; six broadly overlapping, mid-mauve-blue sepals, with the merest hint of rose-pink running from the base to about half way up; reverse has a broad white bar merging towards blue margins; sepals taper to a blunt point, making a very round-looking flower; crown of stamens, which have creamy-white filaments with butter-yellow anthers, contrasts well with the colour of the sepals. ASPECT: any. PRUNING: Group 2 (light).

A strong-growing, compact plant, which is always a 'good doer'. Ideal in a pot.

'Gillian Blades' AGM

Introduced by Jim Fisk in 1975. APPROX. HEIGHT: 6–8ft (2–2.6m). FLOWERS: late spring to early summer, and again in early autumn; almost frilly looking, star-shaped flower, about 6–7in (15–17cm) across; seven to eight overlapping, textured white sepals, with a hint of bluey-mauve along their margins; sepals taper to a point and the edges are crimped; crown of yellow stamens. ASPECT: any. PRUNING: Group 2 (light).

A compact, very beautiful plant that flowers well, is suitable for container cultivation, and deserves to be more widely grown.

'Gipsy Queen' AGM

Introduced by Cripps in 1877. APPROX. HEIGHT: 10–12ft (3.3–4m). FLOWERS: mid-summer to early autumn; 5–5½in (12–14cm) across; very dark purple on first opening, paling slightly as the flower matures; six broad, velvety, slightly reddish-purple sepals which taper to a blunt tip and are narrow at the base, making the flowers appear rather gappy; off-white filaments with dark red anthers. ASPECT: best in some sun. PRUNING: Group 3 (hard).

'Guernsey Cream'

Introduced by Raymond Evison from Guernsey. APPROX. HEIGHT: 6–8ft (2–2.6m). FLOWERS: late spring to early summer, and again in late summer; 5–6in (12–15cm) across; eight sepals overlap and taper to a point to make a very 'full' flower; pale, yellowy-cream on opening, with a slightly deeper bar which, on the early blooms, sometimes has a hint of pale green; colouring pales to cream as the flower matures; beautiful crown of stamens with white filaments and yellow anthers; unfortunately, flowers do not die very gracefully and benefit from dead-heading. ASPECT: best grown in semi-shade to preserve its delicately pretty colour. PRUNING: Group 2 (light).

A compact and very free-flowering variety which is good in a pot.

'Hagley Hybrid'

Raised by Percy Picton when head gardener at Hagley Hall and introduced by Jim Fisk in 1956. APPROX. HEIGHT: 6–8ft (2–2.6m). FLOWERS: early summer to early autumn; 5–6in (12–15cm) across; open a good shell pink but fade quickly if grown in full sun, although even faded to pale pink the effect is still very pleasing; six pointed sepals with a satin sheen and a textured surface; edges of sepals are crimped and incurve slightly; reverse is pale pink with a white bar; stamens have white filaments, merging towards the wine-red anthers. ASPECT: avoid full sun. PRUNING: Group 3 (hard).

Compact, free-flowering and ideal for a pot, this clematis is widely grown and deservedly so.

'Haku Ookan'

Introduced from Japan by Jim Fisk in 1971. This plant's official name is 'Hakuôkan', which means 'The White Royal Crown', referring to the crown of stamens which make its flower look so regal. APPROX. HEIGHT: 6–8ft (2–2.6m). FLOWERS: late spring to early summer, and again in early autumn; occasionally semi-double from the old wood; star-shaped; 6–7in (15–17cm) across; eight overlapping, pointed sepals, each tapering to a sharp point, and with slightly incurving margins; rich royal purple, some-times paler down the centre of the sepal, overlaid by dark purple veins; reverse has wide bars of white, running out to dark purple margins; huge crown of stamens have white filaments and pale primrose-yellow anthers. ASPECT: avoid exposed, north-facing situation. PRUNING: Group 2 (light).

Another excellent candidate for container cultivation, owing to its free-flowering, compact habit.

'Helen Cropper'

Raised by the Dennys of Preston, Lancashire, and introduced in the early 1990s. APPROX. HEIGHT: 6–8ft (2–2.6m). FLOWERS: late spring to early summer, and again in early autumn; 7in (17cm) across; seven or eight large, overlapping sepals with blunt tips, crimped edges and a textured, satiny surface; very pale pink, heavily overlaid with deep, dusky mauve-pink, deepening towards the margins and giving a mottled appearance; reverse is equally as pretty as the face; stamens have white filaments, merging towards deep red anthers. ASPECT: any. PRUNING: Group 2 (light).

'Henryi' AGM

Hybridized by Anderson-Henry of Edinburgh in 1855, this cross between *C. patens* and *C. lanuginosa* was one of the earliest crosses of large-flowered clematis. APPROX. HEIGHT: 10–12ft (3m). FLOWERS: profuse, from early summer to early autumn; a huge 7–8in (17–20cm) across; eight pointed, almost pure white sepals with a satin sheen; when lit from behind, the flower has an almost tissue-paper-like appearance; large crown, 1½in (3cm) across, of white stamens with coffee-coloured anthers. ASPECT: any. PRUNING: Group 2 (light).

A very elegant flower which is still one of the most popular white clematis available.

THE *HERACLEIFOLIA* GROUP

These are all hardy herbaceous plants with thick, woody stems. They vary in height from 2½–4ft (0.75–1.3m). They are clump-forming non-climbers, and flower from late summer to mid-autumn. Flowers: ¾–1½in (2–4cm) long; almost identical to those of the hyacinth; tubular, borne in clusters from the leaf axils, with a large cluster at the top of each stem;

four sepals with a textured surface and crimped edges, becoming broader towards the blunt tips which recurve right back on themselves as the flower opens; yellow stamens with beige anthers. FOLIAGE: coarse, with large, almost hairy-looking leaves of dull green, which have serrated edges.

C. heracleifolia
Introduced from central and northern China in 1837, and was originally known as *C. tubulosa*. Has no apparent scent. APPROX. HEIGHT: 2–3ft (0.6–1m). FLOWERS: bears both male and female on the same plant; tubular; ¾–1in (2–2.5cm) long; sepals are deep, purply-blue, with recurved tips.

C. heracleifolia '**Campanile**'
Has no detectable scent. APPROX. HEIGHT: 3–4ft (1–1.3m). FLOWERS: an individual plant bears both male and female; 1¼in (3cm) long, light mid-blue sepals roll back to reveal pale yellow anthers; sepals have a white bar with blue margins on the inside, the bar disappears towards the tip which is blue.

'**Côte d'Azur**'
Said to be of a deeper shade than 'Campanile', but I believe these could be one and the same plant.

'**Crépuscule**'
Also seen as *C.* x *bonstedtii* 'Crépuscule', this is said by Bean to be a hybrid between *C. heracleifolia* and *C. stans*, raised by Lemoine.

C. heracleifolia var. *davidiana*
Collected by Père David in 1863 near Peking in northern China, this plant is very sweetly scented with a light, fresh perfume similar to that of spring flowers. APPROX. HEIGHT: 3ft (1m). FLOWERS: individual plants bear either male or female flowers; light mauve to grey-blue sepals about 1in (2.5cm) long open to reveal pale yellow anthers.

C. heracleifolia var. *davidiana* '**Wyevale**'
'Wyevale' is also strongly scented; its perfume has been likened to that of the hyacinth. It reminds me of spring flowers, like cowslips, violets and primroses. APPROX. HEIGHT: 3½–4ft (1–1.3m). FLOWERS: deep mid-blue flowers, larger than those previously mentioned.

'**H. F. Young**' AGM
Hybridized and introduced by Pennells of Lincoln in 1962, this clematis has been a favourite of mine for many years. APPROX. HEIGHT: 8–10ft

(3m). FLOWERS: late spring to early summer, and again in early autumn; 7in (17cm) across; eight overlapping sepals of bright, slightly mauvy mid-blue, with rounded edges tapering to pointed tips; on opening, each sepal has a soft pinky bar down the centre that quickly fades as the flower opens; reverse has greenish-white bars radiating into the mauve-blue background; stamens have white filaments with primrose-yellow anthers which help to make this a bright sunny flower. ASPECT: avoid exposed, north-facing situation. PRUNING: Group 2 (light).

H. F. Young is a very reliable variety which always flowers along the whole length of the plant, making it ideal for growing as a specimen in a container.

'Huldine'

Thought to have been raised in France, around the beginning of this century, this clematis received the RHS Award of Merit when shown by Ernest Markham on 14 August 1934. APPROX. HEIGHT: 15ft (5m). FLOWERS: late summer to late autumn; 3–4in (7–10cm) across; six pearl-coloured sepals with a translucent satin sheen on the surface, each tapering to a slightly reflexed point; equally pretty on the reverse, with a deep, dusky reddish-purple bar running along the mid-ribs and paling towards the margins; stamens have white filaments with butter-yellow anthers; ASPECT: best in full sun. PRUNING: optional: Group 2 (light) or Group 3 (hard); a late-flowering variety that normally requires hard pruning; we have found it to flower better after only light pruning, when it begins around mid-August and goes on until the frosts of November.

A vigorous plant which looks good scrambling over substantial medium-to-large shrubs, rather than high up on a wall, when a ladder would be needed to appreciate the flowers!

THE INTEGRIFOLIA GROUP

Introduced in 1573 from Eastern Europe, this group of lovely herb-aceous, non-climbing clematis are clump-forming, extremely hardy, easy to grow and very pretty. APPROX. HEIGHT: all grow to about 2–2½ft (60–80cm) tall. FLOWERS: mid- to late summer, from the current season's wood; bell-shaped; generally smaller than those of the hybrids; deep mid-blue. PRUNING: Group 3 (hard).

The integrifolias are very useful little plants: they can provide colour at the front of a border, between shrubs, amongst rose bushes, or in a herbaceous bed. They take up so little space, one could be planted almost anywhere.

If your garden is open and windy, you may find it necessary to provide these plants with some support. A few twigs pushed into the ground around the integrifolia will keep the growth upright. Alternatively, the stems can be left to scramble along the ground. When the plant has made a substantial clump, it can be lifted and divided at pruning time.

C. integrifolia 'Alba'
FLOWERS: pure white; four deeply ribbed, pointed sepals, 1–1½in (2.5–4cm) long, that turn out and twist slightly as the flower opens to reveal butter-yellow anthers.

C. integrifolia 'Hendersonii'
Slightly scented. FLOWERS: deep mid-blue; the largest flowers of all the integrifolias – the four pointed sepals are 2¼in (5.5cm) long; as the bloom opens, the sepals remain hanging down, but recurve and twist just enough to see the furry looking buttercup-yellow anthers; reverse has raised ribs of a slightly darker blue, which is also seen along the crimped edges.

C. integrifolia 'Olgae'
Slightly perfumed. FLOWERS: clear mid-blue; four pointed, 1¾in (4.5cm)-long sepals, open wide with tips reflexed and slightly twisted to reveal bright yellow anthers; sepals have three distinct raised ribs along the length of the reverse.

C. integrifolia 'Pangbourne Pink'
From Busheyfields Nursery in Kent. FLOWERS: four deeply grooved, 1½ in (3.5cm)-long sepals; very deep, slightly mauve pink; on both the front and the reverse the central bar is deeper in colour than the margins; three distinct ribs run the length of the reverse; sepals are pointed, and twist at the tips as the flower opens to reveal pale yellow stamens.

C. integrifolia 'Pastel Pink'
Introduced by Barry Fretwell in 1986. FLOWERS: four pale pink, deeply grooved, 1¾–2in (4–5cm)-long sepals that recurve and twist as the flower opens to reveal bright yellow anthers.

C. integrifolia 'Rosea'
Slightly scented. FLOWERS: mid-mauve-pink; very similar in shape to integrifolia 'Olgae'; four pointed, 1½in (3.5–4cm)-long sepals that open wide and partially twist, revealing the bright yellow anthers.

'Jackmanii' AGM
Raised in 1858 by Jackman and Sons of Woking and awarded a First Class Certificate on 4 August 1863. The result of a cross between *C. lanuginosa*, *C. eriostemon* 'Hendersonii' and *C. viticella atrorubens*, this has to be one of

the most widely grown clematis, which has adorned many a cottage wall since its introduction in 1863. APPROX. HEIGHT: 8–10ft (3m). FLOWERS: mid-summer to early autumn; 4–5in (10–12cm) across; four, or occasionally, five or six sepals, which are a good bluish-purple with a reddish flush at the bases and have a textured, ribbed surface; pale beige-green stamens. ASPECT: any. PRUNING: Group 3 (hard).

An old favourite which always blooms profusely.

'Jackmanii Alba'

Introduced by Noble in 1878. APPROX. HEIGHT: 10–12ft (3–4m). FLOWERS: double from early to mid-summer, and single in early autumn; 5in (12cm) across; many layers of deeply textured, pointed sepals; outer layers are bluey-mauve with splashes of green, and have green bars on the reverse; paler inner layers, the uppermost rings are a bluey-white; the whole flower turns whiter as it matures; single flowers have five or six bluish-white sepals; stamens have white filaments with light brown anthers; in common with 'Duchess of Edinburgh', there is a ring of distorted leaves approximately 6in (15cm) down the flower stem. ASPECT: any. PRUNING: Group 2 (light).

'Jackmanii Superba'

Introduced by Jackman's of Woking in 1878. APPROX. HEIGHT: 10–12ft (3–4m). FLOWERS: early summer to early autumn; 5–5½in (12–14cm) across; sepals are broader than those of 'Jackmanii'; rich purple on opening, with a reddish bar along the mid-rib that quickly fades as the flower matures; greenish-cream filaments with beige anthers. ASPECT: any. PRUNING: Group 3 (hard).

'James Mason'

Hybridized in 1984 by Barry Fretwell of Peveril's Nursery in Devon, and named after the famous actor who was extremely fond of white flowers. APPROX. HEIGHT: 6–8ft (2–2.6m). FLOWERS: late spring to early summer, and again in early autumn; 7–8in (17–20cm) across; eight overlapping sepals, each of which tapers to a blunt tip, and is deeply grooved along the mid-rib; edges of the sepals are wavy and recurve slightly as the blooms mature; huge crown of dark stamens, with white filaments and dark, wine-red anthers. ASPECT: avoid exposed north-facing situation. PRUNING: Group 2 (light).

Ideal in a container.

'Jan Pawel II' ('John Paul II')

Introduced from Poland in 1982 by Jim Fisk. APPROX. HEIGHT: 8–12ft (2.6–4m). FLOWERS: late summer to late autumn. 5–5½in (12–14cm) across; six broad, overlapping sepals, each tapering to a point, with a textured surface and a pretty satin sheen; pearly, almost translucent white with a hint of pink; on first opening, sepals have a pink bar on both the face and the reverse; as the flower ages, the bar on the surface fades, but that on the reverse still gives a hint of pink through the sepal; stamens have creamy-white filaments and deep wine-red anthers. ASPECT: any. PRUNING: optional: Group 2 (light) or Group 3 (hard); we would normally hard prune this late flowering variety; however, ours had never done very well in the garden until it was lightly pruned – since when it has flourished; even after light pruning our plant does not begin flowering until mid-August.

C. japonica
Originally from Japan – thought to have been introduced during the mid-nineteenth century. APPROX. HEIGHT: 6–8ft (2–2.6m). FLOWERS: late spring to early summer; 1¼in (3cm)-long bell-shaped flowers born from leaf axils amid the foliage; four thick, reddish-brown sepals, whose tips recurve as the flower opens, which it does not do fully. FOLIAGE: large and attractive. ASPECT: any. PRUNING: Group 2 (light).

This species is easy to grow, but it needs to be situated where the small flowers can be admired close to. We grow ours over the arch of a well-used pathway, which makes an unusual, attractive feature.

'John Huxtable'
A chance seedling from 'Comtesse de Bouchaud', this clematis has all its parent's characteristics, but instead of being pink, it is a slightly creamy white. APPROX. HEIGHT: 6–8ft (2–2.6m). FLOWERS: mid- to late summer; 4½–5in (11–12cm) across; six deeply textured sepals with a wonderful satin sheen, each one tapering to a slightly recurved point; stamens have white filaments and bright yellow anthers. ASPECT: any. PRUNING: Group 3 (hard).

Very free flowering, which makes it ideal for growing in containers.

'John Warren'
Hybridized by Walter Pennell of Lincoln. APPROX. HEIGHT: 6–8ft (2–2.6m). FLOWERS: early to late summer; star-shaped, 8in (20cm) across; six or, occasionally, seven sepals; each has lightly crimped edges that taper to a point to form the 'star', and a satin sheen to the surface; unusual base colour of grey-white, heavily overlaid with a deep pinky-red, especially along the mid-rib, as a bar, and also along the margins; white bar on the reverse, merging towards deep pink margins, with deep pink running along the mid-ribs; stamens have white filaments and wine-red anthers. ASPECT: sheltered. PRUNING: Group 2 (light).

C. x *jouiniana* 'Praecox' AGM

A semi-herbaceous, non-clinging clematis, with no perfume as such, but quite a strong pollen smell. APPROX. HEIGHT: 6–10ft (2–3.3m). FLOWERS: mid- to late summer, through to mid- to late autumn; borne in large sprays of around sixty; 1½in (3.5cm) across; four narrow sepals, white at the base, changing to deep bluey-mauve half-way along their length, so that their blunt tips are usually well coloured; colour is much deeper on the reverse; ½in (1cm)-long, prominent stamens with white filaments and primrose-yellow anthers. FOLIAGE: lush, even in a drought. ASPECT: any. PRUNING: optional: Group 2 (light) or Group 3 (hard); we hard prune our jouiniana; it could be lightly pruned to remove the growth which produced flowers in the previous season, and to allow it to grow taller or to cover more ground.

This late-flowering clematis makes excellent ground cover as it has extremely dense growth. It also looks good grown as a climber, but needs to be tied in.

'Kathleen Dunford'

Introduced by Jim Fisk in 1962. APPROX. HEIGHT: 6–8ft (2–2.6m). FLOWERS: semi-double from late spring to early summer, and single in early autumn; 7½in (19cm) across; early flowers are semi-double with two layers; eight narrow, pointed sepals on each layer, the ones on the top layer being a fraction shorter and narrower than the bottom ones; sepals are a lovely deep, purplish mauve-pink, which becomes a mottled, pale lavender blue at the margins; reverse has a white bar merging towards purple margins; stamens have white filaments with wine-red anthers. ASPECT: any. PRUNING: Group 2 (light).

'Kathleen Wheeler'

Hybridized by Walter Pennell of Lincoln. APPROX. HEIGHT: 8–10ft (3m). FLOWERS: very elegant; early to mid-summer, and again in early autumn; 6–8in (15–20cm) across; six to eight very pointed sepals; deep, plummy mauve with a hint of rose pink shading down the central grooved mid-ribs; stamens have same plummy, mauve-pink filaments with pale, primrose-yellow anthers. ASPECT: any. PRUNING: Group 2 (light).

'Ken Donson' AGM

Hybridized by Walter Pennell in 1961. APPROX. HEIGHT: 8–10ft (3m). FLOWERS: early summer to early autumn; 6in (15cm) across; six broad sepals that taper to a point open a rich, deep slightly purply blue; reverse has a white bar melting into deep blue margins; stamens have white filaments and bright yellow anthers, contrasting well against the colour of the sepals. ASPECT: any. PRUNING: Group 2 (light).

'King Edward VII'

Hybridized by Jackman's of Woking in the early 1900s. APPROX. HEIGHT: 6–8ft (2–2.6m). FLOWERS: early to late summer; 7–8½in (17–21cm) across; six overlapping sepals which have a very textured surface and taper to a point; the most wonderful shades of mid-rose-pink produce a mottled effect over the entire sepal, with occasional mottles of white, and fade out to deep mauve margins; stamens have white filaments with light reddish-brown anthers. ASPECT: any. PRUNING: Group 2 (light).

These beautiful flowers show up well when this clematis is planted through a small, dark-leaved shrub such as *Osmanthus* x *burkwoodii*. If I was forced at any time to express a preference between the large-flowered hybrids, I feel sure I would favour this plant.

'King George V'

APPROX. HEIGHT: 8–10ft (3m). FLOWERS: mid- to late summer; 6in (15cm) across; five or six broad sepals of pale pink overlaid by a wide, mottled bar of raspberry-pink; sepals taper to a red-tipped point, and there is a satin sheen over the textured surface and lightly crimped edges; stamens have creamy-white filaments with coffee-coloured anthers; reverse has a white bar, melting into pale pink margins. ASPECT: avoid full sun; unfortunately, the pretty colouring is quickly lost if exposed to strong sunlight; a position in semi- or full shade is best. PRUNING: Group 2 (light).

A good plant for brightening up a dull spot.

'Lady Caroline Nevill'

Hybridized by Cripps of Tunbridge Wells, and awarded a First Class Certificate on 21 August 1866. APPROX. HEIGHT: 8–10ft (3m). FLOWERS: double in early to mid-summer, and single in early autumn; 5–6in (12–15cm) across; three or four layers of bluey-mauve, pointed sepals, each cascading down over the layer below, followed by a display of single flowers later in the season; single flowers have six broad, overlapping sepals which taper to a point; the colour has an almost translucent appearance and a satin sheen; greenish-white bar on the reverse; stamens have creamy-white filaments with coffee-coloured anthers. ASPECT: any. PRUNING: Group 2 (light).

'Lady Londesborough'

Hybridized by Noble of Sunningdale, and awarded a First Class Certificate on 18 May 1869. APPROX. HEIGHT: 6–8ft (2–2.6m). FLOWERS: late spring to early or mid-summer; 6in (15cm) across; eight overlapping, pale pinkish-mauve sepals gradually fade to silvery-mauve as the bloom matures; sepals are round edged, tapering to a point, and have a textured surface with a pretty satin sheen; stamens have white filaments with dark reddish-brown anthers. ASPECT: avoid exposed, north-facing situation. PRUNING: Group 2 (light).

Compact and free-flowering, well suited for a pot.

'Lady Northcliffe'

Hybridized by Jackman in the early 1900s. APPROX. HEIGHT: 5–6ft (1.6–2m). FLOWERS: early summer to early autumn; 5–6in (12–15cm) across; really rich royal blue when first open, paling slightly to a good mid-lavender blue as the flower matures; six broad, overlapping, wavy-edged sepals that each taper to a point and do not open out flat; reverse has a silvery bar, blending into dusky mid-blue; stamens have creamy-white filaments with pale greenish-yellow anthers, which contrast well against the sepals. ASPECT: avoid exposed, north-facing situation. PRUNING: Group 2 (light).

A short, compact clematis which flowers over a long period, and is ideal in a container.

'Lasurstern' AGM

This lovely variety, which puts on a spectacular display early in the season, was introduced by Messrs Goos and Koenemann, of Germany, in 1906. APPROX. HEIGHT: 8–10ft (3m). FLOWERS: late spring to early summer, and again in early autumn; 7–8in (17–20cm) across; rich, slightly mauve mid-blue, with the central bar paling as the bloom matures; seven or eight overlapping sepals, their crimped edges tapering to a point; white bar on reverse; stamens have white filaments with yellow anthers. ASPECT: any. PRUNING: Group 2 (light).

'Lawsoniana'

One of the first large-flowered clematis to have been hybridized, and still worthy of a place in our modern gardens, this clematis, a cross between C. patens and C. lanuginosa, was hybridized by Anderson-Henry of Edinburgh in 1855. APPROX. HEIGHT: 12–16ft (4–5.2m). FLOWERS: early summer to early autumn; a huge 7–9in (17–22cm) across; on first opening, the mid mauve-blue colour is really vibrant, with a hint of pink, but fades to pale lavender-blue as the flower matures; eight pointed, overlapping sepals; huge crown of stamens, some 2in (5cm) across, which have white filaments and beige anthers; reverse has a white bar. ASPECT: any. PRUNING: optional: Group 2 (light) or Group 3 (hard); with light pruning, 'Lawsoniana' grows very tall and bears the majority of its flowers high up on the growth; try hard pruning to keep the overall height lower and the blooms within sight; this will however make the flowering period a few weeks later, and the blooms slightly smaller.

We grow 'Lawsoniana' with the pink climbing rose 'Compassion', the pair making a wonderful combination of subtle colour. Alternatively, it could be grown scrambling over low shrubs, or other features, where the flowers could be admired without straining one's neck.

'Louise Rowe'

From Mrs Jean Rowe. Probably a cross between 'Marie Boisselot' and 'William Kennett', introduced by Jim Fisk in 1984. APPROX. HEIGHT: 4–6ft (1.3–2m). FLOWERS: early to mid-summer, and again in early autumn; this beautiful double clematis is unusual in that it flowers double, semi-double and single all at the same time; 5–6in (12–15cm) across; pale mauve, the shade varies from delicate mauve to pinky-mauve and grey-mauve, depending upon the light at different times of the day; sepals have rounded edges with pointed tips, and have a textured surface with a satin sheen; inner sepals twist slightly, making the flower appear frilly; stamens are primrose-yellow. ASPECT: sheltered. PRUNING: Group 2 (light).

A really lovely clematis which keeps compact, and is very free flowering, making an attractive display in a pot.

THE MACROPETALA GROUP

The species *C. macropetala* was introduced to Britain in 1910. It is a native of Northern China and Siberia, and was originally discovered by the French missionary and botanist D'Incarville, in Northern China in about 1742. APPROX. HEIGHT: 8–10ft (3m). FLOWERS: profuse, from the old, ripened wood, from mid- to late spring; 1½–2½in (3.5–6cm) long; borne on slender stalks about 3in (7.5cm) long; flowers hang like open bells and have four outer sepals, about 1½in (4cm) long and ¾in (2cm) wide, enclosing layers of smaller petaloid stamens, which become progressively smaller towards the centre; outer layers of the sepals taper to a point, and vary in colour from light to mid-violet-blue; the innermost layer is off-white, sometimes flushed with blue; attractive seedheads are produced, and stay on the plant for most of the winter. FOLIAGE: leaves are each divided into three, each division having three leaflets with serrated edges. ASPECT: any; despite the delicate appearance of the flowers, these plants are really tough, and will cope with the harshest of weather. PRUNING: Group 1 (tidy after flowering); it is worth hard pruning one or two stems each year after the plant has flowered, to encourage fresh growth to cover any bare patches, and allow new wood to be produced and to ripen in readiness to flower the following spring.

There are now many hybrid macropetalas, a few of which are described below; they all have the same characteristics as the original species.

C. macropetala 'Jan Lindmark'
One of the earliest spring-flowering macropetalas, this was hybridized by Magnus Johnson of Sweden. FLOWERS: open out almost flat; four pinkish-purple outer sepals, each 2in (5cm) long; inner petaloid stamens are narrower and have white shadings. FOLIAGE: mid-green.

C. macropetala 'Maidwell Hall' AGM
FLOWERS: 2in (5cm) long; very deep mid-blue and, if grown in the shade, almost french navy.

C. macropetala 'Markham's Pink' AGM
Hybridized by Ernest Markham. Occasionally seen labelled as 'Markhamii', which was the name Ernest Markham used. It received the RHS Award of Merit on 5 March 1935. FLOWERS: four outer sepals, 2½in (6cm) long and ¾in (2cm) wide; mid-pink with very dark purply-pink veins on reverse; inner skirt of petaloid stamens which are as long as the outer sepals but much narrower. A wonderful sight when in full flower.

'Rosy O'Grady'
Hybridized by Frank Skinner of Canada in 1964. The result of a cross between *macropetala* and *alpina*. FLOWERS: have a delicate appearance but cope well with bad weather; buds are deep reddish-pink; on opening, the four 2½in (6cm)-long outer sepals are pale to mid-mauve-pink with very deep pink veins on the outside, and pale pink inside; inner layer of petaloid stamens is slightly paler. FOLIAGE: pale green.

The following three macropetalas are white:

C. mac. 'Snowbird'
Hybridized by Barry Fretwell of Devon, in 1969.

C. mac. 'White Lady'
Hybridized by Tage Lundell of Sweden.

'White Swan'
Hybridized by Frank Skinner of Canada in 1961, this is a cross between *macropetala* and *alpina*.

'Madame Baron Veillard'
Introduced by Veillard in 1885. APPROX. HEIGHT: 10–12ft (3.3–4m). FLOWERS: early to mid-autumn; 4–5in (10–12cm) across; six dusky mid-mauve-pink sepals with textured margins and grooves along the mid-ribs; tips of the sepals are blunt, and recurve as the flower matures; greenish-white stamens. ASPECT: in view of its late-flowering nature, this clematis

is best grown in full sun which will encourage it to flower as early as possible; PRUNING: Group 3 (hard), or if, despite a sunny position, it is reluctant to flower, try light pruning to encourage earlier flowering.

A useful clematis for late colour in the garden.

'Madame Edouard André' AGM

Introduced by Veillard in 1893. APPROX. HEIGHT: 6–8ft (2–2.6m). FLOWERS: early summer to early autumn; 4–5in (10–12cm) across; four to six sepals, with rounded edges tapering to a point, that remain slightly cupped; surface is a lovely matt mid-red, lightly mottled with flecks of white, fading to a more mauvy red as the flower matures; reverse has a white bar, melting into dusky red margins; creamy-yellow stamens. ASPECT: any. PRUNING: Group 3 (hard).

A compact plant which flowers well and is suitable for a pot.

'Madame Grangé' AGM

Introduced by Grangé in 1875. APPROX. HEIGHT: 8–12ft (2.6–4m). FLOWERS: mid- to late summer; 5½–6in (13–15cm); four to six sepals of the most gorgeous, rich, velvety reddish-purple along the margins, with a cherry-red bar down the centre-line; sepals turn in along the margins, making a boat shape and revealing the dusky purply-silver reverse; as the flowers age they sometimes flatten out; stamens have light reddish-purple filaments with coffee-coloured anthers. ASPECT: best grown in sun or semi-shade. PRUNING: Group 3 (hard).

Deserves to be more widely grown.

'Margaret Hunt'

From Margaret Hunt of Norwich, Norfolk, and introduced by Jim Fisk in 1969. APPROX. HEIGHT: 8–12ft (2.6–4m). FLOWERS: early summer to early autumn; 4–6in (10–15cm) across; six sepals with rounded edges which taper sharply to a point at both ends; dusky mauve-pink, with a deeper shade forming a half-bar near the centre of the flower, this colour is carried along the crimped margins and through veins across the entire surface; dusky-red bar on reverse of each sepal; stamens have pale yellow filaments with red anthers. ASPECT: any. PRUNING: Group 3 (hard).

Even in poor conditions, this clematis flowers extremely well. It looks wonderful when grown with a cream rose such as 'Albéric Barbier'.

'Marie Boisselot' AGM

Introduced in the early 1900s, this clematis is also sold as 'Madame Le Coultre', and is listed in the *Clematis Index* under its official name, 'Mevrouw Le Coultre'. APPROX. HEIGHT: 8–12ft (2.6–4m). FLOWERS: early summer to early autumn; 6–8in (15–20cm) across; round appearance, owing to the very rounded shape of the eight overlapping pure white sepals, which look creamy-white against the crown of bright yellow stamens; sepals have a textured, satiny surface, with deep grooves along the mid-rib, and sometimes twist as the flower matures; stamens have cream filaments with golden-yellow anthers. ASPECT: any. PRUNING: optional: Group 2 (light) or Group 3 (hard).

This clematis is best grown over low to medium-sized shrubs or through roses, where the blooms can be seen from above. They are held horizontally, looking skyward, so it is difficult to appreciate them if the plant is allowed to climb tall.

'Maureen'

APPROX. HEIGHT: 6–8ft (2–2.6m). FLOWERS: early summer to early autumn; 4½–6in (12–15cm) across; a stunning, velvety shade of intense purply-red, which fades only slightly as the bloom ages; six broad, overlapping sepals, each tapering to a point; bars of pale grey, fading into dusky-red margins on the reverse; the edges of the sepals recurve as the flowers mature; stamens have creamy-white filaments with pale yellow anthers, and look perfect against the deep colour of the sepals. ASPECT: any. PRUNING: optional: Group 2 (light) or Group 3 (hard).

A compact plant that flowers profusely and is therefore ideal to grow in a container.

'Miss Bateman' AGM

Raised by Charles Noble of Sunningdale and awarded a First Class Certificate on 4 May 1869, this is another very early-blooming large-flowered variety, which is still very popular after almost 130 years. APPROX. HEIGHT: 6–8ft (2–2.6m). FLOWERS: late spring to early summer; 5½–6in (13–15cm) across; eight satin-white sepals which overlap and taper to a blunt point, making the flower appear very rounded; large crown of stamens with white filaments and very dark red anthers; sepals of early flowers, particularly if grown in shade, have a pale green bar down the centre. ASPECT: any. PRUNING: Group 2 (light).

A compact, free-flowering variety, ideal for container cultivation.

THE *MONTANA* GROUP

The original *C. montana*, introduced from the Himalayas by Lady Amherst in 1831, was white. There are now many clematis labelled 'montana', but they vary greatly, because over the years they have been grown from seed, and not reproduced vegetatively. APPROX. HEIGHT: the majority make about 20–30ft (7–10m) of growth; some are less rampant, growing to around 15ft (4.5m), while others can reach 40ft (12m) or more. FLOWERS:

produced in abundance from old ripened wood through late spring and early summer, and a modest display is occasionally produced during early autumn; most are single with four sepals, but a few plants bear semi-double; colour varies from white through all shades of pink to almost cherry-red. FOLIAGE: colour also varies with the varieties, from light green to deep purply-bronze; leaves each have three leaflets with serrated edges. PRUNING: because montanas flower from the old wood they should be pruned to tidy them up immediately they have finished flowering. (Group 1)

In view of their rampant nature, montanas are ideal for using to cover eyesores in the garden. Whilst they are not evergreen, they hold their leaves for much of the winter, and while dormant their mass of jumbled stems will soften the outline and disguise a garden shed, garage or barn. If grown on a house wall, they must be pruned and trained vigilantly if they are not to become a nuisance or an untidy mess. They look their best clambering up and over large trees as they would in their natural environment. The flowers will keep for several days in water.

C. montana 'Alexander'

Introduced from northern India by Col R. D. Alexander, this scented variety is not often seen, probably because it takes several years for the plant to settle down to flowering. APPROX. HEIGHT: 20–30ft (7–10m). FLOWERS: 2½in (6cm) across; creamy-white. FOLIAGE: light green. ASPECT: best grown in sunny spot.

C. montana 'Broughton Star'

Raised by Vince and Sylvia Denny of Broughton, Lancashire, in 1988. FLOWERS: semi-double; 2in (5cm) across; very deep plummy-pink, almost resembling those of a macropetala; inner skirts of petaloid stamens stand up like a crown, and are the same deep pink as the sepals. FOLIAGE: deep purply-bronze.

If this very pretty clematis is to be fully appreciated, it is best seen against a light background, or grown in a sunny position.

C. montana 'Elizabeth' AGM

Raised by Jackman in 1958, this clematis has a light vanilla scent. FLOWERS: 2½in (6cm) across; pale pink sepals with a satin sheen and a textured surface; pale yellow stamens. FOLIAGE: young foliage is bronze, turning green as it matures. ASPECT: 'Elizabeth' is best grown in some sun which will enhance its colour; if grown in shade it will be almost white.

C. montana 'Freda' AGM

Raised by Mrs Freda Deacon of Woodbridge, Suffolk, and introduced by Jim Fisk in 1985. FLOWERS: 2½in (6cm) across; the darkest-coloured of all the montanas; sepals are deep cherry-pink, with paler pink bars and almost red margins; surface is textured and has a satin sheen; pale yellow stamens. APPROX. HEIGHT: 20–30ft (7–10m), but growth is not as rampant as that of other montanas.

C. montana 'Grandiflora' AGM

From northern India. Moore and Jackman, describing *montana* in their book of 1872, said: 'A variety called Grandiflora, with flowers twice the size of the original, has also been introduced by Messrs Veitch and Son'. Apparently, it flowered for the first time for Veitch in 1844. APPROX. HEIGHT: this is one of the most rampant montanas, growing to 40ft (12m) or more. FLOWERS: at 4in (10cm) across, these are the largest flowers of all the white montanas available today; brilliant white round-edged sepals; stamens have white filaments and bright yellow anthers, making a very 'sunny' flower. FOLIAGE: very dark green.

A wonderful sight when in full bloom.

C. montana 'Margaret Jones'

A seedling from the garden of Anne Smyth of Hoveton, Norfolk, and named after her mother. Introduced by Thorncroft Clematis in 1991. FLOWERS: semi-double, creamy-white; four main outer sepals that are about 1¼in (3cm) long and ½in (1.25cm) wide; inner layers of between six and twelve shorter, narrower petaloid stamens; stamens are greenish-cream. FOLIAGE: light green.

'Margaret Jones' does not produce flowers quite as profusely as some of the other montanas, but is nevertheless very pretty.

C. montana 'Marjorie'

Raised by Miss Marjorie Free of Suffolk, and introduced by Jim Fisk in 1980. FLOWERS: open a 'grubby' white but, after a few days, a lovely deep salmon-pink spreads across the sepals and petaloid stamens in veins, darkening towards the margins, and the base colour becomes more creamy; four outer sepals are about 1in (2.5cm) long and ½in (1.25cm) wide, making a flower 2½in (6cm) across; inner layer of petaloid stamens, which are much narrower and slightly shorter than the outer sepals. FOLIAGE: light green. ASPECT: avoid planting this in a shady position; our 'Marjorie' is grown on a south-facing wall, in full sun, where the blooms can be seen at their best for a full eight weeks.

C. montana 'Picton's Variety'

Raised by Percy Picton during the 1950s. FLOWERS: about 3in (7cm) across; a glorious deep, mauve-pink; four to six sepals with a satin sheen and a textured surface; stamens have white filaments with yellow anthers, and form a bright central crown to the flowers. FOLIAGE: bronze.

This montana is ideal for the smaller garden, as it only grows to about 15ft (4.5m) tall.

C. montana 'Rubens' AGM

The plants usually sold under this name are not, unfortunately, from the original stock that was introduced to England from China by Wilson in the early 1900s. The plants grown today have a beautiful vanilla scent. They are pale pink, and do not follow the original description of 'rosy-red, as large as 'Grandiflora''. It is to be hoped that, in the near future, stocks of 'Rubens' matching the original description will be freely available. Until this problem is rectified, I will describe the clematis now commonly grown as 'Rubens'. FLOWERS: 3in (7.5cm) across; four pale pink sepals, with even paler pink margins, they have a satin sheen and a textured surface; stamens have white filaments and yellow anthers. FOLIAGE: new foliage is bronze, turning green as it matures.

C. montana 'Tetrarose' AGM

Produced in Holland at the Boskoop Research Station in 1960, 'Tetra-rose' has a delicate, spicy scent. FLOWERS: 3in (7.5cm) across; four deep mauve-pink sepals, with a satin sheen and a textured surface; sepals do not open out flat, but remain cupped, even as the blooms mature; a cluster of golden yellow stamens in the centre. FOLIAGE: bronze, with reddish-brown stems.

C. montana var. wilsonii

The scent of *wilsonii* has been described as being like that of chocolate. As is the case with 'Rubens' (above), the *wilsonii* sold today do not exactly fit the original description. The montana introduced from central China by Wilson in the early 1900s, and named *wilsonii*, was also known as 'the autumn-flowering montana'. While the actual blooms of the *wilsonii* available today follow the original description, they generally only appear a couple of weeks later than those of all other montanas. FLOWERS: four creamy-white sepals, each ½in (1.25cm) wide, make a flower 2½in (6cm) across; stamens with white filaments and pale yellow anthers open out very wide, giving the flower a 'spidery' appearance.

'Mrs Cholmondeley' AGM

Introduced by Charles Noble of Sunningdale in 1873, and pronounced 'Chumley'. APPROX. HEIGHT: 10–16ft (3.3–5.2m). FLOWERS: late spring, semi-continuously to mid-autumn; 6–8in (15–20cm) across; six or seven sepals, which are light blue with a hint of mauve, the paler central bar being overlaid with darker mauve-blue veins; sepals taper to blunt tips at both ends, making a rather gappy-looking flower; stamens have white filaments flushed with blue and pale, coffee-coloured anthers. ASPECT: any. PRUNING: optional: Group 2 (light) or Group 3 (hard); with light pruning 'Mrs Cholmondeley' begins flowering during late spring, whereas with hard pruning, flowering does not begin until mid-summer; it may be preferable to hard prune if the overall height needs to be kept down.

A beautiful old clematis which is easy to grow, always performs well, and flowers over a very long period. It will flower equally as well whether light or hard pruned.

'Mrs George Jackman' AGM

Hybridized by Jackmans of Woking in 1873, this is another very old clematis that has stood the test of time. APPROX. HEIGHT: 6–8ft (2–2.6m). FLOWERS: late spring to early summer, and again in late summer to early autumn; 6in (15cm) across; early flowers are occasionally semi-double, usually with four layers of slightly creamy-white sepals; outer layers are broad and overlapping, each tapers toward a pointed tip and has a textured surface and a satin sheen; single blooms have six to eight sepals, again, broad and overlapping, making a very full flower; crown of stamens with creamy-white filaments and light, pinky-brown anthers is displayed well against the pale background. ASPECT: avoid very exposed situation. PRUNING: Group 2 (light).

'Mrs James Mason'

Hybridized by Barry Fretwell of Peveril Nursery, Devon, in 1984, this is a cross between 'Vyvyan Pennell' and 'Dr. Ruppel'. APPROX. HEIGHT: 8–10ft (2.6–3.3m). FLOWERS: semi-double in late spring to early summer, and single during early autumn; 7in (17.5cm) across; a quite stunning, vibrant violet-blue, with a central velvety dark red bar; outer layer of eight broad sepals that overlap and taper to a point; all of the sepals are 'frilled' along their whole length, and curve inwards to form a boat shape; semi-double blooms have two further layers of sepals, half the length of the outer layer, cream stamens show up very well against the sepals. ASPECT: any. PRUNING: Group 2 (light).

'Mrs N. Thompson'

Hybridized by Walter Pennell of Lincoln. APPROX. HEIGHT: 6–8ft (2–2.6m). FLOWERS: late spring to early summer, and again in early autumn; 5–7in (12–17cm) across; striking, deep purply-blue, overlaid with a rich purply-cerise bar, this colour extending out towards the margins; four to six broad, overlapping sepals that taper to a point and have slightly twisted edges, so that the bloom does not lie flat; reverse has a greenish-cream bar, fading out to pink-purple margins; stamens have pale pink filaments and dark red anthers. ASPECT: any, however some sun does enhance the colour. PRUNING: Group 2 (light).

Flowers prolifically early in the season, but is not a particularly vigorous grower. It looks superb growing over a low variegated shrub, such as euonymus.

'Mrs P. B. Truax'

The history of this clematis is unknown. APPROX. HEIGHT: 6–8ft (2–2.6m). FLOWERS: late spring to early summer and, occasionally, in early autumn; 6in (15cm) across; eight sepals with rounded edges and pointed tips, periwinkle blue on opening, fading to a light blue as the flower matures; the bloom appears a little gappy (not to its disadvantage as it flowers extremely well), owing to the sepals also being pointed where they join the flower stalk; the earliest blooms to open sometimes bear a pale green bar that gradually fades away; stamens have white filaments with cream anthers. ASPECT: does better in some sun. PRUNING: Group 2 (light).

A free-flowering, compact variety which is ideal for a container.

'Mrs Robert Brydon'

A semi-herbaceous, non-clinging, heracleifolia-type clematis. APPROX. HEIGHT: 5–6ft (1.6–2m). FLOWERS: late summer to early autumn; clusters of small white flowers, tinged with grey-mauve; four or five sepals of about 1in (2.5cm) long which are narrow and roll right back on themselves; crown of prominent stamens with yellow anthers. FOLIAGE: coarse leaves. ASPECT: any. PRUNING: Group 3 (hard).

An interesting variety, though it does not make a spectacular display. It requires support or to be allowed to trail.

'Multi Blue'

This very unusual looking clematis is a sport from 'The President', and was discovered in Holland in 1983. APPROX. HEIGHT: 6–8ft (2–2.6m). FLOWERS: late spring to early summer, and again in late summer to early autumn; 4½–5in (11–12cm) across; six to eight outer sepals of a light french navy blue, each with a light green bar on the reverse; 'multi' inner layer of sepals, that are about half the length of the outer ones and very narrow, forms an attractive, spiky crown in the centre of the bloom; the spiky layers are slightly paler in colour than the outer-layers and have pale greenish-cream edges and tips. ASPECT: any, although some sun will enhance the colour. PRUNING: Group 2 (light).

Free-flowering and compact, it is suitable for growing in a container.

'Nelly Moser' AGM

An old variety that has been much scorned over the years, mainly, I feel, because of its inability to cope with bright sunlight, which fades the colour dreadfully. Hybridized by Moser, in France in 1897. APPROX. HEIGHT: 8–10ft (2.6–3.3m). FLOWERS: profusely, in late spring to early summer, and again in early autumn; 7½–8in (19–20cm) across; eight rounded, overlapping sepals which are a little gappy where they join the flower stalk; pale mauve-pink base colour, overlaid by a very deep mauve-pink, almost cerise bar; stamens have white filaments that deepen towards dark burgundy-red anthers. ASPECT: when 'Nelly Moser' is grown in the shade, its colour is spectacular. PRUNING: Group 2 (light).

'Niobe' AGM

Hybridized by Wladyslaw Noll in Poland, and introduced to England by Jim Fisk in 1975. Named after the legendary figure in Greek mythology. APPROX. HEIGHT: 6–8ft (2–2.6m). FLOWERS: early summer to early autumn; very lovely deep red, open, star-shaped bloom, 5in (12cm) across, with six pointed sepals which, upon opening, are such a dark red that they appear almost black; as the flower matures the colour changes to deep mauve-cerise along the margins, though the bar remains quite red; crown of stamens, which have white filaments with shadings of reddish-purple, and butter-coloured anthers that seem to intensify the colour of the sepals. ASPECT: any, although the colour is best seen in some sunlight. PRUNING: optional: Group 2 (light) or Group 3 (hard).

A compact grower, ideal for a pot.

C. orientalis var. *orientalis*

We have grown this clematis for many years as *C. glauca* var. *akebioides*, only to discover that its true identity is probably *C. orientalis* var. *orientalis*!

The *orientalis* group of clematis is terribly muddled, largely because since the introduction of the seeds, and the original naming, many nurserymen have propagated new plants from seed, rather than vegetatively. (A new plant has to be produced by cuttings from the original plant to qualify it to carry the parent plant's name.) Even the true species are best propagated from cuttings, as they so easily cross-pollinate from related, but different, species or sub-species. This group of clematis seems to me to be continually being reclassified and regrouped, which can only lead to even more confusion.

APPROX. HEIGHT: 10–15ft (3.3–5m). FLOWERS: mid- to late summer; 2in (5cm) across; four sepals, mid-greenish-yellow on the face, while the reverse bears purply-brown mottling; as the flower opens fully the tips of the sepals reflex and the flower turns on its side to reveal the dark chocolate-brown stamens, beige anthers and bright yellow stigma.

FOLIAGE: finely cut and glaucous. ASPECT: any. PRUNING: Group 3 (hard).

This lovely species also displays a mass of silvery seedheads in autumn. Prone to suckering, but not invasive.

'Otto Froebel'

A really lovely old flower that was hybridized by M. Lemoine of Nancy and described in Moore and Jackman's book of 1872 as being *C. lanuginosa* x *C. patens*. Re-introduced from France by Caddick's Clematis, Cheshire, in 1990. APPROX. HEIGHT: 7–10ft (2.3–3.3m). FLOWERS: late spring to early summer, and again in late summer to early autumn; 6–8in (15–20cm) across; eight broad, overlapping, wavy edged sepals that taper to blunt tips to make a very 'full' flower; the slightly creamy-white sepals, described in Moore and Jackman's book however as 'greyish-tinted or French-white', make a tremendous background for the huge crown of rich 'plain chocolate'-brown stamens. ASPECT: any. PRUNING: Group 2 (light).

'Paddington'

Raised by the late Frank Watkinson in the 1980s, and given to us in 1991. APPROX. HEIGHT: 6–8ft (2–2.6m). FLOWERS: early summer to early autumn; 6in (15cm) across; six overlapping, pointed sepals with crimped edges are a rich, very reddish purple with deep mauve mottling, and with a vibrant, purply-red bar running down the centre of each; pale mauve on reverse, with dusky red along the mid-rib and reddish-purple along the margins; stamens have white filaments flushed with pink, and wine-red anthers. ASPECT: any, although the colour can be best appreciated in some sun. PRUNING: Group 3 (hard).

An excellent, very free-flowering variety with good sturdy growth.

'Pagoda'

Introduced by Treasures of Tenbury Wells in 1980, the result of a cross between 'Etoile Rose' and *C. viticella*. APPROX. HEIGHT: 6ft (2m). FLOWERS: mid-summer to early autumn; 2½in (6cm)-long bell-shape; four textured white sepals with mauve-pink margins, the pink also colouring the veins; as the sepals open, their pointed tips recurve, producing a likeness of the roof of a Chinese pagoda; reverse has a very deep purply-pink bar and pale pink margins; greenish-cream stamens. ASPECT: any. PRUNING: Group 3 (hard).

A very pretty little flower, but one that sometimes has rather weak, spindly growth. We have 'Pagoda' scrambling over heathers, where it grows and flowers extremely well. It is also suited to container cultivation.

'Pat Coleman'

Introduced by Thorncroft Clematis in 1996. A chance seedling from 'Lasurstern', possibly crossed with 'Miss Bateman'. APPROX. HEIGHT: 8–10ft (2.6–3.3m). FLOWERS: early to mid-summer, and again in early autumn; eight sepals have a textured surface and beautifully crimped margins which overlap and taper to a point, making a very pretty, full flower 6–7in (15–17cm) across; open a pinky-white, with rose-pink shadings down the central mid-rib; crown of stamens with yellowy-white filaments and dark red anthers. ASPECT: any; although the pink shading will be quickly lost if grown in full sun, leaving a beautiful pure white bloom. PRUNING: Group 2 (light).

A charming flower which has inherited all its parents' qualities. The blooms also keep well in water.

'Paul Farges' ('Fargesioides')

The naming of this variety, a cross between *C. potanini* Maximovicx and *C. vitalba*, is still a matter of some dispute as it was named 'Fargesioides' by the hybridists in Yalta, Crimea, in 1964, on account of its similarity to *C. fargesii*. This is complicated by there being some confusion between *C. potanini* and *C. fargesii*, and complicated even further as the name 'Farge-sioides' is now prohibited by the International Code of Nomenclature for Cultivated Plants because it is an artificial Latin form and not a 'fancy name'. The now 'legitimate' name 'Paul Farges' was applied to honour the French missionary and plant collector who was murdered in 1912 by Tibetan monks.

APPROX. HEIGHT: 20ft (6m) or more. FLOWERS: mid-summer to early autumn; star-shaped, 1½in (4cm) across; borne in clusters from the leaf axils; usually has six cream sepals, each narrow and blunt-tipped; huge crown of stamens which are the same colour as the sepals; the outer ring of stamens reaches out almost the length of the sepals. ASPECT: any. PRUNING: optional: Group 2 (light) or Group 3 (hard).

'Perle d'Azur' AGM

Hybridized by Morel in about 1885. APPROX. HEIGHT: 8–12ft (2.6–4m). FLOWERS: mid-summer to early autumn; 4–5in (10–12cm) across, semi-nodding, taking on a very rounded appearance owing to the pointed tips and rounded edges of the sepals recurving; four to six broad, tapered sepals; a good mid-blue on opening, with a hint of rose-pink along the centre-line towards the stamens; as they mature, sepals pale in colour to a slightly pinky azure-blue and lose their pink bar; the deep pink bar on the reverse can be seen through the almost translucent sepals; stamens have creamy-white filaments and pale yellow anthers. ASPECT: any. PRUNING: Group 3 (hard).

Perle d'Azur is a very 'leggy' clematis which flowers only on the top quarter of its growth. To help conceal its bare legs, try growing it with climbing roses, or through shrubs, so that this minor problem will not detract from the attractive flowers. We grow 'Perle d'Azur' with the beautifully scented climbing rose 'Sophie's Perpetual'; the pair make a glorious display together.

'Peveril Pearl'

Hybridized by Barry Fretwell of Peveril Nursery, Devon, in 1979. APPROX. HEIGHT: 6–8ft (2–2.6m). FLOWERS: late spring to early summer, and again in early autumn; 6–8in (15–20cm) across; eight overlapping sepals, each tapering to a point, and with a lightly textured surface that has a pearl-like sheen; in the changing light of day and evening, the colour passes through shades of pale mauve and grey with the merest hint of pink, while grooves along the mid-ribs bear a hint of a rose-pink bar; huge crown of stamens with creamy-white filaments and coffee-coloured anthers. ASPECT: best out of strong sunlight. PRUNING: Group 2 (light).

We grow 'Peveril Pearl' through a purply-bronze-leaved weigela, which makes an excellent background for the pale blooms. Compact and free flowering, ideal for a container.

'Pink Champagne'

Known officially as 'Kakio', and originally from Japan, this clematis underwent a name change, presumably to suit the Western market. APPROX. HEIGHT: 6–8ft (2–2.6m). FLOWERS: late spring to early summer, and again in late summer to early autumn; 6½in (16cm) across; this is another one of the very early-blooming, large-flowered varieties, usually beginning its display in late spring; the eight pointed, overlapping sepals have very deep pink margins that pale towards a mauve bar which is covered by deep pink veins; as the bloom matures the sepals recurve slightly, making the flower appear rounded; brilliant yellow anthers makes this a bright, cheerful flower. FOLIAGE: unfortunately, this always looks a bit yellow, but this should not put you off growing this gorgeous clematis. ASPECT: any. PRUNING: Group 2 (light).

Compact and very free flowering – ideal in a container.

'Pink Fantasy'

A very pretty clematis, introduced from Canada by Jim Fisk in 1975. APPROX. HEIGHT: 6–8ft (2–2.6m). FLOWERS: early summer to early autumn; 4½–5½in (11–14cm) across; pink clematis usually have a hint of mauve or blue in their make-up, 'Pink Fantasy' however, is a slightly peachy-pink; six or seven sepals, each with a deep pink bar that fades out towards the margins and only runs about half the length of the sepal, petering out before reaching the pointed tips; sepals overlap and twist, making a rather irregular-shaped flower; as the bloom matures it flattens out and the colour fades to a very pretty pale pink; stamens have white filaments and very deep dusky-pink anthers. ASPECT: any. PRUNING: optional: Group 2 (light) or Group 3 (hard).

Blooms keep well in water. Ideal for a container, it is compact and very free flowering.

'Prince Charles'

From Alister Keay in New Zealand and introduced by Jim Fisk in 1986. APPROX. HEIGHT: 6–8ft (2–2.6m). FLOWERS: early summer to early autumn; produced from about 2ft (60cm) off the ground, right up to the top of the plant; 4in (10cm) across; during the course of the day the light to mid-blue colouring varies, sometimes appearing an almost greenish, azure blue, while at other moments having a hint of pink, becoming mauve-blue; four to six broad sepals that taper to a point and have a deeply ribbed surface and a satin sheen; as the flowers open the sepals twist slightly; stamens have greenish-yellow filaments with butter-yellow anthers. ASPECT: any. PRUNING: Group 3 (hard).

The flowers keep well in water. This is one of my favourites, and one which I would recommend to anybody. It is compact, free flowering and always reliable. Ideal for growing in a container.

'Proteus'

Raised by Charles Noble of Sunningdale in 1876. APPROX. HEIGHT: 6ft (2m). FLOWERS: double in late spring to early summer, and single in early autumn; 5½–6in (13–15cm) across; outer layer of six sepals of a deep dusky purply-pink with shades of pale green along the mid-rib, and a deeply textured surface; further layers of sepals of a paler mauve-pink, with deep reddish-pink edges that look as though someone has outlined them; inner sepals twist and are frilly, making this a very full double flower; single blooms have six narrow, pointed sepals, of a slightly paler colour than those of the double blooms, and with a pale bar; stamens have white filaments with pale yellow anthers. ASPECT: any, although the colour is best seen when grown in at least partial sun, or against a light background. PRUNING: Group 2 (light).

A lovely old variety whose double blooms combine well with cream roses. It is suitable for container cultivation.

C. recta and C. recta 'Purpurea'

This herbaceous clematis, with its delicate, hawthorn-like scent, was introduced to Britain in 1597 from eastern Europe. APPROX. HEIGHT: 4–5ft (1.3–1.6m). FLOWERS: early to late summer; ¾in (2cm) across; star shaped; borne in clusters from the current season's growth; four narrow creamy-white sepals. FOLIAGE: that of *C. recta* is deep, dull green, but *c. recta* 'Purpurea', as its name implies, has purply-bronze foliage which is particularly striking in the spring; given some support this makes an excellent backdrop for other herbaceous plants. ASPECT: any. PRUNING: Group 3 (hard).

C. rehderiana AGM

A native of western China, and originally collected by Père Aubert in the late 1800s. Wilson introduced it to Britain in 1908, when it was given the name *C. nutans* var. *thyrsoidea*. In 1914 its name was changed by Kew to *C. rehderiana*. Its delicate 'cowslip' scent is at its best on warm, sunny days. APPROX. HEIGHT: 10–15ft (3.3–5m). FLOWERS: early to late autumn; clusters of pale yellow, ¾in (2cm)-long nodding bells appearing from the leaf axils; tips of the four ribbed sepals recurve to reveal pale yellow anthers: FOLIAGE: leaves are made up of seven to nine leaflets, each one hairy on both surfaces, and with coarsely toothed edges. ASPECT: any; in view of its late-flowering nature, however, it is best grown in full sun to encourage it to flower as early as possible. PRUNING: Group 3 (hard); I find this clematis is best hard pruned each year simply to keep it under control. If space is not a problem, you could lightly prune it, or even leave it unpruned.

Sometimes slow to become established, rehderiana will eventually become a very vigorous climber.

'Richard Pennell' AGM

Raised by Walter Pennell of Lincoln in 1974, and named after his son. APPROX. HEIGHT: 8–10ft (2.6–3.3m). FLOWERS: early to late summer; 6–8in (15–20cm) across; six to eight broad, overlapping sepals with pointed tips and crimped margins; dark pinky-lavender, with a hint of deep rose pink down the centre of each sepal, and radiating, in veins, out through the textured surface towards the margins; large crown of stamens with filaments the same deep rose pink as in the sepal, and cream anthers. ASPECT: any. PRUNING: Group 2 (light).

A most beautiful clematis which deserves to be as widely grown as the well known 'Vyvyan Pennell'.

'Rouge Cardinal'

APPROX. HEIGHT: 6–8ft (2–2.6m). FLOWERS: early to late summer; 4–5in (10–12cm) across; rich red, opening a dark, burgundy-wine-red with a wonderful velvety depth to the colour, further enhanced by a satin sheen; as the flower matures, the colour gradually fades, and by sepal fall has reached a deep purply-cerise; the tips of the six sepals taper to a point, and as the flower opens they recurve to make a very round-looking bloom; stamens have creamy-white filaments with coffee-brown anthers. AS-PECT: any. PRUNING: Group 3 (hard).

A compact plant that flowers profusely and is therefore ideal in a pot.

'Royalty' AGM

Introduced by Treasures of Tenbury Wells during the mid-1980s. APPROX. HEIGHT: 6–8ft (2–2.6m). FLOWERS: double in early to mid-summer, and single in early autumn; 4½–5½in (11–14cm) across; eight or nine very rich bluey-purple sepals on the outer layer have rounded edges and overlap; pale mauve bar on each, overlaid by deep purple veins; inner layers are an exact copy of the outer, but sepals are smaller. ASPECT: avoid north-facing situation; best in some sun. PRUNING: Group 2 (light).

Very compact plant – ideal for pot.

'Royal Velvet' (PBR – propagation by licence only)

Introduced by Raymond Evison in 1993. APPROX. HEIGHT: 6–8ft (2–2.6m). FLOWERS: late spring to early summer, and again in late summer to early autumn; 5–6½in (12–16cm) across; six to eight overlapping sepals with lightly crimped margins tapering to blunt tips; sepals are a stunning rich, velvety, reddish-purple colour; each has a bar of purply-red, and this colour radiates out in veins across the surface; stamens have pink filaments and dark red anthers. ASPECT: any. PRUNING: Group 2 (light).

An excellent new variety. The plant is compact and very free flowering – a good doer. Ideal for a container.

'Sealand Gem'

Introduced by Bees of Chester in about 1950. APPROX. HEIGHT: 8–10ft (2.6–3.3m). FLOWERS: late spring to early summer, and again in early autumn; 5in (12cm) across; the eight overlapping sepals twist and turn, and have slightly crimped edges, making flowers appear semi-double; down the centre of each pale, satiny mauve-blue sepal is a delicate rose-pink bar that gradually fades away as it nears the blunt tips; stamens have white filaments with coffee-brown anthers. ASPECT: any. PRUNING: Group 2 (light).

An old favourite of mine, this plant is compact, very free flowering and healthy.

'Serenata'

Raised by Lundell in Sweden in 1960. APPROX. HEIGHT: 8–12ft (2.6–4m). FLOWERS: early summer to early autumn; 5in (12cm) across; six sepals of good, rich reddish-purple, with a deep purply-red bar; sepals are broad and taper to a point at both ends, making the flower a little gappy at the base of the sepals; stamens have white filaments with bright yellow anthers, give the flower grace and charm and brighten up the sepals. ASPECT: any. PRUNING: optional: Group 2 (light) or Group 3 (hard).

I grow this clematis to give some summer interest to *pieris* 'Forest Flame', the clematis looking extremely good against the light green summer foliage of the pieris.

C. serratifolia

A native of Korea, introduced in about 1918, this has a lovely, delicate scent reminiscent of sherbet lemon sweets. APPROX. HEIGHT: 8–10ft (2.6–3.3m). FLOWERS: late summer to mid-autumn; semi-nodding, borne from the leaf axils; 1½–2in (4–5cm) across; four mid-greenish-yellow sepals, each about ½in wide, taper to a point and open out almost flat to reveal the dark reddish-brown stamens and tuft of bright yellow stigma. ASPECT: any. PRUNING: Group 3 (hard).

'Silver Moon' AGM

APPROX. HEIGHT: 6–8ft (2–2.6m). FLOWERS: early summer to early autumn; 4½–5½in (11–14cm) across; six to eight mauve-silvery-grey sepals with a wonderful satin sheen overlap and taper to a blunt tip, making a very full, star-shaped flower; stamens have white filaments and butter-yellow anthers. ASPECT: any – ideal for a shady position. PRUNING: optional: Group 2 (light) or Group 3 (hard).

A lovely bloom which is best seen against a dark background, or used to brighten a shady corner. Compact, ideal for a pot.

'Snow Queen'

From Alister Keay in New Zealand. APPROX. HEIGHT: 6–8ft (2–2.6m). FLOWERS: late spring to early summer, and again in late summer to early autumn; star-shaped, 6–7in (15–17cm) across; six to eight sepals open bluey-white, quickly changing to pure white as the bloom ages; sepals overlap and taper to blunt tips, and have a textured, deeply ribbed surface; the later flowers open a pinky-white but, again, soon clear leaving the blooms pure white. ASPECT: any. PRUNING: Group 2 (light); crown of stamens with pale pink filaments and dark burgundy-red anthers.

Compact and very free flowering – ideal for a container.

'Star of India' AGM

Introduced by Cripps of Tunbridge Wells in 1867 and awarded a First Class Certificate on 1 October, 1867. APPROX. HEIGHT: 10–12ft (3.3–4m). FLOWERS: mid-summer to early autumn; 4–5in (10–12cm) across; four to six rounded-edged sepals, tapering to blunt tips; each sepal is a deep bluey-purple, with a cerise bar running down the centre and radiating out in veins across the textured surface; stamens have creamy-white filaments with beige anthers. ASPECT: any. PRUNING: Group 3 (hard).

A lovely old free-flowering variety which looks wonderful growing through shrubs, roses or small trees.

'Sunset'

From the USA. APPROX. HEIGHT: 6–8ft (2–2.6m). FLOWERS: early to late summer; 4–5in (10–12cm) across; almost fluorescent colouring; sepals are deep purply-pink with a satin cerise bar; each one tapers to a point and has a lightly textured surface; bright yellow anthers enhance the already stunning colour. ASPECT: any. PRUNING: Group 2 (light).

Compact, free flowering, and ideal for a pot.

'Sylvia Denny'

Raised by Vince and Sylvia Denny of Broughton, Lancashire. APPROX. HEIGHT: 8–10ft (2.6–3.3m). FLOWERS: semi-double in late spring to early summer, and single in late summer to early autumn; 4–5in (10–12cm) across; pure white, with no hint of green, and good strong stems; pale yellow anthers help to make a very 'sunny' flower. ASPECT: any. PRUNING: Group 2 (light).

C. tangutica 'Lambton Park'

A much larger flower than the species tangutica, this clematis has a lovely coconut-like perfume. APPROX. HEIGHT: 10–12ft (3.3–4m). FLOWERS: early summer continuously to early autumn; 2in (5cm)-long bells; the four thick, deeply textured, bright buttercup-yellow sepals taper to a point, their edges recurving to reveal beige anthers; a superb display of silky seedheads keeps the plant interesting all winter. ASPECT: any. PRUNING: Group 3 (hard); despite hard pruning our 'Lambton' each year to keep it under control, it begins flowering early in June and carries on right through to September; if space allows, however, it could be simply tidied up at pruning time.

THE *TEXENSIS* GROUP

The species *C. texensis* is native to Texas, USA. Originally called *C. coccinea*, it was introduced to Europe in 1868 and then to England in 1880. FLOWERS: very red and about 1in (2.5cm) long; borne on 6in (15cm) stems; pitcher-shaped, constricted at the mouth; four fleshy sepals, opening out at the pointed tips. FOLIAGE: glaucous, blue-grey.

Jackman was the first to hybridize *C. texensis*, crossing the species with 'Star of India' to produce 'Duchess of Albany' and 'Sir Trevor Lawrence' in 1890.

In France, Morel and Lemoine used *C. texensis* in crosses. 'Gravetye Beauty', perhaps one of the best-known texensis hybrids, was raised by Morel in around 1900 and introduced to England, and subsequently named by William Robinson, in 1914. To me, the prettiest texensis cross is that of 'Etoile Rose', raised in France by Lemoine in about 1903; one of its parents was quoted as being *C. viticella*. 'Etoile Rose' certainly has the characteristics of both the viticella and texensis species.

Four old texensis hybrids listed in Ernest Markham's book of 1935, 'Admiration', 'Countess of Onslow', 'Duchess of York' and 'Grace Darling' appear to be lost to cultivation. This was also apparently the fate of 'Sir Trevor Lawrence', until it was reintroduced by Christopher Lloyd. We may yet see these 'dodos' of the clematis world reappear one day.

In recent years Barry Fretwell from the Peveril Clematis Nursery in Devon has produced two super new texensis crosses. 'The Princess of Wales' and 'Ladybird Johnson' were both introduced in 1984 as the result of crossing *C. texensis* with the large-flowered 'Bees Jubilee'. I hope we will see more new texensis crosses being introduced – there is always a demand for them!

As a group the texensis hybrids have a characteristic growing habit, being semi-herbaceous climbers. During a hard winter the top growth from the previous summer will die down completely and we have to rely on new shoots being produced from below soil level. A good thick mulch during the autumn will ensure this happens. In milder climates, viable buds can be found several feet up the old vines during the spring, but all this old wood needs pruning hard back to about 1ft (30cm) from the ground.

FLOWERS: generally begin during mid-summer and continue to early or mid-autumn; normally four sepals, but occasionally five or six, as is the case with 'Gravetye Beauty'; shaped like lily-flowered tulips, holding themselves erect and looking skywards (the exception is 'Etoile Rose' which has four sepaled, open, nodding bells facing downwards.).

The only real problem with these plants is that they are all prone to mildew. This can of course be controlled by fungicide, and if it is applied at the first signs, there need not be a major disaster. When grown in an 'open' aspect they are less susceptible to mildew.

These texensis hybrids are very sociable climbers, and I feel that they display their flowers best if grown in association with other climbers or shrubs, when they can be left to scramble freely over their hosts. Growing them as companions to other plants seems to enhance their natural beauty. Each one could be grown in a container if required, although 'The Princess of Wales' is the most suitable for this, being compact and very free flowering. They all prefer an aspect which is not too exposed. As they all have such similar characteristics and cultural needs, they are listed together; however they are not strictly texensis species as they are invariably the result of a cross.

'Duchess of Albany' AGM
APPROX. HEIGHT: 8–10ft (2.6–3.3m). FLOWERS: very elegant; 2in (5cm) long; candy pink with a satin sheen; there is a deep pink bar on the inside of each sepal.

'Etoile Rose'
APPROX. HEIGHT: 6–8ft (2–2.6m). FLOWERS: open and nodding; about 2 ½in (6cm) across; four deeply textured sepals, each with a broad bar of vibrant, almost scarlet, pink, paling along the margins; as the bloom opens, the serrated edges of the sepals recurve and the tip turns out to reveal pale yellow anthers.

A most exquisite old variety which is much sought after.

'Gravetye Beauty'
APPROX. HEIGHT: 8–10ft (2.6–3.3m). FLOWERS: 2½in (6cm) long; four to six very deep, rich, red sepals that taper to a point and have incurving margins; after a few days the tight, trumpet-shaped blooms open to resemble fingers pointing skyward.

'Ladybird Johnson'
APPROX. HEIGHT: 6–8ft (2–2.6m). FLOWERS: 1¾in (4cm) long; four sepals of deep purply-red with a brighter, almost crimson, bar and a deeply textured surface; the tips open out to reveal cream anthers.

'Sir Trevor Lawrence'
APPROX. HEIGHT: 8–10ft (2.6–3.3m). FLOWERS: 2in (5cm) long; the inside of each sepal has a scarlet bar with margins of dusky purply-red; on opening, the tips of the sepals roll back on themselves to reveal yellow anthers.

'The Princess of Wales'
APPROX. HEIGHT: 6–8ft (2–2.6m). FLOWERS: 2½in (6cm) long; one of the most luminous pinks seen in the clematis world; each of the four sepals has a deep vibrant pink bar on the inside, changing as it nears the margins to a slightly mauve, deep pink.

'The President' AGM
Raised by Charles Noble of Sunningdale in 1876. APPROX. HEIGHT: 8–10ft (2.6–3.3m). FLOWERS: late spring to early summer, and again in late

summer to early autumn; borne in profusion from the old wood; a wonderfully full star shape, 7in (17cm) across; eight overlapping sepals of a rich purply-blue, that each taper to a point; reverse has a white bar, which appears illuninated when the flower is viewed with sun behind it; stamens have white filaments with deep pink shading, and very dark red anthers. FOLIAGE: young foliage is purply-bronze; it becomes dark green with age. ASPECT: any. PRUNING: Group 2 (light).

A very old variety still worthy of space in any garden.

C. tibetana ssp. vernayi Ludlow and Sherriff

A charming clematis that was brought back from an expedition to Tibet in 1947 by Ludlow, Sherriff and Elliot. APPROX. HEIGHT: 10–15ft (3.3–5m). FLOWERS: mid- to late summer, to mid-autumn; 2in (5cm) across; four sepals, $\frac{1}{10}$in (0.25cm) thick and just over 1in (2.5cm) long, taper to a point forming an open, nodding flower; the outside of each sepal is a deep, dull yellow, while the inside is bright buttercup yellow and deeply grooved; sepals open out almost flat to reveal dark reddish-brown stamens and beige anthers; leaves splendid, silky seedheads for winter interest. FOLIAGE: very attractive, almost fern-like and slightly glaucous. ASPECT: any. PRUNING: Group 3 (hard).

C. x triternata 'Rubromarginata' AGM

Sometimes seen as C. flammula 'Rubromarginata'. Thought to be C. flammula x C. viticella. It has a wonderful, almond-like perfume. APPROX. HEIGHT: 10–15ft (3.3–5m). FLOWERS: mid- or late summer to early autumn; borne in such profusion that there is a mass of blossom; star-like, 1–2in (2.5–5cm) across; four narrow sepals of white, becoming a rich red at the tips, with pale yellow stamens. ASPECT: any. PRUNING: Group 3 (hard).

An excellent candidate to plant near a seat in the garden.

'Twilight'

APPROX. HEIGHT: 6–8ft (2–2.6m). FLOWERS: late spring to late summer; 5½in (14cm) across; eight overlapping sepals that taper to blunt tips, making a very round-looking bloom; open a deep mauve-pink, with bright pink shading at the centre of each sepal close to the stamens; gradually fade to light mauve-pink. ASPECT: any. PRUNING: Group 2 (light).

A very compact, free-flowering clematis, ideal for a pot.

'Veronica's Choice'

A cross between 'Vyvyan Pennell' and 'Percy Lake'. Hybridized by Walter Pennell of Lincoln in 1973 and named after one of his daughters. APPROX. HEIGHT: 6–8ft (2–2.6m). FLOWERS: double in late spring to ly summer, and single in early autumn; 6–7in (15–17cm) across; sepals of the outer ring are large and overlapping and have blunt tips; pale mauve with flushes of rose-pink and pale lavender; all sepals have a very textured surface and crimped edges, and all reflex, making the flower look like a frilly ball; touches of green on the sepal tips of some of the earliest flowers to open; golden yellow stamens. ASPECT: avoid open, exposed aspect. PRUNING: Group 2 (light).

A compact plant, ideal for a container.

'Victoria'

Raised by Cripps of Tunbridge Wells, and awarded a First Class Certificate on 17 August 1870. APPROX. HEIGHT: 10–15ft (3.3–5m). FLOWERS: mid-summer to early autumn; 5½in (14cm) across; usually six overlapping sepals, but occasionally four or five; sepals are wide, taper to a point and have a heavily textured surface and crimped margins; open a rich, deep pinky-mauve, with a strong hint of rose pink along the central mid-rib, fading towards the margins; sepals lose some of the pinkiness as they mature, and by sepal fall have turned to light mauve; colour variations in shade are most attractive, and this clematis is highly recommended for the colour and abundance of its flowers; stamens have greenish-white filaments with dusky-yellow anthers. ASPECT: any. PRUNING: Group 3 (hard).

This is one of the best clematis to provide colour in the garden during late summer and early autumn.

'Ville de Lyon'

Raised by Morel in 1899. Its origin was described to the RHS by the raiser as a cross of *C. coccinea* (*C. texensis*) with a large-flowered clematis named 'Viviand Morel' although, he admitted, the wind or insects could have caused additional pollination. We have to assume therefore that 'Ville de Lyon' was an 'illegitimate' hybrid. APPROX. HEIGHT: 8–12ft (2.6–4m). FLOWERS: early summer to early autumn; 5½in (14cm) across; the six overlapping sepals are rounded and have blunt tips, making the flower appear very round; sepals are vibrant cherry-red, with a wide mid-pink bar, heavily overlaid with the cherry-red in veins; as the bloom opens, the margins and tips of the sepals recurve slightly; stamens have creamy-white filaments with yellow anthers. ASPECT: any. PRUNING: Group 3 (hard).

A beautiful flower with one disadvantage – the stems. It grows quite tall, and early in the summer the bottom leaves brown off and leave unsightly bare legs, hard pruning is therefore essential. Rather than growing it alone, if it is given the companionship of a host shrub as a disguise, its flowers can be enjoyed without distraction.

'Vino' (PBR – propagation by licence only)
From Denmark, and introduced in 1993. APPROX. HEIGHT: 8–10ft (2.6–3.3m). FLOWERS: late spring to early summer, and again in late summer; 7in (18cm) across; eight broad, overlapping sepals, each tapering to a point; magenta red, slightly deeper down the central bar, against which the rich creamy-yellow stamens stand out in marked contrast. ASPECT: any. PRUNING: Group 2 (light).

A compact, free-flowering variety.

THE *VITICELLA* GROUP

The species *C. viticella* was introduced to Britain from Spain in 1569, and was known at the time as the 'Purple Virgin's Bower'. (Clematis were then commonly known as 'Virgin's Bower', in recognition of Queen Elizabeth I 'The Virgin Queen').

In general terms, the viticella group are small-flowered, they all flower from the current season's growth and therefore require hard pruning. Most will then make approximately 8–10ft (3m) of growth. They tend not to be susceptible to clematis wilt, and all are easy to grow.

The flowers, which keep well in water, vary in size from 1½in to 4in (3.75–10cm) across, with the plants compensating for having small flowers by producing a mass of bloom. All of the plants in this group flower profusely, seemingly regardless of what the elements or gardeners do to them, beginning during mid-summer and continuing to early autumn.

They are very versatile, and can be used as specimen climbers, grown through climbing roses, over shrubs, or simply left to scramble over low-growing plants.

Over the years *C. viticella* has been used to produce countless new clematis. Some resemble the species while others take on quite different characteristics. It is not strictly correct to include some of these varieties in the viticella group, yet I think it justified as this is the group under which they can most commonly be found. When searching therefore for a particular variety, check under its hybrid name as well as its group name. For example: for *C. viticella* 'Margot Koster', check also for 'Margot Koster'.

C. viticella

FLOWERS: open, nodding and bell shaped; four deeply textured sepals, 1½in (3.75cm) long by just over ¾in (2cm) wide, with crimped edges and pointed tips; the margins are a very dark dusky blue, with a paler bar that has darker veins running through it; the reverse, which is clearly visible, is not quite as dark and the margins have a grey satin look; greenish-cream stamens.

The species viticella is very variable in bloom, as many have been propagated over the years by seed.

vit. 'Abundance'

From Ernest Markham and introduced by Jackman, but possibly raised by Morel, in France. FLOWERS: 3in (7cm) across; deep pink with heavily textured sepals and a deeper cherry pink running through the veins; sepals recurve along the margins and the pointed tips curl back; flowers tend to hang down, showing the reverse which is pale mauve-pink; stamens are bright yellow.

vit. 'Alba Luxurians' AGM

Bean suggested that this was probably raised at Veitch's Coombe Wood Nursery. FLOWERS: bell-shaped; about 3in (7cm) across; the first to open always have huge splashes of green on the sepals; on closer inspection the sepals appear to be half sepal and half leaf; later flowers, and those exposed to full sun, are completely white (this greening is caused by lack of sunlight, so if this effect is desired, grow this clematis in a very shady position and you will retain this unusual look); four broad, 1½in (4cm)-long sepals remain cupped rather than opening out flat, and they curl their blunt tips back as the flower opens to reveal the short stamens which have purply-black anthers; reverse has a hint of mauve with a pale green bar along the mid-rib.

'Betty Corning'

From the USA. In about 1933 Betty Corning, the daughter of a clematis gardener, discovered this clematis, which has a delicate perfume, growing on 'an Albany side street'. She acquired a division, and it was eventually named after her. FLOWERS: bell-shaped; four deeply textured sepals with serrated edges; insides are light pinky-mauve, and there is a hint of a white bar at the base of each; reverse is slightly paler and nearer to a pale pinky-blue colour; stamens are yellow.

'Etoile Violette' AGM

Raised by Morel in about 1885. FLOWERS: 3½in (9cm) across; four to six rich, slightly reddish-purple sepals with a textured surface; sepal edges reflex as the flower opens, making it look very round; reverse of each sepal is pale pinky-mauve, deepening towards the margins; pale greenish-yellow-stamens contrast well with the dark background.

vit. 'Kermesina'

Raised by Lemoine in France. FLOWERS: 2½in (6cm) across; four sepals that recurve along the edges as the bloom opens; rich, deep red, with a large white spot at the base of each sepal, near the dark brown stamens.

'Madame Julia Correvon' AGM

Raised by Morel in about 1900, this is a spectacular sight when in full bloom. APPROX. HEIGHT: 6–8ft (2–2.6m). FLOWERS: 4in (10cm) across; four to six sepals of a rich, vibrant red, which recurve at the tips and twist as the flower matures; reverse has a pale pink, almost white, bar along the central mid-rib; stamens have white filaments with pale yellow anthers.

Free flowering, compact and ideal for a container.

'Margot Koster'

FLOWERS: unusual, rather dishevelled-looking, but produced in great numbers; 4in (10cm) across; four to six sepals of a strong, deep mauve-pink; the colour is maintained up to sepal fall, even if grown in full sun; sepals have rounded edges which taper to a point; as the flowers opens fully the margins roll right back on themselves, and the tips recurve.

An asset to any garden.

vit. 'Mary Rose'

The 'double purple Virgin's Bower' was re-introduced by Barry Fretwell in 1981. The plant has a very old pedigree and is believed to be of great antiquity. Its new name, that of Henry VIII's flagship, was in recognition of the fact that both the clematis and ship were 'resurrected' in the same year. FLOWERS: double, from new wood; about 1½–2in (3–5cm) across; the most subtle shade of 'smoky-amethyst', each flower having many layers of spiky sepals. ASPECT: best grown in a sunny position or against a pale background, where its beauty can be appreciated.

vit. 'Minuet' AGM

Possibly from Morel, in France. FLOWERS: 2½in (6cm) across; four blunt-tipped sepals of satin white, with veins and margins of dusky purply-red; pale pinky-mauve reverse; stamens have pale greenish-yellow filaments with cream anthers.

vit. 'Purpurea Plena Elegans' AGM

Thought to be very old and probably of French origin. FLOWERS: double, from new wood; long-lived, and up to 2½in (5–6cm) across; many layers of dusky magenta sepals, which recurve and twist as the flowers open to show the dusky pale pink reverse.

Flowers keep well in water.

vit. 'Royal Velours' AGM

Possibly from Morel in France. FLOWERS: 3in (7cm) across; four rounded sepals with slightly recurved tips, a textured surface and a satin sheen; deep reddish-purple, with a hint of mauve down the centre-line, overlaid by the darker colour, especially through the veins; stamens have greenish-cream filaments with anthers of greenish-black. ASPECT: best grown in some sun, where the colour can be seen to perfection.

vit. 'Rubra'
FLOWERS: 2½in (6cm) across; four sepals with rounded tips, and edges that roll back as the bloom opens; deep red with a velvety sheen; stamens have light green filaments with brown anthers; *vit.* 'Rubra' does not possess the white spot at the base of the sepals which identifies *vit.* 'Kermesina'.

vit. 'Tango'
Hybridized by Barry Fretwell, Devon, in 1986. FLOWERS: almost identical to those of *vit.* 'Minuet', but fractionally larger, being 2½in (6cm) across, and tending to hold their colour better; four greenish-cream, round-ended sepals, with deep mauve-pink running through veins to wide margins of the same shade; greenish-cream bar on reverse with dusky pink margins; stamens have light green filaments with dark red anthers.

'Venosa Violacea' AGM
One of the largest-flowered viticellas, this one was hybridized by Lemoine, in France. FLOWERS: 4in (10cm) across; from central white bars, purple radiates out towards the margins in veins, increasing in depth of colour as it goes, so that the broad margins are a very deep purple; between four and six slightly overlapping sepals, with rounded edges tapering towards blunt tips; stamens have cream filaments with black anthers.

'Vyvyan Pennell' AGM
APPROX. HEIGHT: 8–10ft (2.6–3.3m). Hybridized by Walter Pennell of Lincoln and named after his wife. Parentage 'Daniel Deronda' x 'Beauty of Worcester'. FLOWERS: double in late spring to early summer, and single in early autumn; 7–8in (17–20cm) across; double flowers have an outer layer of eight pointed sepals with pronounced, reddish-purple tips; open a deep rosy-lavender which fades pleasantly to a deep lilac-mauve; many layers of shorter pointed sepals make up a very double flower; deep mauve-pink reverse of the sepals is visible where the sepals twist and turn; large, single blooms of deep lilac-mauve follow on new growth; stamens have white filaments with beige anthers. ASPECT: 'Vyvyan Pennell' will often burst into spring growth far too early, before the winter weather is over, so grow this where it will be sheltered from the elements. It is also helpful to drape some garden fleece around the plant if a severe late frost is forecast. PRUNING: Group 2 (light).

'Wada's Primrose'

Occasionally seen as 'Yellow Queen', this clematis came from Manchuria and was originally named 'Manshu-Kii' (Manchuria Yellow). It was given to Koichiro Wada, a Japanese nurseryman, in 1933. Thought to be a wild 'yellow patens-type', it was introduced to Europe in 1965 by Mr Wada. APPROX. HEIGHT: 8–10ft (2.6–3.3m). FLOWERS: late spring to early summer; 6–7in (15–17cm) across; the eight sepals are a delicate primrose-yellow, the colour being deeper along the central bar; sepals taper to a point and have a lightly textured surface; huge crown of creamy-yellow stamens. ASPECT: best in shade; if grown in the sun, the yellow colouring will be quickly lost. PRUNING: Group 2 (light).

Ideal to brighten a shady corner.

'Warsaw Nike'

Officially known as 'Warszawska Nike', pronounced 'nee-ka', this clematis is named after the Polish goddess of victory and was introduced from Poland in 1986 by Jim Fisk. APPROX. HEIGHT: 8–10ft (2.6–3.3m). FLOWERS: mid-summer to early autumn; 5–5½in (12–13cm) across; the richest, most velvety reddish-purple; six slightly overlapping sepals, each with deep ribs running down the centre towards the tip; sepal edges are lightly crimped and tend to twist as the bloom opens; reverse is silvery; stamens are a bright primrose-yellow. ASPECT: any, although best seen in some sun. PRUNING: Group 3 (hard).

Flowers profusely.

'W. E. Gladstone'

Raised by Noble of Sunningdale, in 1881. APPROX. HEIGHT: 8–12ft (2.6–4m). FLOWERS: early summer to early autumn; a massive 10in (25cm) across; six or seven mid-bluey-mauve sepals; on opening, the round-ended sepals have rose-pink shadings down the central mid-rib, which fade as the bloom matures; surface of the sepals has satin sheen, and has veins of a slightly deeper mauve; stamens have cream filaments and light reddish-brown anthers. ASPECT: avoid exposed situation. PRUNING: optional: Group 2 (light) or Group 3 (hard).

'Will Goodwin' AGM

Hybridized by Walter Pennell of Lincoln. APPROX. HEIGHT: 8–10ft (2.6–3.3m). FLOWERS: profuse, from early summer to early autumn; 6–7in (15–17cm) across; good, clear mid-blue, paling to light blue; seven sepals overlap and taper to a point, with very crimped, almost frilly, margins; stamens have creamy-white filaments and bright yellow anthers. ASPECT: any. PRUNING: Group 2 (light).

A very pretty clematis which deserves to be more widely grown.

'William Kennett'

Recorded in 1875; hybridist unknown. APPROX. HEIGHT: 10–12ft (3.3–4m). FLOWERS: early to mid-summer, and again in early autumn; 7in (17cm) across; eight broad sepals overlap and taper to a point; the deep textured satiny surface is a mid-mauve-blue and has rose-pink shadings along the central bar; the margins are crimped; reverse is light blue with creamy-white bars; stamens have white filaments with dark burgundy-red anthers. ASPECT: any. PRUNING: Group 2 (light).

A beautiful old clematis.

APPENDICES

I SOCIETIES

British Clematis Society
Richard Stothard
[Secretary]
4 Springfield
Lightwater, Surrey GU18 5XP

International Clematis Society
Fiona Woolfenden
[Secretary]
115 Belmont Road
Harrow, Middlesex, HA3 7PL

II SUPPLIERS

Clematis
Caddick's Clematis
Lymm Road
Thelwall
Warrington, Cheshire WA13 0UF

Thorncroft Clematis Nursery
The Lings
Reymerston
Norwich, Norfolk NR9 4QG

Fisk's Clematis Nursery
Westleton
Saxmundham, Suffolk IP17 3AJ

Valley Clematis Nursery
Willingham Road
Hainton, Lincoln LN3 6LN

Old Fashioned Roses
Peter Beale's Roses
London Road
Attleborough, Norfolk NR17 1AY

III BIBLIOGRAPHY

Markham, Ernest *Clematis* (Country Life Ltd, 1935, revised 1939 and 1951).
Moore, Thomas and Jackman, George *The Clematis as a Garden Flower*,
(John Murray, Albermarle Street, London, 1872).
Snoeijer, Wim *Clematis Index* 1991(Jan Fopma, PO Box 13, 2770 AA,
Boskoop, The Netherlands, 1991).
Howells, Dr John (Editor) *The Clematis 1994* (British Clematis Society).
The Concise Oxford English Dictionary (Oxford University Press, 1964).

INDEX

Page numbers in **bold** refer to the page of the full description in Clematis Profiles.